Exploring Gypsiness

POWER, EXCHANGE AND INTERDEPENDENCE IN A TRANSYLVANIAN VILLAGE

Ada I. Engebrigtsen

Berghahn Books
New York • Oxford

First published in 2007 by

Berghahn Books
www.berghahnbooks.com

© 2007 Ada I. Engebrigtsen

Library of Congress Cataloging-in-Publication Data

Engebrigtsen, Ada I.
  Exploring gypsiness : power, exchange and interdependence in a
Transylvanian village / Ada I. Engebrigtsen.
    p. cm.
  Includes bibliographical references and index.
  ISBN 1-84545-229-1 (alk. paper)
    1. Romanies--Romania--Transylvania--Social life and customs. 2.
Transylvania (Romania)--Ethnic relations. I. Title.

DX224.E64 2007
305.891'49704984--dc22

2006019282

British Library Cataloguing in Publication Data

A catalogue record for this book is available
from the British Library

Printed in the United States on acid-free paper

ISBN-10: 1-84545-229-1 (hbk)
ISBN-13: 978-1-84545-229-2 (hbk)

Contents

Preface

My first visit to the hamlet Roma was in April 1993. It was a cold and rainy day and I had just arrived in the village to visit my husband who had spent a month there already. I remember the strange, muddy streets of the village, the horse-drawn wagons driven by men dressed like Brügel's peasants in medieval Flanders. The wild-looking, mud-soaked hamlet with its inhabitants all appeared like clichés of Gypsies from my childhood's fairytale books. It seemed another world. We entered the house of Kurva and Joska and found the main room crammed with people of all ages gathered around the TV set with entranced expressions on their faces. Joska and Kurva tore themselves away from the screen with difficulty to perform the prescribed rituals of hospitality, and asked us questions about our well-being and my journey. Then the screen absorbed me too. The film we were all watching was a Romanian cartoon version of 'The Wonderful Journey of Nils Holgersson' by the Swedish author Selma Lagerlöf. This story about a small, adventurous village boy in Sweden who jumped up on the back of a migrating goose and followed the flock on its long journey northwards had captured my imagination as a child as it had captured my children's and was now capturing this audience of Roma of all ages in a muddy hamlet in Transylvania. This experience evoked strong feelings of the psychic unity of mankind and the power of imagination as basic features for the transportation of stories as well as the endeavour of anthropology.

On the last days of my fieldwork in the hamlet in June 1997 Kurva sat down with me on the grass outside her house, sighing with contentment. She had just watched an Indian video (with love and violence – *kamikaske hai marimaske*) for the twentieth time and exclaimed in high spirits: 'Of all people in the world I like Indians most. They are just like us, they wear their hair and their skirts long and they really know how to dance and play. They have shame just like we have.' To me this again very well expresses the power of stories to capture people across different cosmologies, languages and daily lives, but it also reflects what I experienced as the hamlet Roma's open-mindedness to imagination and to different life worlds.

Acknowledgements

First I would like to emphasise the importance of the the work of previous Gypsy researchers in the U.S.A. and in Europe for my understanding of the Rom/villager relationship in Transylvania. The work of Judith Okely on Travellers in Britain (1983), of Patrick Williams on Rom and Manouches in France (1985, 1993) and of Michael Stewart on Roma in Hungary (1997) have played particularly important roles in my own analysis

Next I would like to express my debt to the people of the village and hamlet. I can never pay back the warm and emotionally fulfilling experience of laughing, joking and sometimes crying in overcrowded and overheated Rom houses and in more densely populated and somewhat under-heated Romanian kitchens. Neither can I pay back the intellectual stimulation of participating in people's lives and writing about it afterwards. I can only thank the Roma and Romanians in the village and hamlet for receiving us with warmth and enthusiasm and for sharing their food, space and company with us. All the names used in this book are my inventions, in order to preserve my informants anonymity.

I want to thank my husband Lars Gjerde, for conducting fieldwork with me in Romania, as an interpreter and a colleague. I believe our co-operation doubled the scope of my observations and enriched my analysis. His transcribed tape recordings from our fieldwork have been part of my data and some have been presented in my text. I also thank him for endlessly reading through chapters of this book, for his analytical suggestiveness, for his criticism and for his praise. I also want to extend my gratitude to Mr Viorel Achim for receiving Lars Gjerde and myself at his Bucharešti office and discussing his work with us, and for his helpful reply to my e-mails. I thank Michael Stewart, who is, in his way, responsible for this book by encouraging me to rewrite my thesis, for his support.

I want to thank Signe Howell and many of my colleagues at the Department of Anthropology who have read parts of this book. A special thanks to Benedicte Brøgger and Axel Borchgrevink, together with Anne

Waldrop and Elisabeth L'orange Fürst, who have read and commented on several chapters and given me valuable feedback.

Equal thanks go to *Norwegian Social Research*, NOVA and *Norsk faglitterær forfatter- og oversetterforening*, NFF, for financial support. A special thank you to my colleague at NOVA Kirsten Danielsen for reading the manuscript and suggesting necessary changes. Thanks to my friend Aurora Kanbar, who corrected the Romanian text, and to Lars Gjerde for the Romanes text, and to Marion Berghahn for her support and patience.

And last but not least I send warm thoughts to Mona Mørtl for her courage, humour and stamina and for making the village and hamlet accessible to us.

Transcriptions, Pronunciations and Vocabulary

Several words in the text with the same meaning and pronounciation are spelled in Romanian and Romanes according to context. Examples are the Romanian *naţie*, spelled as *nacie* in Romanes. In these vocabularies only important words or words that accur often are included. I have only included plural forms when they appear in the text.

Romanes Pronuncation

For Romanes orthography I have used the scheme suggested by Lars Gjerde (1994) for the *Ćurara* dialect in Norway:

C	*ts*
Č	as *ch* in *church*
Dj	as *g* in *German*
J	as *y* in *yes*
K	unaspirated
Kh	aspirated
P	unaspirated
Ph	aspirated
Š	as in *she*
X	as *ch* in German *acht*
Ž	as in *measure*

Romanes Vocabulary

Amare phure	Our old folks and/or ancestors
Bax	Luck, chance, prosperity
Beng	The Devil
Biav	(pl. a) Wedding
Bilažavesko	Shameless
Bibi	Aunt, polite address to women older than oneself
Bibax	Unluck, misfortune
Bori (pl. a)	Rom daughter-in-law

Bulibaša	Rom headman
čačo (adj.)	Real, true, good
Cigan (pl. i)	Rom (sometimes used as self-ascription towards non-Roma)
Ciganie	The Rom community (local or global)
Coxa	Long Gypsy skirt
Čuternara	Group of Roma (sewage makers)
Čurara	Group of Roma (sievemakers)
Dikhlo	Headskarf of married Gypsy women
Duna	Featherbed
Familia (pl. i)	Close and extended family
Gažo(pl. e)	Non-Rom man
Gaži (pl. e)	Non-Romni (Gypy woman)
Gažikano (adj)	Non-Rom
Gažikanes (adv)	Non-Rom
Ikona	Pretty picture
Kako	Uncle, polite address to people older than oneself
Kaštale	Group of non-Roma Gypsies (wood carvers)
Kelderara	Group of Roma (coppersmiths)
Komnati	In-laws
Kris Romano	Traditional judicial system
Lašo (adj)	Good, kind, pretty
Lažav	Shame
Lažal pe	To be ashamed
Mahrime	Set apart, defiled
Mahril pe	To set oneself apart, to defile oneself
Manuš (pl. a)	Human being, neutral
Melalo (adj)	Dirty
Mesali	Table, a meal in honour of someone
Nacie (pl. i)	Ethnic group, nation
Njam (pl. njamuri)	Relativ
Paramiča (pl. i)	Story
Pačiv (pl. a)	Honour and meal (party) given in hounour of someone
Pačivalo	Hounorable
Phral (pl. a)	Brother
Phej (pl. a)	Sister
Rasa	Ethnic group, (also subgroup of Roma)
Respeto	Respect
Rom (pl. a)	Married Rom- Gypsy man, Gypsies in general
Romano adj	Rom-like
Romanes (adv)	Rom language, Rom way of life
Romanimo	Rom culture, traditions, cosmology
Romni (pl. romnja)	Married Rom-Gypsy woman
šav (pl.e)	Rom boy
šei (pl.a)	Rom girl
šei bari	Marriable Rom girl
šogoro	Brother-in-law
Sokro/sokra	Father in law/mother-in-law
Straica	Beggin bag
T'aves baxtalo	Good day (lit. may you come with luck)
Te xoxavav le gažen	To beg from non-Roma (lit. to lie)
Vero/verišoara	Cousin
Vurdonara	Group og Roma (lit. of wagons)
Xanamik	The relation between to men exchanging

(pl. xanamikuri)   children in marriage
žamutro   Son-in-law
Zor   Power, strength
žungalo   Ugly, also used about menstruation

Romanian Vocabulary

A face curat   To clean
Deochi   The evil eye
Bizniţa   Business
Bine aranjată   Groomed, proper about a woman
Bulibaşa   Gypsy leader
Cinste   Honour, ritual gift
Ciubuc   Small gift (bribe)
Civilizaţie   Civilisation
Cuib   Birdsnest
Cunoscuţi   Aquaintances
Curat   Clean and spiritually pure
Familie   Family
Gospodăriă   family farm, household
Harnică   Industrious (referring to a woman)
Mită   Bribe
Naţio (pl. e)   Ethnic group, nation
Neam (pl. neamuri)   Relative
Om   Man, person, decent person
Om de trăabă   Honourable hardworking man
Pregătire   Education (lit. preparation)
Român   Romanian (masc.)
Românca   Romanian girl, woman
Rob   Slave
Sărut mâna   Greeting tyo a woman (Lit. I kiss your hand)
Spurcat   Impure, polluted in a religious sense
Străin (pl.i)   Stranger
ţâra româneăscă   The old Romanian territories Wallachia and Moldova
ţigăn (pl. i)   Gypsy man
ţigănca (pl. i)   Gypsy woman
ţiganesc   Gypsy-like

Introduction

This book is about the relation between Rom Gypsies and peasants in a village in Transylvania. The term *gypsiness* will refer to what I see as the Rom-Gypsy mode of existence that implies their relationship to non-Gypsies and the mutual ideas that govern this relationship. Gypsiness as a social form is a creation of specific social processes in time and space. Gypsiness in this study does not refer to a community, but to the particular social form created by the interdependence of Gypsies and non-Gypsies *(gaze pl.)* – here the hamlet Roma and peasants in a village in Transylvania. I see this form to be one local example of gypsiness that is expressed in different ways in different localities. I opt for a view of Gypsies and gypsiness as a relationship that is flexible, changing and explorative in adaptation to the surrounding populations. This book is an effort to combine an ethnographic description and analysis of one Rom Gypsy community with an analysis of its relations to the peasant community it is part of and dependent on.

Joska, the *bulibaša* (headman) of the Rom hamlet, is the protagonist of this story. In Part I of this book we follow him and his family through different aspects of everyday life, which will reveal the complex and changing relations between Roma and villagers in present-day Romania. It will also demonstrate the complex strategic situation Joska accommodates to by balancing his loyalties with his ambitions. The second part of the book discusses the exchanges, interdependencies and power relations between Roma and villagers and the place of the Roma in the Romanian figuration.

Background

Gypsies, Roma and Ţigani

Gypsy is the English denomination for a vast and diverse category of people consisting of several culturally different ethnic categories and groups. The term *Gypsy* represents a specific European discourse of power and certain romantic ideas and sentiments of freedom that have been interpreted differently in different times and in different places. Gypsy and 'Gypsy-like' generally refers to categories of people who are considered in some way to oppose the majority's way of life and world view as expressed in names like bohemians, travellers and tinkers (Lucassen and Cottaar, 1998: 1). The majority of these groups and categories speak different languages and do not admit any affinity to each other.

The Roma form one category of Gypsies consisting of groups speaking dialects of *Romanes* (referred to as Romany in English). Roma constitute the largest minority population in Europe. The most numerous and widely dispersed category of Roma is often referred to as Vlach Roma and consists of several groups that occupy slightly different economic niches and constitute what they themselves call *nacie* or *rasa* which in local *Čurara* dialect, is almost synonymous with ethnic group (Voiculescu, 2002). These groups refer to themselves as Roma often with a more specific name for what they see as their nacie. *Vlach* is a linguistic term that refers to speakers of vlach Romanes. *Vlach Romanes* today refers to the variant of Romanes that is significantly influenced by Romanian vocabulary (Matras, 2002). A common language enables Vlach Rom from all parts of the world to communicate.

Ţigani[1] is the Romanian term for Gypsy, but ţigani have had a different position and a different history in Romania than in other European countries and the term is not at all synonymous with Gypsy. In feudal times ţigan was synonymous with craftsman or slave (Achim, 2004), whereas today the term covers a great variety of meanings in colloquial Romanian. It is a derogatory term often referring to dark-skinned people with a bad reputation in general and also to a vaguely alleged ethnic category. Ţigani are estimated to constitute somewhere between 1.8 percent and 10 percent of the Romanian population of about twenty-three million.[2] As for minority populations in general, the problem of definition is at the core of these discrepancies. Nonetheless, Romania has the largest Gypsy population in Europe and the largest percentage of Gypsies who together with Hungarians (around 7 percent), constitute the two largest minorities in Romania.[3] Ţigani is an ascription that covers a wide range of categories, groups and individuals with different self-ascriptions. In this book I will be mentioning some of these such as *the Čurara, the Kelderara* and *the Kaštale* – who at least from a Rom point of view are different ethnic groups (nacie/rasa).

Roma/Ţigani have lived in what is today Romanian territory for about six centuries after emigrating into the area from the late fourteenth century, probably in connection with wars. Although ţigani have not suffered genocide in the same way as Gypsies in other European countries, they suffered a harsh fate as slaves and service serfs until the abolishment of feudalism in the mid-1880s. In spite of this and because of their incorporation in the feudal system as slaves and serfs, țigani in Romania have coexisted with other ethnic groups, such as Romanians and Slovaks, at the bottom of the rural society governed by Hungarian, German and Romanian feudal lords. Today țigani, or Roma as they prefer to be called, can be found on all economic levels of Romanian society from the overwhelmingly rich business people in the cities to the nomads who still roam the countryside in horse-drawn wagons crammed full of half-naked children and half-wild dogs. The majority, however, are to be found among the poorest segments of the rural and urban population, most often on the outskirts of villages. This book will use the term Gypsy to refer to Gypsies in general and to the Western European ethnic discourse of Gypsies. The term țigani (pl.) will be used without capital letter to denote its derogatory connotation, to refer to Gypsies from the general Romanian perspective, and the terms Roma and hamlet Roma (pl.) will be used to refer to Roma's own perspective. I am aware that this may seem somewhat confusing, but I find it necessary to highlight different perspectives and different aspects of gypsiness in this way. I apologise for any apparent inconsistencies.

Transylvania

Romania has always been and still is a multi-ethnic area in the sense that people with different languages, religions and cultural practices have lived together and in the sense that ethnicity has played an important political role. Transylvania, "the land beyond the forest", or Ardeal to Romanians and Erdely to Hungarians, has played a special role in the formation of Romanian national lore and identity because it was in this area the national question was experienced as most urgent due to its history and ethnic diversity and the large percentage of Hungarians. Relations between the Hungarian minority and the Romanian state have been a continuous political struggle throughout the two last centuries. Transylvania today has the greatest percentage of minority populations such as Hungarians, Germans and Roma. The relation between Hungarians and Romanians is not the primary concern of this book, but will be discussed in the last chapter.

The Village

The location for this book is a Romanian village in Transylvania. The first written account of the village is from the thirteenth century, when it was mentioned in a crown document because of its salt mines and being the crossing point of the big river.[4] The whole area was part of a Hungarian estate until about 1918 when Transylvania became part of the Romanian nation. Land reforms in the 1870s and 1921 ensured the Romanian population a minimum of land for subsistence, but this period was remembered by my informants as the poorest and most critical in the history of the people of the Ardeal. A census from 1930 shows that the Romanian and Hungarian population has been remarkably stable since then, while the number of Roma has increased considerably. The Jewish population was either deported during the Second World War or they left, none returning after the war.[5]

The village is typically Transylvanian, consisting mainly of subsistence farmers, some shopkeepers, schoolteachers, factory and railway workers and a few administration clerks. The population in 1996 consisted of about 2,500 inhabitants: about 750 Hungarian and 1,550 Romanian in the main village, and about 250 Roma on the hilltop in a settlement of their own but still considered part of the village. It is a beautiful village, with its gardens and orchards blooming in springtime and full of fruit in the autumn. The villagers say that the air is particularly clean and invigorating here and that it is the prettiest village in Romania. A vital river runs through the village with Romanians and Hungarians settled on either side, connected by a bridge. The village is surrounded by hillsides covered with huge, old beech woods and pastures with grazing cows, horses, sheep and goats. The area is densely populated, and the next village starts about 500 feet from where the first ends. Every house has its courtyard facing onto the street but locked behind tall, iron gates. For the visitor, the village seems at the same time both inviting and beautiful and somewhat barren and forbidding.

On top of the hill live the Roma in their more-or-less shanty town houses. The Roma are relative newcomers to this village, as are most sedentary Rom populations in Transylvanian villages. Before the Second World War, the Roma of this area were mainly nomadic. They travelled through the villages in spring, summer and autumn and used to spend the winter on the outskirts of villages in earth huts dug out of the ground. The ancestors of hamlet Roma thus used the village as their winter quarters. The hamlet Roma call themselves Čurara and *Vurdonara* (lit. of wagons). In the 1950s the Communist regime banned nomadism so all travellers were forced to sell their wagons, set up permanent houses and send their children to school, and all men were forced to work as state employees. Although the hamlet is seen as separate from the village, the last house in the Romanian village is only about 100 feet from the first house in the Rom hamlet and the most peripheral house in the hamlet is only about 20 feet from the first house in the next Romanian village.

All ethnic groups are Romanian citizens, but they present themselves as Roma, Hungarians and Romanians. Relations between Romanians and Hungarians are ambiguous, peaceful and friendly in everyday interaction when political matters are avoided as they generally are. In ethnically segregated settings both groups tend to talk of each other in slightly derogatory terms and when the conversation turns towards politics, controversy and aggression surfaces. It is the political position of the Hungarian minority that is the problematic issue, but many villagers also have bad memories from the Hungarian occupation of Transylvania in the last years of the Second World War. The stories of deportations, imprisonment and violence from the Hungarian soldiers were often told and lamented. Like most Romanian villagers the hamlet Roma are Romanian Orthodox, while Hungarian villagers are Protestants, but several other churches are also present in the village. During the Ceauşescu era most villagers worked on the co-operative farms and in state-owned enterprises, but today most families have land and are dependent on it for their living in addition to other kinds of income.

To make it easier for the reader to distinguish between the Hungarian and Romanian villagers on the one hand and the hamlet Roma on the other, the terms *villagers* and *peasants* will be used to refer to both Hungarians and Romanians in the village and area, if nothing more precise is necessary for the context.

Fieldwork

My first visit to the village was in 1993 when my husband, Lars Gjerde, was assigned as a Romanes interpreter by a NGO that was involved there. Because of his work we already had contacts among villagers and hamlet Roma, when we came to do fieldwork in August 1996. Lars Gjerde worked with a linguistic project, I on my Ph.D. in anthropology. My husband spoke the Čurara dialect of Vlach Romanes and we had both worked for several years with Rom in Norway before going to Romania. As I was not fluent in the language, I was dependent on my husband as an interpreter, especially in the first months. Our discussions about the interpretations of different events and pieces of information were thus extremely fruitful. The interviews he recorded and transcribed for his own research are part of my material and some are directly referred to in this book. We brought a video camera in order to use video recording as a method for the production of data. It turned out to be successful as all families wanted their pictures taken individually and in groups, thus making it easier to classify the relationships between individuals.

Fieldwork as Intervention

Most traditional monographs open by presenting a landscape where the social life of 'the people' unfolds. The biogeographical landscape is often seen as a natural constant in a shifting social landscape (Hirsh and O'Hanlon, 1995: 2). But field sites are not what they used to be. Most processes that anthropologists study cover several 'places' and the meaning of place has changed and widened, and has perhaps become more flexible and even more vague than it once was (Appadurai, 1996; Fardon, 1990; Gupta and Ferguson, 1997; Hann, 1996; Fog Olwig and Hastrup, 1997; Godelier, 1999,) The concept of multisited ethnography (Marcus, 1995) is based on the idea at that the world is changing and that global processes have local implications. In this open terrain, multisited fieldwork implies that the researcher moves according to the movements of her subject and objects of study. Multisitedness may, however, imply many forms of movement. Marcus points out that every field covers many sites and that any fieldwork in principle may be multisited. The conventional understanding of the field none the less tends to be guided by theoretical limitations that have reduced it to a more or less one-dimensional 'place' (Marcus, 1995: 100).

The Geographical Terrain

This more or less one-dimensional, innocent understanding of places as naturally bounded guided my first encounter with the village. I caught the first glimpse and then overview of the village from my seat by the train window on my first visit in 1993. When I tried to describe the village later, I discovered that the description was from some imaginary spot about 16 feet above the train window. I had created an imaginary and very clear overview of what appeared to be the natural landscape with its obviously natural boundaries, shaped by rivers, bridges, heights and space between groups of houses. From here the village appeared as a separate, central entity with the Rom hamlet as a natural expansion, while the neighbouring villages came out as 'secondary' compared to the 'primary' village. This first external geographical perspective was, however, later supplemented by the internal perspective of our Romanian host family. When we settled down in the village in 1996 we stayed for the first months in a cramped room inside the family bedroom, inside the closed courtyard, behind the tall gates that protected the houses in the village. Inside these gates the daily life was centred on the kitchen and courtyard – the area of women and children – while the men where in the more dirty back areas, where the animals and the workshop were situated, or out at work. Most conversation in the kitchen and courtyard concerned events and people outside the gates, such as neighbours, Hungarians and țigani at the margins of the Romanian village community. This perspective, that I think of as from the inside and from below, was the Romanian peasant perspective. This perspective covered a geographical area from the outskirts of the village to the Orthodox church and the market and to the administrative centre on the other side of the river. That was the Hungarian part, there was nothing wrong with it from our hostess Florica's perspective; it was just not an area she usually frequented. The fields outside the village, where the peasants grew their crops, represented, however, the most significant terrain from the peasant's point of view. The open, spacious fields, that Florica loved, represented a contrast to the closed and dense atmosphere in the village. These two terrains, the domestic and closed courtyard and house, and the open, but private fields were the only good places from a Romanian peasant perspective. Outside these terrains was the uncontrollable and natural landscape of the strangers, the țigani and the woods. Whenever we left the house to visit the Roma, our hosts shook their heads and told us to look out and always be back before dark. The Romanian peasant perspective was closed around the family and the farm, from this perspective the rest of the village was dangerous and some parts even inaccessible.

After living for some months with the family, we moved to a rented peasant house situated at the outskirts of the village towards the Rom hamlet. The house was on 'țigani street', the street where the Roma walked every day on their daily business. Now the village changed in several ways: geographically, because the Roma came closer as they now could visit us at home, but also because other parts of the village became accessible to us in new ways. We discovered new paths and roads, and people that we had been cautioned about by Florica revealed new perspectives of the village. The Hungarian families we came to know had other perspectives of the village and of villagers than the Romanians we knew. Our own perspective as foreigners living in our new house may be comparable to the Hungarian view as minority and may be called a view from below and outside. From this perspective the village also expanded socially and mentally and became more open and less threatening than from the Romanian peasant perspective. The Hungarian perspective was however never really accessible to us as we did not speak Hungarian and knew only a few Hungarian families.

The third geographical perspective can be characterised as a view of the village from above and the outside. This was the Rom perspective and was quite different from those of the peasants and the Hungarians. The Rom terrain was unordered compared to the peasant terrain. People, pigs and horses, men, women and children, neighbours and kin all mixed in the space between the houses and in the surrounding pastures. No gates or fences created boundaries between house, people or animals. This apparent disorder made the hamlet seem more open and less threatening than the village and in turn made the village appear even more closed and dense. The Rom hamlet is placed on a hilltop overlooking the village and surrounded by the village communal pastures, a site that made village life look distant and a bit unreal. From the hilltop and from this unbounded perspective the village boundaries came out as social boundaries and not natural ones. In the same way, the physical openness of the Rom hamlet made visible the symbolic boundaries between individuals and families there.

Because the Roma, especially the women, are mobile and spend most of their time outside the hamlet and village and have kin in villages all over the area, this perspective changed the village from a naturally bounded entity to a more heterogeneous place with connections to other villages by mud tracks and paths. From here we also discovered that what we from the train and village perspective had seen as the neighbouring village of B, could just as well be seen as the main village, with 'our' village as the neighbour. I discovered that the Roma used the village B in a different way than they used our village and had other relations to people there. If I had been situated physically in B instead of in our village, my data on gypsiness would probably have been different. So by being situated in different geographical places I had access to different productions of locality in the sense of aspects of social life (Appadurai, 1996). The different life worlds, practices and social positions of Romanian peasants, Hungarian villagers and Roma in the village community represent different types of sociability, use of the physical environment and belonging to the same terrain that I had mistaken for one place: our village.

The Moral Terrain

Our life and movement in the village did, however, not only change our own perspective; to some extent it also changed the perspective of Romanians, Hungarians and Roma. When we crossed boundaries drawn by peasants, their perspective on what was morally and socially possible also changed. When we visited Rom houses in broad daylight and opened our house to Roma, we crossed some tacit boundaries and created confusion by questioning what had not previously been questioned. If educated, well off Europeans such as ourselves could mix with ţigani, why not Romanian peasants? Of course most boundaries were crossed also by villagers, but in secrecy or for 'good' reasons. Our explicit border crossings questioned the validity of the boundaries. The Rom hamlet was in these contexts cut loose from the wild forest and approached the civilized village. And every geographical site implied an ethnic and moral position. In village discourse there were no middle positions in this terrain, but the change of focus revealed that crossing boundaries was vital for the village to present itself as one village. By crossing boundaries openly and challenging the social terrain of the village, I also challenged the ideal of the discrete and considerate anthropologist. This was a deliberate choice and a painful experience for us and for villagers and sometimes for Roma. I will characterise this breach as an intervention in the field that turned us into anomalies and put our social position under constant scrutiny. Of course all fieldwork is intervention, but I consciously exploited my position in the field to gain new insight into hidden domains. By moving between different ethnic groups and by not presenting myself as aligned to any of them, I raised suspicion, but I also opened up opportunities for intimate confidence and for exploitation. The uncertainty that followed from my ambiguous position allowed for different interpretations of my experiences, than if I had identified closely with one group.

Our border crossings also caused pain for villagers and Roma. When we walked through the village with our Rom friends, our Romanian friends were caught in ambivalence; should they greet us and stop for a chat like they usually did or should they walk passed us? The power of language added to the frustration. When we were with Roma we talked Romanes, signalling our belonging to them; but when we were with Romanians we talked Romanian, which they took as a sign that we were 'on their side'. By meeting Romanians in the village when we were with a group of Roma talking Romanes together, we signalled that we were Roma and distanced ourselves from Romanians. In such a situation we all felt ashamed, not knowing how to handle it. Our Romanian friends felt caught between their desire to show us, their friends, politeness and thus to accept our friends, or to follow the village norm and reject the ţigani and us altogether. We were torn between the urge to respect our Romanian friends, which would mean rejecting our Roma friends, and the other way around. The Roma felt uncomfortable by seeing the bewilderment of the Romanians. Something similar happened when I was out walking with Rom children and met Romanian friends. Rom children walking alone in the village are used to abuse from villagers and they answer with cursing and dirty language. Thus they appear to be relatively protected from internalising village contempt. When they were with me they presented themselves very differently: they were friendly, open and affective; sweet children. One day I brought a girl of about eleven years down to our car in the village to give her a pair of shoes that she had asked for. As we approached the car we saw five or six village women, whom I knew well, seated on a bench near by. It was too late to turn around. When they saw the girl and understood that I wanted to give her a pair of shoes, they started scolding her and calling her a lousy beggar and a good for nothing, etc. She instantly turned purple and lost her voice. Caught between the wish to defend herself in the Rom manner and present herself as a 'bad' girl in the eyes of non-Roma, and the wish to present her friendly, polite self as a 'nice' girl towards me, her defences were down and she felt shamed. Thus we brought Roma and villagers together in new and unknown ways that were disagreeable to all parties and that highlighted the social and moral boundaries that were challenged.

Our position as an anomaly also opened up a rich source of gossip and confidences, but was also a source of exploitation for Roma and villagers. We had access to scandalous family stories, secret crimes and slander, even about those whom we regarded our close friends. But this position also rendered us much more vulnerable to people asking for loans, financial support and other services. Our position betwixt and between opened up social fields that would have been difficult to access, had we been tied more closely to one family or one group. We were present in Florica's courtyard when *Romnja* came in to beg or exchange. Because most Romnja knew us they sometimes ran two parallel conversations, one a polite discussion in Romanian with Florica about the transaction they were about to make, and the other a contemptuous conversation with us about Florica and how bad and stingy she was: 'How can you stand living with this hag, come and live with me instead, we cook much better than these stingy Romanians'.

Situations like this one also revealed to us that the village was permeated by a perpetual flow of exchange that engaged all villagers to different degrees. The discrepancy between the village discourse about the bad and uncivilised ţigani and the exchange practices helped us understand that the village discourse was primarily about the villagers' moral habitus. Our presence made it necessary to legitimie the exchange by an explicit condemnation of ţigani and in that way persuade us, the foreigners, that villagers are different and morally superior to ţigani.

This hostile discourse did, however, influence our life and whereabouts, because we only understood the legitimizing aspect towards the end of our stay. Thus even though we challenged village boundaries, we also developed all kinds of discrete ways of handling them. Whenever villagers meet they ask each other series of questions that act as polite interest: 'Where are you going? What are you doing there?' etc. When we walked up the streets towards the Rom hamlet, villagers sitting outside their houses always asked us where we were going, and knowing we were crossing boundaries we answered rather vaguely. They immediately helped us out of our embarrassment by stating: 'Oh yes, you are going up to get some fresh air'. We consented thankfully to this euphemism and this became the way we talked about visiting the hamlet. When we later decided to move up and live in the hamlet, we were nervous and postponed it several times partly because we anticipated that it would mean total rejection from the villagers. When we eventually did move in and lived in our van, the reaction proved to be a surprise like everything else. The first morning we walked down to the village after our first night in the hamlet and met some villagers, we answered a bit stupidly that we had taken fresh air. As it was seven o'clock in the morning, we realised we had to put an end to this nonsense. Going back to the hamlet that day we stopped and chatted with some villagers and told them that we had moved in with the ţigani. They all laughed with gusto, clasped their hands and said: that was really amusing and how did we like it? After this confrontation encounters were easier for us and for them, as all parties let go of our masks and the pantomime we had been performing to each other for months. I suggest that the fact that we actually lived with the ţigani showed the villagers that we accepted what they regarded as the most shameful aspect of the village as a social place. By accepting and even liking ţigani, we demonstrated that we accepted and even liked the village as it is, with its shameful aspects. After that we could all let our hear down and call a spade a spade without being ashamed.

The Anthropological Terrain

My theoretical interest and understanding also changed by changing sites. I became more interested in the relations between groups and entities and the transgression of boundaries, than in the substance of the boundaries and categories themselves. I became more and more aware of how individuals and groups create each other by mirroring each other. But this pushed other perspectives in the background. As long as I saw everything as exchange, power structures tended to vanish while complementarity in all relations became very significant. All that did not circulate and that was not complementary became my blind spot during parts of my fieldwork, for good and for worse. This changed the political perspective of rather rigid minority/majority relations and structures of domination that I had had on the outset. Instead I discovered patterns and interpreted relations that were much less absolute and one-dimensional than anticipated. Thus my oscillation between sites and minority and majority positions hindered any uncritical identification with the 'subaltern' (Marcus, 1995: 101) and allowed for a much more dynamic interpretation of relations of domination.

Theoretical Considerations

Marginality and Modernity

Much literature on Gypsies takes for granted their marginal position in society both politically, economically and socially (Lucassen, Willems and Cottaar, 1998; Okely, 1994; Willems, 1995). The idea that one may identify one 'centre' – be it political, economical or social – of a society contains the idea of a 'periphery', and almost naturally implies that the powerful are in the centre and the powerless at the margins. Of course, it is possible to analyse categories of people and even groups that are the most active decision-makers concerning economic or political issues with relevance far outside their own 'group' at a given time in a given society. Of course, one can identify institutions that control vital resources (material and/or symbolic) for all citizens, for instance in a state, but does the analysis of 'economic/political centres' necessary imply margins, and marginality and powerlessness in face-to-face relations? One might ask how to identify margins in an economic and political landscape that is only to a certain degree national and bounded, where there are several centres with overlapping interests.

Gypsies are often described as marginal because they are generally poor and illiterate, often nomadic and perceived as traditional and 'uncivilized'. The semi-nomadic Norwegian Roma are portrayed that way in official accounts, as are Gypsies in most European countries. In spite of being illiterate, Roma in Norway have economic and social connections all over Europe and religious co-operation with Roma on other continents.[6] They do not participate in competition for political positions in Norwegian society, but they do compete for economic resources and this competition is based on and creates networks of alliances both in Norwegian society, abroad and in the diverse European Rom societies. In Romania, rural Roma obtain their living in close relations with villagers and are dependent on this exchange. Many participate in the general competition for resources in rural Romania, but in addition their lack of land makes them able to exploit more distant and changing resources not available to land-bound peasants. The social structure of the Roma ensures that most individuals and communities have networks of connections outside their own area. In addition, as many Roma are migratory, these connections expand even to the rest of Europe and America. The Romanians complain that the only people who migrate from Romania to Western Europe are ţigani, thus ruining the reputation of decent Romanians. The 'poor beggars' in my study have, precisely because they are Roma, access to international relief organisations that supply them with goods that are exchanged in wide circles in their own society.

In this book I argue that ţigani in Romania play an integral part in the economy, politics and consciousness of ordinary Romanians, and that the discourse on marginality should be discussed as an ongoing process of differentiation and of 'otherness' that creates the national and cosmological order (Tsing, 1993: 26). In the political discourse about ţigani as marginal, we find implied series of dichotomies about marginality, illiteracy, tradition and powerlessness versus centrality, literacy, modernity and power (Achim, 2004; Chelcea, 1944; Crowe and Kolsti, 1991). Illiteracy among many Gypsy populations is seen as an examplenof the 'lack' of modernity resulting from marginality and causing that marginality. I argue that illiteracy also is a conscious strategy that Roma use in their struggle for cultural and political autonomy. The idea that the ţigani as a social category will soon disappear, together with all other reminiscences of the premodern era, is thus misconceived. Modernity may be seen to contain several partial, overlapping and interconnected discourses that are enacted differently in different contexts (Ewing, 1997:4). Discourses of modernity as well as modern technologies are incorporated into Gypsy modes of existence without rendering them less 'different' than before and thus less marginal in the eyes of many Western analysts.

Authenticity and Figurations

Marginality is related to ideas of isolation but also of 'otherness'. This inherent otherness of Gypsies is linked to the idea of the Roma as a 'foreign people' who emigrated from India and who never quite integrated into majority society. The idea is often paired with one of an 'original Indian culture' that is more or less 'lost' in contact with host societies in Europe and elsewhere (Hübschmannová, 1998). This idea also often expresses a view of continuing degradation, something like: *the Gypsies, although stigmatised, were once proud and valuable contributors to their host societies economically and culturally, but industrialisation has pressed them to the margins of modern society where their culture is slowly degrading* (see Williams, 1983). The idea of original, authentic societies is no longer an issue in anthropology, but it is to political activists and intellectuals who try to restore 'Gypsy identity and culture' for political purposes. These processes are important and necessary, but such interpretation of Gypsy culture should be understood as an expression of contemporary relations and not as historical 'truth'. I see the Roma as a fundamentally European people (Okely, 1994).Without questioning their Indian origin,[7] it is in Europe they are constituted as *Gypsies, țigani, Sigøynere, Gitanos, Zigeuner, Tsiganes etc.* (Lucassen, Willems and Cottaar, 1998; Okely, 1983; Willems, 1995; Williams, 1993). As the past is not made socially relevant for identity formation among the Roma I have studied, there is no collective memory of any Indian origin (Stewart, 1997). I suggest it to be essential to see both aspects: the Roma as an integral part of European societies and as exotic strangers (Williams, 1993: 52). It is this double position that constitutes their identity and culture in the Romanian figuration.

De-centred Society – De-centred Subjects

By seeing social practices and discourses from different points of view: that of Roma, those of villagers, and my own interpretations, I wish to convey a notion of society as plural, multicentred and if not unbounded, then contextually bounded. This does not imply an idea of free-floating relations that are not structured in any particular way, but a notion of society that is multicentred and where boundaries overlap. I suggest that everyone experiences their own network of relations as somehow circling around themselves as centres, and their community as central in their own practices. The notion of society, community and culture as bounded, whole entities is not only an academic illusion; it is an integral part of people's conceptualisation of wholeness and completeness. The experience of wholeness, says Katherine Ewing, should be understood as a necessary reification of the flux of experience that people imagine in order to make them objects of reflection (Ewing, 1990: 263).

Studying Rom communities has very forcefully challenged my somewhat unconscious expectation that the classification people apply to their social world is directly reflected in their actions. I was constantly looking for a consistency between what I experienced as people saying something in one context and the opposite in another. I was constantly frustrated by trying to make sense of the discrepancies between people's discourse and their actions. What confused me was not only the seeming contradictions, but the apparent lack of preoccupation with them. It did not seem that people were bothered by what I experienced as lack of consistency. For instance, when the conversation touched upon the Jews who used to live in the village, our Romanian host would always claim that they were nasty people who never worked. In another context he would tell a nice story about one of them who had been a colleague of his at work. The villagers always said that they never had anything to do with the ţiganii and at the same time we could observe a ţigan family working on their fields. When I confronted people I knew well with my observations they looked surprised and did not see the problem. The point here is not that this incongruity existed, but that it was not perceived as such by people themselves. What I interpreted as inconsistency between action and discourse and in discourse itself, led me to see ambivalence and uncertainty at the base of people's interaction. However, ambivalence does not seem to be the right term as I seemed to be the only one to be confused. The notion of ambivalence then has as its precondition that people expect 'to agree with themselves', and that internal disagreement is seen as dysfunctional. The idea of the integrated self is one of the founding ideas for self-consciousness among modern, urban academics like myself. A modern self is balanced, so that one's ideas, values and feelings are consistent with the way one acts and speaks. In line with this assumption, different and opposing feelings lead to a conflict that may block action (Giddens, 1991: 75). Of course, most people know that handling practical reality implies choices that do not always harmonise with one's feelings or moral values; the point is that such harmony is an ideal. Katherine Ewing (1990) and Henrietta Moore (1994) have, among others, challenged this Western concept of self as an analytical tool in anthropology. Based on ideas of 'the heterogeneous selves' (Kristeva, 1982; Lacan, 1977), they developed notions of a self that is *'experienced contextually and relationally'* (Ewing, 1990: 253). Moore argues for the notion of embodied, multiple and competing subjectivity:

> Thus, gendered subjectivity does not have to be conceived of as a fixed and singular identity, but can be seen instead as one based on a series of subject positions, some conflicting or mutually contradictory, that are offered by various discourses (Moore, 1994: 4).

She further argues that this view of identity, as expressed by subject positions, presupposes some degree of strategic, conscious and self-reflexive agents that are able to identify positions available to them, reject some and chooses others dependent on context and interest. It also implies the existence of multiple competing discourses, and the role of desire and fantasy, for the formation of a sense of self that makes agents comply or resist different discourses. Ewing presents much the same argument about people's multiple, inconsistent and context-bound self-representations, which she refers to as shifting selves (Ewing, 1990), but stresses that people everywhere none the less strive to experience themselves as whole and consistent. She maintains that even if the experience of wholeness is illusionary it is not to be dismissed, but should be understood as an important trait of selfhood:

> An experience of wholeness and coherence is encapsulated in a self-representation, in a semiotic process that highlights and organizes certain fragments of experience. I argue that, although such wholes are actually fleeting, they are experienced as timeless (Ewing, 1990: 263).

Ewing further argues that processes whereby people experience whole cohesive selves derive from a symbolic constitution of the self and 'may be' universal (Ewing, 1990).

Unpredictability and the Experience of Wholeness

A theory of self that implies multiplicity, partiality and contradictions is suited to analysing agents coping with the multi-ethnic, unpredictable and constantly changing social world of rural Romania. Multi-ethnicity means that every individual is involved in relationships of some sort with people of another religion, with another language and with other moral values. One even has to relate closely to people one despises and fears in order to survive. Unpredictability means that one's livelihood is dependent on a variety of people and factors that one cannot trust. Due to political and economic chaos, Romanian factory workers may not know when they will receive their next wage and what regulations will be decided upon. Peasants received private land in the 1930s, lost it to collectivisation in the 1950s and got some of it back again in the 1990s. Although they own their land now, for how long will that last? And most of the other things they rely on for their material and social life are provided by very fragile exchange systems. The constantly changing social world does not mean that people move but that their opinions do. Changing political leadership requires the peasants to change their (public) viewpoints and statements to accord with the ever-changing political rhetoric. This is a situation of multiple, contrasting and competing discourses, hegemonies, languages and sign systems which demands shifting self-representations that would be very difficult to handle with the idea of a consistent, whole self that is the same in all contexts. Villagers and Roma also see 'self' as an entity one can consciously work on to develop; but they none the less handle life's challenges as best they can and by different representations of self in different contexts in accordance with their interests, their desires and the expectations of others. In such a cultural environment, being "the same", in the sense of saying and acting according to some well defined principles, does not create continuity and wholeness. On the contrary it may create conflict, anxiety and feelings of inadequacy.

This does not mean that people do not experience themselves as whole and coherent, but that religion, among other symbolic systems, plays an important role in constituting this wholeness that contribute to consistency. In Orthodox Christianity man is an image of God, and although 'the gift of rationality' is an aspect of human existence, the self and soul are elements of the struggle between God and the devil (Yannaras, 1991, 57, 58). It is in prayer, by fasting and by attending religious rituals that these themes are reflected upon, not about how to act in concordance with oneself, but with the wish of God. The different ethnic cosmologies, with their different power structures, ethnic hierarchies and sign systems, are other examples of the struggle to form coherent wholes, and the discourse of modernity is yet another. These and many more symbolic orders are domains in relation to which people position themselves, and by shifting allegiance with shifting contexts (or rather by positioning themselves in accordance with their interests, desires and the requirements of others), there are many possibilities for shifting selves.

What I perceived as ambivalence was probably not experienced by my informants as a dysfunction of an integrated whole self, nor as a categorical indeterminacy, but as the ability to act in the world in situations where two contradictory options are perceived as equally important and necessary. Such contradictory situations may or may not be experienced as ambivalent. When Joska's (the headman's) eldest son is supposed to obey his father according to the norms of kinship and seniority and to oppose him according to the norms of manhood and equality, this is handled very well when in contexts where only his father, mother and sisters are present. But sometimes the values are mutually exclusive; in the presence of his wife the two demands become ambivalent, and he may have to choose to be a man in eyes of his wife or a son in the eyes of his parents. One solution is to avoid the presence of both together, and that is what young couples generally do. Little by little I came to see ambiguity combined with uncertainty and certainty simultaneously structuring social life and cultural conceptions, and how people coped with this through shifting self-presentations.

My own idea of identity and selfhood did not cope very well with the social diversity and antagonism of the village, partly because I expected my solutions to moral dilemmas to be congruent and to overcome ambivalence in that way. I always opted for 'either/or' solutions where most people opted for 'both/and' solutions. An example was the social use of our car. People always asked us to drive all over the region for minor and major tasks. We often agreed and saw it as a way of paying back people's hospitality. Refusing to go was, however, always a problem because we never really thought we had a good reason. The only way of coping with this dilemma and keeping our self-respect was to tell people the truth: we did not want to go. This was, however, a direct rejection that we feared would be interpreted as very rude by villagers. So very often we just tried to avoid giving an answer at all, which was a bad solution as some people never gave in. The Roma did not understand our problem. 'Just say that your car has broken down, say you have no petrol, just lie' was their advice. When we answered that everybody knew we always had money for petrol and that people saw we were using the car and would know we were lying, the Roma laughed and said that of course everybody knew it was a lie, but then they would know that we did not want to go. This made us reflect upon how impossible it was for us to tell a lie that everybody knew was a lie; it was contradictory to our self-perception as honest and integrated persons. When we told the Roma that we could not lie in that way, they laughed their heads off and wondered how one could get on in this world by sticking to the truth. The point here is again not that Romanians tell more lies that Norwegians, but the way our culturally defined self-perception is suited to cope differently with different social environments.

The Concept of Figuration and Civilization

Norbert Elias's ideas of the social human, and of social formations and the process of civilization have been important for my understanding of the relations I studied in Romania (Elias, 2000; Elias, 2001). Elias uses the concept of figuration to denote certain social, political and psychological formations of interdependent individuals and groups. Inspired by these ideas, I see the Romanian figuration as multilevelled, one level being the specific village figuration, another, what we could call the Transylvanian figuration and yet another, the national figuration in a specific time; all interdependent. The strength of these ideas for my material is that they enable me to discuss the present structural relationship between social classes as an instant in a dynamic pattern of relationships that have evolved for centuries. Thus it may shed light over the relationship between individual motivations and behaviour at the village level and the structural relations on a national level. I will discuss the interdependence of ethnic categories in the Romanian society in terms of a social figuration resulting from a specific civilizing process whereby different social groups defined by ethnic, economic and political criteria have been involved in constant power struggles. The Romanian discourse of civilization, *civilizaţie*, is meaningful to all classes when referring to the relationship between groups in the Romanian ethnic hierarchy and about the ratio of power between them. This locally constituted discourse on civilization is thus to be understood as an expression of the civilizing process that constitutes both the village and the national figuration. These concepts will be discussed more thoroughly in the next chapter and later in this book.

The Nomadic Metaphor – Transition and Duality

This leads to the last theoretical point of this introduction: relations of power between the Rom hamlet and the peasant village as interdependent communities modelled by different but interdependent ideologies. I will argue for the metaphor of 'nomadism' to understand the relations between Roma and the state, represented by villagers and local power holders. Gilles Deleuze and Félix Guattari have developed what they call a 'nomadology' to understand the relations between 'stasis', represented by state formation, and 'movement', represented by a 'nomadic mode of existence' (Deleuze and Guattari, 1985). These ideas are based on relations between what are seen as the difference and interdependence of systems of power – the centralised, normative and standardised system of state power and modes of existence on the one hand and the 'un-rooted', flexible and decentralised power they see as inherent in what they term 'nomadism' on the other. They discuss the relation between these systems or principles, and claim that nomadism challenges the power of the state by its mere existence as it is not controlled or incorporated by state power and resists such incorporation. First, they claim nomadism to be based on a very different relation to space from sedentarism and state power. Nomads relate to places in terms of points or resting places on their paths; their mode is mobility. While the State territorialises space by dividing it into portions, distributes it and sets up lines of communication between territories thereby creating 'striated space', nomadic modes use the land as open, unstriated and infinite space. This represents the spatial uncontrollability of nomads. Second, in contrast to state power, the power structure of nomadism is not centralised or fixed but flexible, contested every time it tries to establish itself, always only a potential. The French sociologist Pierre Clastres's ideas about 'society against the state' (Clastres, 1977) are central to this argument. Third, they claim nomadism to be organised in a numerical way. This I take to denote an organisation that is based on solidarity groups that are linked together by kinship or other kin-like relations, that have no centre and no periphery, but that may be fused when necessary. In short, the argument is that nomadism as a mode of existence resists and even negates, ideologically and in practice, the standardisation, fixation and control of state power as a system while coexisting with it. The nomadic mode is exterior to the state mode and is not appropriated by it. It is in the exteriority to state power, say Deleuze and Guattari, that the nomadic mode is termed 'a war machine against the state'. Not by waging war, but because it is not appropriated and because it is in itself the opposition and thus inherent destruction of the state mode. Nomadic existence is thus a metaphor for different modes of social life 'outside' the state:

> The outside appears simultaneously in two directions: huge world wide machines branched out over the entire ecumenon at any given moment, which enjoy a large measure of autonomy in relation to the state (for example commercial organisations of the 'multinational' type, or industrial complexes, or even religious formations like Christianity, Islam, certain prophetic or messianic movements, etc.) but also the local mechanisms of bands, margins, minorities, that continue to affirm the rights of segmentary societies in opposition to the organs of State power (Deleuze and Guattari, 1985: 16).

Still they see 'nomadism' and 'state' as systems of power that are interdependent and coexisting and that transform into each other. The nomadic is transformed into state and vice versa, thus forming a continuous field of interaction and interdependence.

Deleuze and Guattari's perspective is highly suggestive, but also slippery and may be misinterpreted in terms of nomadism as representing ideologies of freedom, resistance and revolution, as a 'liberating' and thus good power. The state may thus be equated with repression, domination and enslavement, with 'law and order' in a bad sense only (Jameson, 2000). I do not wish to convey this rather normative stand, but emphasise what I see as the core of this philosophy: different systems of power as the condition for creative and dynamic interdependence, represented by the dualism of nomadism and the state (Østerberg, 2000).

Agency, Duality and Figuration

The notions of shifting selves and subject positions are basic to the understanding of agency in this book. I see agency as the outcome of people that self-reflexively and consciously strive to follow their interests and desires in compliance with and/or opposition to their social environment by taking up different subject positions offered them by different social practices and discourses (Ewing, 1997; Moore, 1994). I thus imply a strategic view of people, but this should not be misinterpreted as seeing humans as rational beings calculating risk and opportunity in an economic manner. Self-reflexivity and consciousness imply interest and desire, desire implying both the conscious and the subconscious, and 'shifting selves' implies the social as an inherent trait of self. Interest and desires are often contradictory, and even if I insist that people are reflexive and conscious and make choices, they cannot always foresee the outcome of their actions. Agency, strategy and consciousness are also structured by the inherent interdependence of social actors – what Elias calls social figurations (Elias, 2000). Forming societies together implies negotiating values, norms, rules and ideas to guide and evaluate social practice, which is 'part of the game'. Thus experiences of ambiguity, uncertainty and ambivalence are all aspects of agency, self-reflexivity and strategy that influence it and contribute to make the outcome of actions different from that anticipated. This perspective of agency implies what I have termed duality as the mutuality of seemingly opposed values. The theory of subject positioning and multiple selves supports, in my understanding, the idea of people relating to values and value systems that may appear contradictory in one context, but that in other contexts may be experienced and expressed as axes of a continuum. The idea expressed in Elias's term *'homines aperti'*, is of the person as 'open' in the sense that self and other are not clearly bounded and that the interdependence between social actors is a precondition for individuality and personhood (Mennell and Goudsblom, 1998b: 33; Elias 2001). The figurational approach to society thus denies in my view the construction of absolute boundaries and dichotomies between individuals and groups as between systems of knowledge, and opts for a view of persons as relations in process. The perspective of figuration based on ideas of interdependence and of the unbounded traits of social persons that stress process and flexibility as central to the formation of society is also, in my view, consistent with my basic idea of duality as the interdependence of bipolar, but not contradictory values, emotions and ideas. Duality in this sense is parallel to my understanding of Deleuze and Guattari's philosophy of difference, co-existence and interdependence as metaphorically represented by 'the nomad' and 'the state'.

Notes

1. See Romanes vocabulary.
2. More precisely 22,455,500 in 1999.
3. The lowest figures are from the official census in 1992 and rely on self-ascription as ţigani, while the highest are estimates made by the Gypsy Research Centre at the René Descartes University in Paris in 1994.
4. This information is from a historical overview made for me by a Romanian high school teacher and neighbour with knowledge of and interest in local history.

5. There were 3,017 people living in the village, about 2,200 being of Romanian nationality (this is the term used for the different categories), 730 Hungarian, 4 German, 20 Slovac, 55 Hebrew and no țigani. The language census shows, however, 5 țigani speaking villagers at that time (Recensamantul dîn 1930).

6 Several men are priests: *pasteuri* in the Rom Pentecostal church and travel abroad for religious meetings.

7 I see no scientific reason to contest the theory of the Gypsies' Indian origin. Romanes itself strongly supports this theory. The Indian origin is, however, socially relevant primarily to Gypsy scholars and ethnopoliticians. The emigration from India probably took place from the ninth century and onwards and any Indian cultural roots have undergone such transformations as to be quite uninteresting as such. The Roma I know see the alleged Indian origin as something quite exotic, amusing and/or disgusting. It is their actual social relations and their economic involvement in different nations in the world that constitute Gypsy identity and culture.

8. The book referred to is a discussion of Orthodoxy by Christos Yannaras, a Greek professor of Theologyand Philosophy at la Faculté des Lettres de Paris (Sorbonne) and the Faculty of Théology de Thessalonique. Personal communication with the village Orthodox priest, and villagers' own theological interpretations revealed that the devil plays a more important role for development of the soul and the idea of personal choice than is discussed by Yannaras.

Part I
The Rom World

Chapter 1
Roma in the Romanian Figuration

Introduction

The aim of this opening chapter is to highlight the significance of Roma as the social and ethnic category: *Gypsies* in the Romanian figuration. I will develop my argument by exploring the notion of 'civilizaţie' in the discourse of Romanianness and the theory and concept of civilization developed by the sociologist Norbert Elias (Elias, 2000). The Romanian concept of 'civilizaţie' is interpreted in different ways by different socio-economic groups and ethnic groups, but I suggest that a common denominator of the colloquial use is that it refers primarily to the behaviour of people in society and especially 'their outward bodily propriety', bodily carriage, gestures, dress, facial expressions – in short, outward behaviour as expressions of 'the inner self' (Elias, 2000: 49). Civilizaţie generally also contains ideas of technical progress and certain moral virtues such as work ethic, honesty and religious piety. The most significant feature of the meaning of civilizaţie is its inseparability from the Romanian idea of *naţie* both in the sense of ethnic group and that of nation-state.[1] The discourse of civilizaţie is common for all ethnic groups in Romania and its main focus is the gradation of different ethnic categories, naţie and nations in what is seen as a natural hierarchy (see also Berge, 1997). Thus the discourse of civilizaţie is a discourse of domination and hegemony portraying interesting aspects of the power relations of Romanian society. The hierarchy also applies to nationstates: Scandinavia and Germany are placed at the top of the civilization ladder and Turkey and the Arab countries at the bottom. It thus also mirrors the historical relations between two major empires, the Habsburg and the Ottoman, fighting for control over the area. The 'low' position of Romanians and Romania on the 'civilization ladder' points to the ambiguity of the concept, an ambiguity that is expressed quite explicitly by most Romanians, contrasting civilizaţie to 'inner' values and personality traits such as warmth, hospitality, vitality and cheerfulness. This ambiguity may be seen as a response to historical power relations in Romania where the ruling classes always have been made up of 'foreigners' to the Romanian-speaking peasantry. Thus civilizație has also been interpreted as an instrument of domination towards Romanian serfs by a foreign ruling 'nation'. The concept of civilizație thus reflects both the inferiority complex of the Romanians as naţie in relation to other naţie in and outside Romania, as well as the resistance to a civilizing process forced upon them by their former rulers. The Romanian idea of civilization reflects the general ambiguity towards both 'uncivilized ţigani' and 'civilized strangers'.

The Figurational Approach and the Civilizing Process

The Civilizing Process

Norbert Elias' (2000) suggests analysing social formations as figurations of more or less interdependent individuals and social groups. He used dance as an analogy describing how all dancers are interdependent for their movements and how the relationships between these interdependent actors are in constant change. He saw a dance floor as a social figuration analogous to larger figurations such as those we call societies. The dance floor is like other social figurations, relatively independent of the specific individuals performing their dance, but not of individuals as such. Social figurations in Elias's sense are to be seen as formations of interdependent actors that imply political, economic and psychological aspects. Thus a social figuration links long-term structural developments of societies with changes in people's socially constituted personality and their social behaviour that Elias termed 'habitus'. Elias saw emotions such as shame as socially constituted and linked to structures of society such as power relations. He thus emphasised the interdependence between changes in society and changes in the individual sentiments and moral habitus (Mennell, 1998a:15). Elias underlined that although interdependence is a trait of all social relations, a process of civilization increases this interdependence as it increases social complexity.

Elias claimed that the French concept of civilité, as the Western folk model of civilization and, I would add, the Romanian folk model of civilizație, are moral discourses and vehicles for the domination of one social group over others. In Elias's words: 'this concept expresses the self-consciousness of the West' (Mennell, 1998a: 5). Thus the discourse of civilization in the West is one of domination whereby incorporated classes, peoples and nations are positioned in relations of dependence and relative subordination towards a certain hegemonic class and/or nation. By studying the history of manners, etiquette and the social discourse on civilité, Elias suggested that the process of political incorporation and centralisation is dependent on a process of bodily control, increased physical discipline and general drive economy that enables the relatively peaceful coexistence and interchange of groups and individuals. His argument is that the increased interdependence between social groups demands and creates a certain feeling and experience of security that again demands restraint of individual gratification. In contrast to folk models, Elias's model of civilization does not imply an idea of inevitable progress (Mennell, 1998a). On the contrary, one of Elias's main points is that although violence is experienced to be controlled, it continues to play a decisive part even in the most civilized, peaceful societies, but as also Foucault (1976) and others have pointed out, it becomes more hidden. Elias refers to 'civilized conduct as an armour' (in Mennell, 1998a: 20) that would disappear, if for instance, the levels of insecurity in society were to rise to the levels of earlier times. Elias did not see the civilizing process as a lineal evolution but as the result of political and economic relations in social figurations that are constantly changing, so that processes of decivilization counteract processes of civilization. Wars and other social breakdowns are results of decivilizing processes that temporary change the relations between parties in social figurations (Elias, 2000).

Elias's theory of the civilizing process illuminates the central aspects of the idea of a 'civilization ladder' that structure the discourse on ethnicity, class and power in Romania. I am thus discussing civilization on two levels, one as a political process that influences individual habitus and identity, the other as a Romanian moral discourse of power and interethnic relations. The Romanian discourse on civilizaţie is thus treated as an instrument for the civilizing process in Elias's sense. I have no intention of trying to trace the historical process of Romanian civilization in any detail, but to use Elias's theory of the civilizing process and the notion of social figuration (Elias, 2000; Mennell, 1998b), together with the folk model of civilizaţie, to discuss the role of the ţigan for Romanian collective identity.

Aspects of Transylvanian History

Civilizing the 'Vlach'

The economic, political and psychological relationship between the naţie of Romania can not be understood without some insight into the history of this region. From the early feudal times, Transylvania had a relatively free position under the Ottoman Empire and came under Hungarian rule and later that of the Habsburg Empire in the late seventeenth century, while Wallachia and Moldovia were vassal states under the Ottoman Empire until the late nineteenth century. The ethnic, political and economic figuration of Transylvania was slightly different from that of Wallachia and Moldovia, but had many similarities (Achim, 2004). The peasant serfs, called Vlach were predominantly Romanian-speaking in both regions, and the ţigani were in both regions itinerant craftsmen, serfs and slaves. Until the late nineteenth century, then, the feudal states of Transylvania, Wallachia and Moldova were composed of interdependent but ethnically, culturally, politically and economically different categories of people. *Lord* was synonymous with *Hungarian, Saxon* or *Greek, peasant* and *serf* with *Vlach*, and *slave* or *artisan serf* with *ţigan*. A naţio was the nomination of a group associated with a territory, its members holding a particular legal status as citizens. Contrary to subjects, members of a naţio were considered noble (Verdery, 1983: 83).

The Catholic and Calvinist Magyar, the Szekler and the Lutheran Saxon made up the three naţie of Transylavania. Romanian-speaking people, although a numerical majority, were not considered a naţio and were thus not citizens. Vlachs and ţigani were positioned as social groups, not as 'nations', and social mobility meant ethnic assimilation. To acquire an education, a position and citizenship, wealthy Vlachs changed their 'nationality' and their religion and turned German or Magyar. This is parallel to how ţigani still become Romanian, Magyar or German to better their social position in society (Seim, 1998; Verdery, 1983).

From the eighteenth century the Hapsburg regents Maria Thereza and Josef II started a process of centralisation and homogenisation of the vast empire to strengthen, control and increase its tax revenues (Verdery, 1983). I will here only point to the civilizing strategies applied by the Habsburg Empire in terms of religious, linguistic and cultural cohesion in Transylvania, and to the resistance and compliance by the Romanians serfs.[2] According to Verdery (1983) the economic and political strategies for controlling Transylvania were primarily felt as an obstruction by the gentry, while the serfs in many instances experienced them as a protection against exploitation. When the serfs opposed the strategies for cultural integration it was primarily questions of religion. The Uniate Church, a hybrid of the Roman Catholic and Orthodox faiths, was introduced by the Habsburg Government to ease the transition to Catholicism, and represented a means for Vlachs and other non-nations to acquire certain privileges and possibilities to rise to noble status. Although this strategy had some success in the beginning, the serfs soon left and rejected the Uniate Church in great numbers supported by their Magyar masters who had no reason to rejoice in the transformation of Vlach serfs into nobles. This religious opposition was paired with an increased awareness among the Magyar nobles of the empire's effort towards the Germanisation of state bureaucracy. To counteract this effort, an emerging nationalist awareness among Magyar nobles developed, followed by strategies of Magyarisation of Transylvania that culminated in the revolution of 1848 and the proclamation of a Hungarian state including Transylvania in 1867. In this process 'naţio' was confirmed as a concept of group affiliation based on ethnicity and class, and this meaning was appropriated and kept by large also by the non-naţie populations of Transylvania (Verdery, 1983). Only Magyars would be part of the new nation that embraced a territory with almost 50 percent non-Magyar population. This again prompted a rising Romanian nationalism, based on the same logic of creating a nation of Romanians. The Uniate Church created by the Habsburg Empire as a state-building strategy was now becoming an important element in developing the Romanian nation. The clergy's access to higher education and their knowledge of Latin and History helped them develop the profound basis of Romanian national ideology – that of Roman ancestry. The idea of Roman ancestry later developed into theories of Dacian/Roman ancestry that provided Romanian nationalism with an imperial and noble past like that claimed by the Hungarians, but linking the Romanians to the West in opposition to the Hungarians (Verdery, 1983).

After Transylvania was united with Hungary in the established dual monarchy in 1867 and Hungarian was recognised as the only nation, an active programme of Magyarisation was implemented as a response to the rising national awareness of minorities (Georgescu, 1991, Verdery, 1983). A series of laws gradually replaced minority languages with Hungarian in educational institutions, and laws were implemented to repress all nationalist agitation and opposition. Not until the last decade of the dual monarchy reign in Transylvania did Romanians gain some political representation, but it was too late. The Romanian nationalist struggle in Transylvania did eventually lead to the unification of Transylvania with Romania after World War I, and only then did the Romanians of Transylvania become full citizens of their state (Verdery, 1983).

From Vlach to Romanian

After the incorporation of Transylvania in Romania after World War I and the implementation of the agrarian law,[3] all inhabitants of Romania became citizens with equal rights independent of their ethnic identity. In the interwar period, Romanians in great numbers were transformed from 'peasants to gentlemen' (Verdery 1983: 273). Not only was much of the land transferred from Magyars and Germans to Romanians, but higher education was a possibility for the children of former Vlach serfs, and they suddenly represented the political majority of Great Romania. A Romanian middle class was beginning to develop beside the minorities that had constituted it. Both Magyars and Germans suffered losses both in ownership and in political influence. Hungarians, Greeks, Saxons and other former rulers left the region in great numbers, and those who remained had lost many of their possessions and their political power. These changes were most prominent for Transylvania, but in Wallachia and Moldovia the middle and upper classes had long been dominated by Greek- and Turkish-speaking minorities (Verdery, 1983). The economic dependence of the power-holders as well as the peasants on ţigani craftsmanship and slave labour decreased steadily towards the twentieth century. Industrialisation and the emerging class of Romanian artisans made many of the ţigani's services unwanted all over Romania, but in spite of this ţigani as such did not disappear but their economic niches changed. Although the abolishment of slavery and serfdom and several civilizing and settlement campaigns helped to increase the number of ţigani assimilated into the Romanian and Hungarian population in the twentieth century, the number of ţigani in Romania did not seem to decrease significantly (Achim, 2004).

The golden age of Romanian nationalism, from the mid-nineteenth century to the 1970s was focused on the symbolic battle between Hungary and Romania over the birthright to Transylvania. This issue became a cause for the whole nation to prove the historical roots of Romanian civilization. The civilization ladder, a legacy from the feudal times, must have been confirmed in this period. Different versions of a theory of Roman/Dacian ancestry developed during the past centuries was to form the basis of the ideology of the new nation (Verdery, 1991). According to these theories Romanians are descendants of an amalgamation of the remnants of the Roman Emperor Trajan's soldiers, who conquered an indigenous Dacian empire in the second century B.C., and the defeated Dacian population. The Daco-Roman inheritance positioned the earlier Vlach serfs as descendants of powerful ancient civilisations; it rooted Romanian collective identity in the Western civilization and what was to be seen as an indigenous Dacian civilization (Verdery, 1991: 31–34). The oscillation between these two 'civilizations' for the formation of Romanian national ideology and identity has been a constant trait of the elite's nationalist rhetoric in Romania ever since (Verdery, 1991).[4] The Romanian discourse on civilization is thus an expression of what Norbert Elias discussd as the German attitude towards what he terms the antithesis between *'Kultur und Zivilisation'* (2000).[5] The nationalist rhetoric of this period created the Romanian peasant as the sturdy survival of centuries of exploitation by foreigners. The exploration of 'the national essence' and some inherent 'spiritual Romanianness' was a concern in this nationalist period and was by many thought to be found in the peasantry, the villages thus being idealised space for authentic Romanianness (Verdery, 1991: 29). Romania and the Romanian people were portrayed by scholars and artists as continuous victims of exploitation by foreigners,[6] a well known theme in other East European countries (van de Port, 1998: 123). This national discourse was expressed locally by villagers telling us how Romania had paid the price of poverty and thus a low level of civilizaţie for protecting Western Europe, first from the Ottoman empire and then from communism.

The cultivation of the 'peasants into gentlemen' (Verdery, 1983: 273) in this period was by means of education and refinement of language and manners defined by the Hungarian and German noble classes, but also probably inspired by the French ideas of civilité. Many Romanian intellectuals had been educated abroad in France and Italy, and French and Italian culture was an inspiration in the development of Romanian nationalism (Achim, 2004: 85). I suggest that this aspect of the process of civilization in this period constituted an amalgamation of values from the old ruling classes and the new ideology of the idealised Romanian peasantry. In Elias's words:

> Here we come upon one of the most remarkable characteristics of the civilizing process: the people of the rising class develop within themselves a 'super-ego' modelled on the superior, colonizing upper class. But on a closer inspection this super-ego is in many respects very different from its model. It is less balanced and therefore often much more severe. It always reveals the immense effort which individual social advancement requires; and it shows equally the constant threat from below as from above, the crossfire from all sides to which individuals are exposed in their social rise (Elias, 2000: 431).

This ambiguity is clearly represented in the discourse of indigenous Romanianness and civilizaţie. The role of the foreigner in this national discourse is quite significant (Verdery, 1983; Verdery 1991). Prominent representatives of the Romanian elite claimed that Romanianness should be developed by rejecting all foreign influence and by cultivating the inherent virtues of Romanians expressed by the simple people who had cultivated the land and protected the culture from the foreign rulers. Others opted for an amalgamation of inherent Romanian virtues and Western influence in the development of the Romanian nation. The double bind relationship between the former serfs and their rulers is, however, expressed by the morally significant notion of civilizaţie as an inescapable, hegemonic model for social mobility. The Hungarians – although a threat to the Romanian state – were placed towards the top of the ladder of civilizaţie.

In this national rhetoric it was foremost the Jews who were seen as enemies of the new Romania: they have historically represented foreignness, money and modernity, all threats to the new nation (Verdery, 1996: 99). At the same time the social distance from the non-civilized ţigani increased. As the majority of village ţigani, who still performed their old and new services, did not participate in this transformation, I suggest that they were not regarded as a threat to Romanian nationalism in the same way as the Jews.

Omul Nou – the New Romanian

After the Second World War and the establishment of the socialist government in Romania, the figuration changed rapidly once again. After the first, unsteady years, Ceaușescu confirmed his power, and new strategies were developed to transform the population. There was no longer talk about different nations in Romania; the only nation was represented by the state and was Romanian. The development of the new Romanian citizen: *Omul nou*, based on Marxist ideology, was one of the aims of the Ceaușescu regime. The new person was expressed as 'a multilaterally developed human (omul multilateral dezvoltat)' (Naterstad, 1996: 71, my translation). This idea implies the combination of artistic and practical skills as necessary for human development. 'Omul nou should preferably be a doctor, a farmer and a musician at the same time' (Naterstad, 1996; 71, my translation) and artists of all crafts were employed by the government to develop this new personality (Verdery, 1991: 155). Culture, and specially the development of folk culture, was to spread the socialist gospel and increase the economic development of Romania. Peasants and workers were the heroes of the new nation who were to change Romania under the leadership of the Party and Ceaușescu. Patriotic poetry and literature together with the support of Romanian traditional culture were expected to transform the inherently foreign Communist Party into an indigenous part of the nation in Romanian consciousness (Naterstad, 1996).

Țigani and other minorities were in the first few years offered special possibilities and positions in the new government, not as ethnic minorities, but because they were seen as the poorest segment of the population (Achim, 2004). Hungarians and Saxons, for their part, lost more of their old privileges, such as education in their own language. As in the nationalist period between the wars, the idea of the new person was apparently moulded on a combination of peasant virtues and the ideal of a civilized person: a Magyar or Saxon. Art, music and poetry that praised the nobleness of the Romanian nation and higher education were all means to achieve the developed person, while the industrious peasant, representing the essential indigenous Romanian, was the basis of this development. Evolutionary ideas, expressed as 'the staircase of history and civilization' and the rejection of everything reminding of the old days in favour of spiritual and technological progress were all traits of this ideological campaign that was to transform Romania into a modern socialist state (Naterstad, 1996: 129). The țigan position in this process seems to have been confirmed more and more as the negation of the 'new person', and as reminiscence of the exploited past. Dressed in their traditional clothes modelled on seventeenth century peasant costumes, living in houses of dried earth and even in hovels, mostly illiterate, many still travelling the countryside with their wagons and horses, they must have expressed everything the socialist government did not want. The last effort at assimilation was carried out in the 1960s and up to the late 1970s, when it was estimated that 65,000 țigani were still nomadic or seminomadic (Achim, 2004: 191). Forced settlement and forced labour changed the life of most of Romanian țigani in these years, but still the bulk of them did not become Romanian – neither in the eyes of the peasants nor to themselves. Towards the end of socialist rule in Romania, țigani made up a greater part of the population than in many previous periods; although the majority seemed to be settled, they were not yet 'civilized' (Achim, 2004).

Even though țigani probably constitute the second largest minority in Romania, they have generally been omitted from the romantic public celebrations of Romania as a nation of 'coinhabiting nationalities' (Beck, 1986). To most foreign observers, such as human rights organisations, the Gypsies' alleged marginality and cultural, economic and political insignificance is explained by their stigmatised position, thus strengthening the idea of their insignificance for the understanding of Romanian society in public discourse. My argument here is that the different social groups of Romania constitute a specific ethnic figuration that is crucial for the understanding of power relations and ethnic identity in the region, and that țigani hold a significant position in the Romanian figuration and in the collective identity of Romanians as ambiguous and stigmatised 'others'.

The Țigani in the History of the Romanians

The people without history, in Wolf's sense (Wolf, 1982), are the peoples incorporated into a hegemonic historiography so as to render them invisible as separate categories with a political impact. The Romanian țigani are people without history in this sense. Nowhere in Romanian historiography do they appear as Roma, thus contributing to the formation of the past and present Romanian figuration. If they appear at all in Romanian historiography, they do so as slaves, serfs and țigani. Serfs play a part in Romanian historiography, as the Romanian peasantry, but slaves do not. The țigani have not historically been considered an ethnic category in line with Romanians, Jews, Saxons, Hungarians or Turks. The immigration of the țigan population into the Balkans has, however, been an issue of some interest in Romanian historiography in certain periods. The Romanian historian Viorel Achim is the only scholar to present a comprehensive reconstruction of the ţigan past from their probable immigration to the northern parts of the Danube until the present. The following account rests almost entirely on his book: *The Roma in Romanian History* (Achim, 2004). In compliance with the English translation, I will here use the term Gypsies instead of the term ţigani.

The First Appearance of Gypsies in Romania

The emigration of peoples, later called Ţigani in Romania,[7] from India towards Europe is estimated to cover the period from the ninth century to the fourteenth century. The advent of the Gypsies into the Byzantine Empire is generally connected to the raids of the Turkish warriors in Armenia in the middle of the eleventh century. From their probable arrival in Trachea that marks their entry in European history, they spread at the beginning of the fourteenth century in all directions.[8] The greatest part of the Gypsy population remained in the Turk- and Hungarian-dominated territories of Moldavia, Wallachia and Transylvania, where the percentage of Gypsies in the majority population has been the greatest in the world up to the present time. Accounts of Gypsies are first documented in connection with donations between local princes and monasteries; these donations become more and more frequent, and in the fourteenth century most of the monasteries and great feudal lords (*boieri*) owned Gypsy slaves.

Slavery was a part of the social system in the Ottoman Empire and in the Romanian principalities. Tigani soon 'monopolised' this institution, and from the second half of the fifteenth century they were the only slaves in the territory. The term *ţigan* became synonymous with the term *slave*; *rob* in colloquial Romanian. Gypsy slavery played an important role in the economy of medieval Romania due to their skills as artisans, most prominently blacksmiths, and due to other socio-economic developments in that time (Achim, 2004: 15–34; Beck, 1989).

Legal Status of Slaves in the Romanian and Moldovian Principalities

Although the Gypsies were not a homogenous population, they made up a large and distinct ethnic category apart from the majority population in the Romanian territory. This category was divided into groups specialised in different tasks, with different cultural traits and speaking to a certain degree different dialects of Romanes. Their occupation and way of life were the basic criteria of classification. There have always been sedentary Gypsies living on the properties of their owners as well as nomadic Gypsies who roamed the countryside, and all of them were slaves. The serfs in the Romanian principality were Romanian, and they were not free in the modern sense of the word as they were dependants of their feudal lords. Achim underlines that it was the lack of juridical rights that defined the position of slaves – they were not legal subjects, – rather than their lack of personal freedom. Slaves were part of their owners' general, moveable property that he could dispose of as he liked, put to whatever service he wished, that he could sell, give away, exchange for other items and use as payment for debts (Achim, 2004: 35).

Marriage between serfs and slaves was either prohibited or such mixed marriages turned the serf spouse and the offspring into slaves thus increasing the property of the owner. In 1766, a law was passed that banned the separation of slave children from their parents by sale or by similar means. Achim notes that this was the first sign of a change in the general public view on slavery and Gypsies. Slaves could, however, also be given freedom by their masters and thus become Romanians, a practice that was a widespread in the last period of slavery in Romania (Achim, 2004: 34–65).

Royal Serfs in Transylvania

Transylvania was an autonomous principality under Hungarian rule from the mid- sixteenth century until the late seventeenth century when it was merged with the Hapsburg Empire. From their appearance in this territory in the late fourteenth century, the Gypsies were appropriated as 'royal serfs'. They formed one of several ethnic categories in Transylvania and made up a much higher percentage of the population than in the rest of the Hungarian Empire. As their conditions as serfs in Transylvania were generally better that that of a slave in the principalities, there was a constant migration of Gypsies into Transylvania and to the rest of Hungary. They depended directly on the king who gave the different groups permission to travel around the country, and the only obligations they had were towards the crown. The Gypsies could attach themselves to a certain landowner with the permission of the king. Apart from being directly dependent on the crown, they could not be judged by the local legal system but were legally under the exclusive jurisdiction of their own leaders, called *voivod* or *bulibaša*. Theoretically, Achim notes, the administrative authorities had no authority over Gypsies. The freedom to roam the country or to settle on crown property, the internal autonomy of the Gypsy groups, their obligations towards the state (very few in comparison with the peasant population), their exemption from military service, and the tolerance of the authorities concerning the non-Christian faith of most Gypsies, were all privileges that set them against the Romanian peasantry they lived among. After the Ottoman occupation of Buda in 1541 and the end of Hungarian reign, a special administrative system was set up to regulate the relations between the state and the

Gypsy serfs. Every Gypsy serf was to pay tax, collected by the appointed leader, to the local state administration (half of the peasants' amount). The process of linguistic and cultural assimilation into the Romanian-speaking serf population was a general trait of Gypsies who settled down in villages in this time, but much less among those that settled down in cities. Although sedentarisation and assimilation into the peasant serf segment of the population was significant, a large number of the Gypsies continued their nomadic life (Achim, 2004: 42–46).

Socio-economic Relations

The Gypsy slaves and serfs played important roles in the economy of the principalities and that of Transylvania from the fifteenth century. Achim refers to a foreign traveller who attributed the profession of blacksmiths to Gypsies, and notes that: 'Slaves working as blacksmiths were indispensable to any feudal economy and they existed in large numbers' (Achim, 2004: 46, 47). Achim notes that in 1756 all mechanical tasks in a certain area were in the hands of Gypsies and other 'strangers'. Apart from being blacksmiths, locksmiths, weapon- and tool-smiths, and horseshoe-smiths, they were also bricklayers, wood carvers, musicians, bear trainers, cooks etc. Some slaves worked in workshops at the princely court, others worked on the estates of their owners or in the cities, and still others had their own workshops (Achim, 2004: 47). The major part of all categories of slaves was, however, nomadic. They followed certain paths, settled down on the outskirts of villages and cities offering their services and selling their products, usually for money, for a period before travelling on. Some settled permanently and served the village or area. All iron tools used in agriculture and in the household were crafted by Gypsies.

Nomadic Gypsy slaves were organised in extended family groups. Achim notes that agriculture performed by Romanian resident peasants and serfs, and crafts performed by nomadic Gypsy slaves, were perceived as antagonistic activities and ways of life. But he underlines that nomadism – although in opposition to residency – was not seen as destructive, and there was never a real conflict between the two modes. Nomadism was regulated, limited and controlled; nomads travelled the same routes during summer serving their owner's territory, and lived on his land during winter. In contrast to most of Europe, where nomadism was forbidden, it was tolerated or even encouraged in the principalities and in Transylvania for certain strata of the population: the Gypsies. Achim notes that the Gypsies held the lowest social position in feudal society and were considered to be outside society (Achim, 2004: 55).

From the sixteenth century the social distance between Romanian serfs and Gypsy slaves in the principalities did, however, decrease. Serfs could not move or travel without the consent of their owner, they were increasingly burdened and tied to the soil and children were even sold separately from their parents, like slaves (Achim, 2004: 42–65).

Forced Sedentarisation and Assimilation

In the late eighteenth century the Habsburg Empress Maria Theresa issued three decrees about the sedentarisation of Gypsies in the kingdom of Hungary including Transylvania and the Banat. This was the first systematised policy of sedentarisation of Gypsies. In 1783 her son the Emperor Josef II issued a special decree concerning the Gypsies of Transylvania, the '*De Regulatione Zingarorum*', that regulated their conditions down to the last detail. Among other things it was prohibited for Gypsies to live in tents. They lost their traditional internal autonomy. Children were to be separated from their parents and raised by peasants. Nomadism was forbidden and Gypsies were not allowed to keep horses for sale, only for agricultural use. All aspects of their lives where to be regulated and cleansed of Gypsy traits. Issued by the Hapsburg emperors, these regulations mark the first consistent policy towards Gypsies in Transylvania. Achim notes that the aims of these regulations were not reached, however, due to lack of interest from the local government, the great regional differences and the fact that the population was not ready to accept Gypsies as ordinary citizens (Achim, 2004: 69–79).

Abolishment of Slavery and Feudalism

The social and economic modernisation of the Romanian society (Wallachia and Moldavia) began in the mid nineteenth century, but the institution of slavery, like that of serfdom, did not change with a new constitution in 1831. The institution was, on the contrary, confirmed by establishing the slave's fiscal obligations and launching a policy of sedentarisation. Gypsies thus entered the capitalist economy as commodities that were turned into profitable capital and advertised for sale in the big newspapers. This was the prime move towards the increased sedentarisation and changes in the Gypsies population. Only in the late nineteenth century did ideas of abolishment take root in Romanian society, with intellectuals educated in Western countries contributing to this new awareness. In 1856 the final law was passed that emancipated all slaves in the principalities. Through these legal processes Achim estimates that about 250.000 people were liberated from slavery and given citizenship (Achim, 2004: 112).

All emancipated slaves were to be given land by their former owner and were to settle on their land, but many resisted as the conditions of serfs often put them in a worse position than earlier, as they had to pay more tax and they lost their internal political autonomy. The policy of forced settlement was strengthened, and troublesome Gypsy communities were dispersed among Romanian villages. This period saw the greatest assimilation of Gypsies into the Romanian population and society.

Achim notes that the emancipation of slaves and serfs had another important effect: that of mass emigration of Gypsies westwards in search of better economic and social opportunities. This has been termed The Second Great Migration of the Gypsies and led to the spread of this population to all parts of the world (Achim, 2004: 120). These Gypsies, often referred to as Romanian Gypsies or Vlach in their new countries, called themselves Roma. They belonged mainly to the *Lovara* (horse dealers), *Kelderara* (coppersmiths) and *Čurara* (sieve makers) groups. They had different linguistic, cultural and organisational features from the local Gypsy populations in Europe that had migrated in the Middle Ages. Culturally and linguistically influenced by living for centuries with Romanians, the newcomers formed a distinct, new Gypsy population that is now to be found in all European countries, on the American continent, in Australia and beyond. As Roma they make up the single largest cultural and linguistic category of Gypsies today (and probably the single largest minority).

In Transylvania, Achim states, a great majority of the Gypsy population had become sedentary in the nineteenth century and had settled down among Romanians, Magyars, Szekeler and Saxons. A census from 1893 shows that in Transylvania 105,034 persons, that is 4.67 percent of the population, declared themselves Gypsies. Only about 40 percent of these declared that Romanes was their mother tongue, 39 percent spoke Romanian, 19 percent Hungarian and 0.2 percent German (Achim, 2004: 136). Apparently the nomadic Gypsies were reduced to a minority. But even if one may question how reliable these figures are, they illustrate that the Gypsies of Transylvania have kept their linguistic and ethnic traits to a much larger extent than in Hungary. Figures from this census show that while almost half of the Gypsy population lived separately from the rest of the Transylvania population in their own neighbourhoods, about 40 percent lived in mixed settlements alongside other villagers (Achim, 2004: 135). This demographic situation may explain the relatively high percentage of Romanes-speaking Gypsies in Transylvania, together with the very conscious creation of ethnic differences by all ethnic groups, differences that were strengthened in the nationalistic century to come (Achim, 2004: 87–127).

The Interwar Period

By the peace treaty in 1918, Transylvania (Bucovina and Bessarabia) with the principalities became the modern Romania and Gypsies in all the former principalities became citizens of Great Romania (Achim, 2004: 145). In the interwar period the Gypsies lost their monopoly over rural crafts due to industrialisation and the education of Romanian craftsmen. Achim states further that in public opinion among Romanians in general, the Gypsy population was expected to become completely assimilated in a short time (Achim, 2004: 151).

The 1930s also saw some of the early attempts of ethnic organisation of Gypsies in Romania[10] much as a result of the coming of a new elite of educated people, of artists and successful businessmen of Gypsy origin. Several organisations were formed and the first congress was held the same year where Gypsies from all over the country participated. Achim notes that the achievement of this movement was modest – they were mostly one-man organisations – but that it succeeded in drawing public attention to the social problems of the Gypsies (Achim, 2004: 146–162).

Scientific Racism and Deportation

Achim claims that there was never a 'Gypsy problem' in Romania after the emancipation in the way that there was a 'Jewish problem': Gypsies were regarded as marginal social groups rather than as an ethnic minority. This changed, however, with the rising 'scientific' interest in race theory of that time. Romanian representatives of biopolitics labelled Gypsies 'an inferior ethnic group' associated with Jews and warned the authorities of the danger of ethnic assimilation as 'a bioethnic danger, a "plague" to the Romanian society, etc.' (Achim, 2004: 163–64). Based on these ideas the new state policy under general Antonescu, towards Jews and Gypsies was formed. The most significant measure of this policy was the deportation of Gypsies and Jews as 'colonisers' to the province of Transnistria, a territory between Bug and the Dnjestr river, then part of the Soviet Ukraine, occupied by the Germans and Romanians in 1941. Over the next two years, from June 1942 to autumn 1944, Achim claims that 25,000 Gypsies were deported.[11] Once in Transnistria they were more or less left to themselves, and about half of the deported died during the three-year period until Romania was liberated by Russia in 1944 and the deported were evacuated (Achim, 2004: 163–88).

Gypsies in the Communist Era and the Present Day

Achim notes that it is difficult to reconstruct the history of the Gypsies in the communist period, as state policy that was developed towards the

Gypsies after the Second World War has not been made public (Achim, 2004: 189). Not until the mid-1970s did the authorities concern themselves with the Gypsies, and there was no specific minority policy towards them. In the first decades of the communist period, Gypsies in large numbers were, however, engaged in the party apparatus, in the army, the militia and the security organisations – a new phenomenon in Romania. Gypsies without land or with little land were among the first to enrol in the collective farms, and as the new regime favoured the rise of the poor, many Gypsies profited from this policy and even reached superior ranks in the party organisation (Achim, 2004: 190). Housing, health and education were also improved for Gypsies during this period, but there were also negative developments. Their old skills as blacksmiths were not in demand anymore and large parts of the Gypsy population had to adapt to modern occupations. Those that did not make this transformation joined the lot of the urban poor or lived on the on the outskirts of villages and towns, surviving on the marginal resources they could find as they always had. From the early 1960s, the authorities appointed fixed settlements for nomadic Gypsies, but the result was not as anticipated. Many accepted their houses but continued to live in their tents in the yard and used the house as a stall for their horses. As soon as summer approached, they continued to travel around the country, performing their crafts or business. Achim argues that despite some material improvements the most significant change during communism was the polarisation of the Gypsy population. While a minority profited from the policies for social improvement, the bulk remained at or were demoted to the bottom rung of the social ladder (Achim, 2004: 197). In 1977 the number of people still living as nomads was estimated at 65,000 (Achim, 2004: 189–203).

Hamlet Roma in the Romanian Figuration

The hamlet Roma discussed in this book are examples of Roma that did not assimilate, but were forced or chose to settle down in the late 1950s. Their own stories indicate that their forefathers travelled in these areas during summer as artisans, petty traders and beggars and settled down in hovels in the outskirts of the villages during winter. They have more or less perpetuated the economic practices, political organisation and cultural traits of their forefathers now on a sedentary basis in close interaction with Romanian and Hungarian villagers. They constitute one local expression of the ethnic relationships that constitute the Romanian figuration.

Notes

1. On the development of the concept of 'naţio' in Romania, see Verdery (1983).
2. For a discussion of these processes see Verdery 1983, part 2.
3. This land reform, implemented from about 1921, changed the power structure of Romanian society. In Transylvania it meant distributing the former Hungarian gentry's land among their former Romanian serfs. According to Verdery (1983) this was the most radical land reform in Eastern Europe and no doubt partly a response to the peasant uprising in 1907.
4. See Verdery (199???) Part 1 chapter 1 for an interesting account of the Daco/Roman discourse in Romania.
5. See also Susan Gal (1991) about national rhetoric in Hungary.
6. See, for instance, the national poet Mihai Eminescu (1999) for an interesting sample.
7. *Gypsies, Tsiganes, sigøynere, Gitanos*, etc. in other countries.
8. They probably spread in three main directions: towards the south, through the Greek continent and the Ionic islands; towards the west, into Hungary and later to central Europe; and towards the north, over the Danube and into Ţăra Românească (Wallachia and Moldova). The great flux from these regions towards Europe did not happen until the mid- nineteenth century when slavery and serfdom were abolished (Achim, 2004).
9. Achim notes that *ţigani* in certain periods and districts in Transylvania were slaves in this period.
10. David Crowe and John Kolsti (1991; 52–61) point to a conference in Kisfalu in Hungary where political and civil rights for Gypsies were discussed as an early inspiration to ethnic self-awareness in the region.

Chapter 2

Cultivating and Harvesting
Social Environment

Introduction

With Joska and Kurva

It is six o'clock in the morning and the bulibaša household is starting the new day, as are all the thirty-two households in the Rom hamlet.[1] *Bulibaša* is the Slavic term for a Rom headman, but it is as Joska, the male head of the household, that I will introduce him in this chapter. Joska and Kurva his wife, *Romni*,[2] are the first to get up in the morning while the rest of the household still are asleep in the main room of the house. There are three big beds in the room, a stove where the household's meals are prepared, and a small table for the TV set. Joska and Kurva sleep in one bed with their youngest son of five years and other children who will creep up into the bed during the night. In the next bed sleep their four unmarried sons aged from seven to fourteen years. The third bed is usually for the two unmarried daughters and one grandson of five years who lives with his grandparents. This 'girls' bed' is also used by the household's married daughters when they are visiting. The house has three rooms and a hall where food, clothes and other items are stored. Only two of these rooms have a stove, and the household's oldest married son, Teddi, and his wife Violetta, the *bori* (daughter-in-law),[3] sleep in the other with their two children. The third room has no stove and is mostly used for storage in the cold season. It will soon be prepared for the next bori, the eldest unmarried son's wife-to-be. Joska and Kurva have three more daughters who are not part of this family household. Mariora, the eldest, is married to the son of Joska's cousin in town, Claudia is married to her cousin (Joska's brother's son) in the hamlet and lives two huts away, and Kasablanka is living with a young man in his parents' household in the hamlet. All the rooms in the house are decorated with the traditional

Romanian carpets with religious motifs or nature scenes and with peasant finery decorated with embroidered shawls.[4] Different types of religious pictures, together with photographs of more or less undressed pin-ups cut out of magazines and other 'pretty pictures' (*ikona*),[5] adorn the walls.

During the winter Kurva will start making a fire and possibly leave the sleeping children alone or with Joska and visit other households of the *familia* (extended family). In summer the Roma from different households will meet in the space between the houses or on the open pastures and chat until the daily chores split them up. Just as the sun comes up, the grazing horses that seek shelter between the houses at night come drifting towards the open slopes around the Rom hamlet.

Meanwhile the young bori Violetta is preparing herself and her baby for the train journey into town to collect from the dustbins bread to feed the family pigs and items to barter in the village. She is often accompanied by Maria, the eldest daughter in the household, while the youngest girl, Dana, is still sleeping. Violetta dresses the baby, ties a small feather quilt (*duna*), tight around his body and secures it with a red ribbon;[6] swaddling babies is a common practice in Romania. Then she puts the 'parcel' in a big flowered headscarf that she carries across her chest as a sling. Another big piece of dirty cloth or an old headscarf is brought to carry what is gathered from the gutter. She arranges her own hair in two braids with red ribbons, ties them together at her neck, puts on her flowered headscarf and is ready.

From April to October the household is engaged as herders of the cattle of the neighbouring village. This work is mainly carried out by the males of the household, with Joska as the person in charge, Teddi as the main actual herder, and the four younger boys as assistants. So by half past seven Joska or Teddi walk over to lead the cattle to the pastures. As the young boys, Pepe, Joska jr. and Milionaru wake up, they take turns herding the cattle, and Teddi and/or Joska come back to the hamlet. Then the small ones, Titi, Josef and Lalo dress and feed themselves on a loaf of bread or the cold soup from yesterday. The boys who are not herding chop up the firewood or fetch dry branches from the woods for storage. Dana, the girl still at home, walks to the nearby stream for drinking water. Then she sweeps the floors and arranges the beds. She, the boys or Joska gives the pigs water and lets them out to feed on the pastures.

In wintertime, providing firewood for heating and cooking is the main occupation of the males of the household as for all other males in the hamlet. The young girls and women often help the men and boys by gathering dry branches in the woods. Kurva, as a grandmother in her mid-forties and as the household's female head, does not engage in this work. Neither does Kurva go scavenging in town. Her main tasks are cooking, looking after the household's smallest children and her other grandchildren and bartering; *te phires* or *te xoxaves le gažen* (lit.: to go walking or to cheat the non-Roma), expressions used for begging and bartering in the village. Kurva, like most married women in the hamlet, has exchange relations with many villagers in the area. In summer she collects the daily food payment for herding cattle[7] and she visits her regular villagers. She might have something to sell, or exchange or she may receive food etc. in exchange for promises for the future. Almost every day Kurva and Joska walk together to the village to buy food, take a drink at a bar, to call on some villager etc. They usually also walk home from the village together, Joska carrying the groceries.

When Kurva and Joska visit the villagers where they are engaged as herders to collect their weekly payment of food; they are let into the kitchen of the house and are often served food or a drink. Contrary to the hamlet where there are no gates or fences between houses, every house in the village is entered from the street through a tall iron gate. This gate is kept locked and usually guarded by a dog. Inside this gate is an open courtyard with walls on all sides, as every house is built onto the next. The kitchen is the daily 'reception room' that is entered directly from the court. Joska points out that most Roma are only let in to the courtyard and are seldom offered anything to eat by villagers. He emphasises that he is respected in the village and is considered more civilized and trustworthy than other Roma. 'You see, people in our family are clean and we do not steal', Kurva adds as an explanation. Kurva and Joska generally spend much time together. Kurva often joins Joska when he is herding to keep him company or just because they seem to like being together.

As soon as they come back from the village it is time to prepare the daily meal. When there is plenty, for example when the allocation money has just come, the clothes from the relief organisation have been sold,[8] when there are plenty of mushrooms in the woods and a good price for them, or when Joska or Teddi have made a profitable bargain, Kurva will prepare two main meals a day. Like the villagers, the Roma do not consider themselves satisfied without a soup first and a second dish of meat with bread. When food is really scarce, usually in March and April, a potato soup with some cabbage and bread and perhaps a bit of lard is the daily ration. Every day is a new day when it comes to food; the produce from the gardens is pickled and stored, but only lasts for a few months. The rest of the year the food to be consumed by the household is daily bartered, begged or bought if there is money. Whatever Kurva has at her disposal, she has to prepare for her own household of fifteen persons, and there should always be enough to serve any guest or family member that turns up at the meals. If her daughter Claudia is in town and her children are not fed by their father, Kurva will feed them as well. This holds for any family member outside the household, especially small children. One chicken feeds seventeen persons when prepared in a soup with potatoes, noodles and cabbage.

Meanwhile, Violetta and Maria have caught the train to town. From every household in the hamlet some women go to town every day. In wintertime the women will make a fire at the station while waiting for the train. Romanians spread all over the station while the *Romnja* (pl. of Romni) are gathered in one corner around a fire or around the station bar. The children run around playing, fighting and laughing and the whole group is extremely colourful, noisy and from many Romanians' point of view also irritating. Some villagers smile and even laugh at the noise and the unconventional dress[9] of many Rom children, but villagers and Roma usually leave each other in peace. When the train arrives most of the Roma hurry to the last wagon while the villagers spread all over the train. The last wagons are by some silent agreement left for the Romnja and their children with exception of ignorant travellers from other places. Rom men usually sit among other passengers. After a while the ticket collector appears and a daily 'mocking relationship' is staged. He asks for tickets. The Romnja laugh and say their husbands have them, or their sisters, mothers etc., in other parts of the train. The ticket collector then says in a tired sort of way that they cannot travel without a ticket and that he will have to throw them off the train at the next station. They all scream or laugh and say they are all pregnant or have newborn babies and he cannot be that cruel. Usually he just laughs or sighs and withdraws; he knows them and does not really care. Often this performance is for us 'the foreigners', and as we signal that we do not care whether they have tickets or not, we all laugh together. Sometimes, however, there are police officers from other districts checking tickets, and passengers without tickets have to leave. The Romnja scream and laugh as they are thrown off the train accompanied by streams of dirty language in Romanes. They may have to walk to town that day or walk back to the village. This drama or comedy is repeated every day with different ticket collectors who are either considered 'a devil' or 'nice' (*beng vai lašo*). Scenes like this one function as a public circus enjoyed by some passengers while others are annoyed. One thing is certain – in spite of the chance of being thrown off the train, very few Romnja buy a train ticket when they go scavenging.

The train runs past villages all the way to town, but only at some stations do other Roma enter. These are mostly women with children and gathering bags like the ones from the hamlet and they are all relatives, friends or enemies. Together they form a large band of women and children flowing into town every morning. The women and children spend about 6–8 hours in town. How often they go depends on the household's available women and the number of pigs they raise. In most households all women – young and old – go scavenging in town. In others the household heads stay at home while the younger women go. Some women and many of the children beg in the streets after they have finished searching the containers. The girls usually sit somewhere near their mothers or sisters, while the boys roam the town on their own. Many make small posters with the text 'No mother, no father, please help', others find small jobs in shops, wash car windows or steal. But the women also have time for pleasure, walking in small groups through town looking at people, sometimes shopping at the market and even taking a coffee or a drink in a bar.

Five Romnja in the hamlet go to town almost every day, not as scavengers, but 'to steal', as some of them bluntly express. They go to bars and restaurants in the suburbs and meet 'men that need women'. Laughing they tell me that they promise the men sex, talk softly to them, sit with them and drink with them. When the men are completely drunk they steal their money. These women usually do not mix with the scavengers as they say they smell too bad.

Back in the hamlet Kurva and Dana have prepared the first meal and everybody gets a plate as long as there are plates available. The children eat from the grown-ups' plates or are given a plate to share. Regardless of how many are present and how little there is, everyone will be offered food. The meals are seldom fixed, and every household member eats as he/she comes in. The boys and girls are expected to go to the pastures with food for the herders. Any child of the household and every child belonging to the familia may be asked to perform this or any other task. If one child refuses, another is asked, and usually someone agrees to go in the end. When no child volunteers, Kurva will explode in fury; 'Go eat The Lord's prick, let the cancer eat your knuckles in the hospital (*Te xas le devlesko kar! Te xal tu o kanšero če kokola ando kurhauso!*)'. If this does not work, Joska may offer some reward such as money or sweets.

After the meal the dishes are washed with cold water in the pan where the food was cooked and the water is then given the dogs, cats or pigs. This is the usual way to wash dishes in the village as well. In most Rom households, however, dishes are not used, as everybody eats out of the pan with one or two spoons, forks or knives to share. The Roma say they prefer eating from the same dish as it is '*Romanes*' – the Rom way.

While the women are in town scavenging or in the village bartering, men, elderly women and toddlers stay in the hamlet. Some men are away doing business or working in the village or in nearby villages, some are spending the day in one of the village bars, some are producing bricks, pans or other items to sell or barter in the village, but sitting together, chatting playing cards or telling jokes and keeping an eye on the playing children, the grazing horses and pigs are the main occupations of many hamlet men.

In summer the afternoon is hot and is usually spent relaxing, talking and perhaps sleeping. Kurva and Joska will spread out a blanket on the grass somewhere in the shade where they may spend hours chatting and sleeping, while the children and grandchildren play and tumble around them. Other family members may come along and the afternoon will be spent in sleepy relaxation. In the wintertime the same scene takes place inside the house.

Then as the evening approaches and the bori is expected home, it is time for Kurva to prepare the next meal. The women returning from town marks the beginning of evening in the hamlet. On the top of the steep hill that looks down on the village and station, the small children sit waiting for their mothers. As the heavily burdened women climb the roads of the village towards home, young sons and sometimes husbands come along to help. Unloading the backpack and showing what has been found, stolen or bought today and discussing how it was obtained is always a moment of expectancy and is always done inside the houses. The small children expect a snack, the older ones are waiting for the bread to feed the pigs and the grown-ups are perhaps expecting some groceries for the evening meal.

When there is plenty of money and food and a big meal is prepared, Joska will help Kurva with the heavy tasks such as pouring the hot soup from the chicken for the noodles, or even plucking the chicken. The children are sent to other households or to the store to fetch what Kurva might lack – salt, bread, seasonings etc. Joska will lay the table when guests from Norway (anthropologists or aid organisations) are expected. Joska likes everything concerning preparing meals, as does the rest of the household, so he often hangs around the kitchen assisting Kurva, just as the room is always full of playing children when Kurva is cooking.

After dark the Roma only seldom leave their hamlet. On bright summer evenings, however, youngsters (boys) and young men often go to the village to have a drink at a bar, to play billiards or even sometimes to the local weekend disco. Grown men who have spent the day drinking in the village will usually come home before their wives come from town; only the really drunk ones swing home after dark. As the sun sets in spring and summer and night approaches, the playing children gather on the high slopes outside the circle of huts and houses, singing and dancing, running and playing as the sun disappears behind the hills. In winter, evening comes early and is long. Joska and Kurva spend the evening on the bed in their house with the children or with other familia members, chatting and watching TV. Sometimes they visit some other household to watch a new Indian video or to sit and chat. At nine or ten o'clock the children start falling asleep and so do Kurva and Joska.

In summer most households make fires outside, where families and neighbours gather. Then Joska and Kurva usually go visiting the fire outside one of Kurva's brothers' houses, in the centre of the hamlet. Children and young people make their own fires and their distant singing can be heard as they dance and laugh in the dark. As the night gets chillier the fires burn out and the hamlet goes to sleep. In the warmest months of summer Kurva and

Joska and some of the children take their mattresses or blankets outside and sleep in the open. 'We always slept like that in summer when I was a child and we were still travelling in wagons', Joska laughs.

In the night the hamlet's many dogs take charge. Some gather together and go hunting in the woods during the night, others guard the houses and chase the horses that seek shelter among the humans. The sounds of barking dogs and of horses thundering through the hamlet echo through the silence of night until dawn comes and the sounds of humans take over.

The Family Household

In this chapter I will start to explore the first circle of relatedness among Roma; the familia. The hamlet Roma use the term *familia* not only about people who live together in the same house, but also about their larger extended family. This larger, extended family is best described as a cognatic kindred group that is quite flexible in composition, consisting of several two-to-three generation families living in separate houses, that are more or less interdependent. *Familia* may in practice also signify any part of one's kin-group in and outside the hamlet, dependent on context, as will be discussed in more depth in the next chapter. I will refer to the segment of the familia that live together in the same house and work together as a group, pooling resources, as the family household, and the larger, extended group will be referred to as familia. Most familia contain several family households, some living in one main house, others in huts or small houses nearby. The main house generally contains the oldest living couple in the extended family and is regarded by Roma as the local core.[11] Main houses and huts contain households at different stages of the household cycle. Joska and Kurva's household represent a middle stage of this cycle in the hamlet. There were about 230 people living in the hamlet, around 170 of them under the age of eighteen. The hamlet consisted of ten main houses; the remaining twenty-two houses are to be considered as huts.

The family household among hamlet Roma is a basic social unit for production, reproduction and consumption, but it is also the basic political unit in Rom organisation. Being a member of a family household means pooling resources and working together, but the physical structure of the house does not form the limits of the people working together for the common good; sons and daughters living in their own houses with their spouse and children may or may not be economically dependent on their parents, although they may have their own fire and sleep separately. The permeability of the family household as an economic as well as an emotional unit is thus a feature of Roma hamlet organisation. Although the familia among Roma is charged with strong moral and emotional value, and although the Roma present their family household and familia as a haven of trust and unity, the individual interests of its members as well as interests based on gender and age are diverse and sometimes conflicting. The complexity and fluidity of the Rom family challenges the idea of family households as collective agents. It highlights the fact that relations of power, domination and resistance are aspects of these relations and that interdependency and authority as well as co-operation and loyalty are not naturally given, but contested, disputed and negotiated by their members (Harris, 1981; Moore, 1994; Waldrop, 1997).

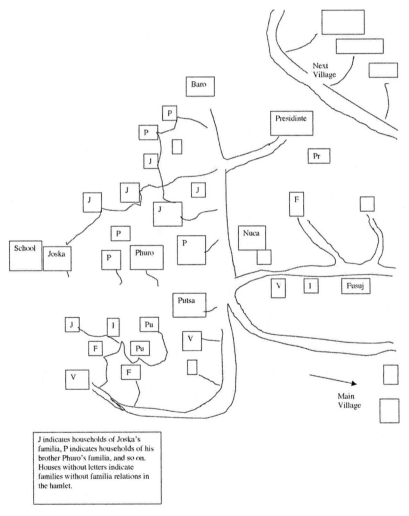

J indicates households of Joska's familia, P indicates households of his brother Phuro's familia, and so on. Houses without letters indicate families without familia relations in the hamlet.

Figure 2.1 *The Rom Hamlet*

Production for Subsistence

Every family household in the hamlet scraped a living out of a multitude of resources. I say 'scraped' because although most households managed fairly well, the Roma told us that some people did not eat every day. This meant that they did not always get a hot meal but had to eat bread. As pigs are an asset to be converted into cash for ritual purposes they were rarely sold. Both men and women complained about the hardship of life in Romania just like the peasants did and it is hard to understand how a family of twelve could live on a herder's income or on selling some pans and whips, on occasional paid labour, bartering and begging and a little allocation money. But they did. Gypsy groups, and the hamlet Roma in this case, are not directly dependent on their natural environment, but rather on their social environment (Piasere, 1987). As the hamlet Roma depend economically on the villagers, the agrarian cycle that plays a fundamental role in structuring work, symbols and rituals among peasants in general, figures among the Roma only as an indicator of the peasants' needs and the Roma's opportunities. Their economic strategy is to exploit the surplus of peasant production, by gathering, begging, exchange, petty barter and/or trade. Their 'means of production' are to a large extent their collective and individual ability to monopolise material and symbolic resources in exchange for the peasants' products. The domestic mode of production and the moral model of sharing and equality between kin and between hamlet Roma tends to destroy the accumulation of surplus that would allow the Roma to invest in goods in a capitalist way. Although some hamlet Roma own horses and contract for work with peasants, the balance of individual/domestic accumulation and the honour of sharing tend to make them distribute their wealth and invest it in symbolic capital, such as social networks and honour, rather that in material capital.

As peasants' dependency on Rom production is questionable, the personal ability of every individual Rom to cultivate customers is crucial. The basic skill required for this type of economic adaptation is to present themselves and their goods and services as indispensable or desirable to *gaže* (non-Gypsies); like all groups offering services and goods, they must know how to cultivate relationships in order to have customers. To reproduce themselves as a distinct social group they must also create and maintain boundaries towards others. In the Rom case the cultural value of self-sufficiency, implying that every family household is a self-sufficient economic and political unit, paired with strong ideals of autonomy, necessitates the exploitation of a variety of economic resources by both men and women. This heterogeneity makes possible a flexible adaptation to environmental changes (Piasere, 1987). The cultural value of co-operation and sharing are simultaneously preconditions for group formation outside the family household and for the relative social and economic integration of hamlet Roma.

Barter and Exchange

Most hamlet families grew some vegetables for consumption in their back yards, but as their plots were small the produce only lasted a few months. For their daily provisions women bought, exchanged, bartered and/or begged for food in the village. As will be discussed in Part Two of this book, exchange relations with peasant women in the village together with scavenging for pig fodder in town were basic subsistence strategies for hamlet women. Some women had specialised in stealing from drunken men in town and many of the old women were sorcerers and told fortunes. The women were responsible for the daily provisions for the family household. This responsibility took them out of the hamlet and the plains to the village, into the houses of gaže (non-Roma) and even to town. Scavenging, the only regular task that was performed in town, was only performed by women and children. Through trade and barter, begging and sorcery women are thus much more exposed to the social world of the gaže than their men are (Okely, 1975).

Most men produced some sort of household tools used by peasants such as pans and brooms, buckets, baking moulds, baskets or even whips for sale at the market or for the women to barter in the village. Clay-bricks were made regularly by one couple and their children, mostly for sale to villagers, just as most family households had developed their own subsistence speciality. Some raised horses for sale and also for transport jobs for villagers, most young men took on construction work, repairing roads and farm work in the village, others specialised in different sorts of business transactions in the village and even in town. All men were, however, involved in whatever business was available, such as currency exchange and bartering stolen items like gold and jewellery or firewood. A few family households herded cattle for the neighbouring peasants like Joska's household did; this work occupied most male members of those family households for parts of each day from April to November. And then quite a few men did not appear to engage in any form of economic activity. In contrast to women, most of the men's daily activities were performed in the hamlet and in the forest. Only some men went regularly to town, but most of them spent time in the village bars a few times a week. Men did not beg; the only exceptions were the hamlet's drunkard who begged on the trains and the oldest man in the hamlet, said to be over ninety, who travelled to town by train now and then, where he sat the whole day singing sad songs and begging. So the general picture is that the women and older children leave home in order to provide for the household's daily needs while the men and the old people stay at home looking after the house, the pigs and the younger children. When one visited the hamlet in the early afternoon the only people at home were often men, children and the elderly.

Pigs and Horses

Every household kept pigs, and to raise them women and children went to the nearby town to scavenge among the rubbish bins outside the apartment areas for bread to feed them. Pigs roamed freely in the hamlet and grazed on the village pastures. Pork was divided up between close kin and exchanged between distantly related households in return for money. Pigs and horses were the only things that were sold openly between hamlet Roma, but as a woman explained: 'They are supposed to pay me 15,000 lei a kilo, but they never have money, so they pay months later or when they slaughter a pig themselves or not at all.' As people slaughtered at different times meat was often available. Whenever a pig was slaughtered some Roma always waited outside the household holding rights to shares of the meat. Horses were raised by men for pleasure, for transport and for sale, and have great economic and symbolic value. Only few families in the hamlet had horses and they were prestigious objects that were handled with respect, and by men.

'What Can We Do, We Have to Eat'

Nobody ever told us that Roma work for peasants in the fields at harvest time. On the contrary, most villagers denied that they employed ţigani and Roma firmly denied working for peasants. I suppose both parties were slightly ashamed; the villagers did not like to reveal any dependence on ţigan labour, and the Roma did not want to admit they had sometimes to work like peasants. We would never have known of this if we had not gone ourselves to harvest corn with our Romanian host Florica and her family, and met some hamlet Roma picking corn like ourselves. No hamlet Rom was regularly employed, but both men and women worked on the peasants' land as day labourers at harvest time and in springtime. Later we realised that the hamlet men are hired on a short-term basis for all sorts of unskilled manual labour in and around the village. The Roma thus constituted a pool of cheap labour, not only to peasants, but to all sorts of contractors in the area. Several of the men migrated to Turkey to work in construction, on roads and other sorts of manual labour. One villager told us he had 'my own crew (*equipul meu*)' of 'ten ţigan boys', all from the hamlet, that he contracted in and around the village. He told us they were cheap labour and they were young and strong. He emphasised that many villagers were sceptical of using ţigani, but that they were good workers as long as 'they are properly treated and disciplined' (they had to be kept on a tight rope). The Roma who had horses did different sorts of work in the village and surrounding villages. Selling firewood, transporting materials and all sorts of transport work was available as horses were important in agriculture in this part of Romania, where they were scarce (Romanians ironically refer to them as the Romanian's tractor – tractorul românului).[12] As this is men's work it was generally paid in cash, but could also serve as a repayment in a barter transaction.

Most mature men did, however, complain of the fact that they sometimes had to work for the peasants and if anything more prestigious or rewarding appeared, few men would take on wage labour. Whenever we met a Rom in the village digging a trench or unloading a truck and commented on their work, they sighed regretfully and said, 'What can we do? We have to eat (*so te keras? trubul te xas)'*. Manual or wage labour is not expressed as shameful by hamlet Roma, but it does not enhance a man's honour or respect and is generally not performed by household heads (Stewart, 1997). The Roma engaged as herders were often ridiculed by others in the hamlet for working for gaže. It is wage labour per se that is conceived of as degrading to the Rom sense of dignity and self, but like most moral notions this one is also ambiguous. Joska the bulibaša would often brag about the fact that all hamlet Roma were employed during the Ceauşescu period and he would add that they were considered very good workers. But then he would add: 'but now we have *šaumage* (unemployment) and we are free!'.

Market Exchange

The Roma did occasionally sell pigs and horses at the weekly market in the village. The market was the main supplier of clothes, vegetables, furniture and house equipment as well as of livestock both for villagers and Roma. There were only a few shops and the choice was limited. Apart from the shops and the market, the village was visited by itinerant merchants and artisans. Most of these were Roma of different subgroups. The itinerant Rom tinsmiths – the *Čuternara* – usually came by car and walked from house to house offering their services. Others, often called *Biznicara*, had the trunk of their cars filled with carpets that they offered by door-t-o-door selling or they cried out their merchandise street by street. *Bombakara* sold material for clothes and curtains etc. All sorts of items were offered in this way, mostly from Roma to villagers. This exchange was of an immediate type that differed from that between villagers and between villagers and Roma.

The Relief Gift

The most important economic resource for the hamlet Roma since the revolution is the annual arrival of clothes and other luxury items from a West European NGO. Most of this gift is sold and bartered to peasants, thus strengthening already established exchange relations. The female head is in charge of this exchange on behalf of the family household. As this gift has arrived every year at the same time for twelve years it has transformed the economic conditions of the Roma to a substantial degree and has established a new season to the Roma's work cycle: the arrival of the gift. This exchange will be discussed in the second part of the book.

To sum up this section about production, the hamlet Roma exploited a variety of resources dependent on relative movement over a limited area. The women generally only went to the nearby villages and to the closest big town, while some also travelled further when necessary. The men were engaged in subsistence production for shorter periods than women, but could travel further, such as when they occasionally went on business trips to different big towns in the area. After we had left the hamlet some men left to work in Turkey for six months. What characterises this economy is its flexibility and variety of available resources where new resources are exploited whenever they are accessible (Piasere, 1987). It is also characterised by its dependence on mobility and a relatively numerous customer population, and last by the amount of leisure it makes possible, at least for men. In short it has many of the characteristics of 'original affluent society' where only a small part of people's daily lives were occupied with economic activity (Sahlins, 1988).

Gender and Age, the Organisation of Tasks

Children and unmarried young people performed, in principle, the same tasks as the adults, mostly as assistants. However, looking after their younger siblings, getting water for their household, running errands and collecting dry branches in the woods were children's special tasks. Children were anybody's servants, but even if every child could be asked to perform a service for any adult, they were usually only asked by members of their own family household or familia. Kurva had stopped scavenging, that work was now carried out by her bori and daughters. Although Joska still herded cattle, he left all the real work to his sons. Joska generally lay down and fell asleep once the cattle were brought to their right pastures. The older people grow, the more grown children and bora they have, the less they perform tasks both in and outside the household. After the age of fifty, people are considered old. They often have health problems and prefer to sit and chat. Most elderly women did, however, perform sorcery, but this was hard work as the customers were dispersed all over the village and neighbouring villages and walking was the only way of getting there. It might have been the case that younger women were unwilling to admit that they did this kind of work; it might also have been that the young generation in the village did not not use sorcerers so that it was a dying occupation.

Table 2.1 illustrates quite clearly the principle of gendered tasks, but also of co-operation in most tasks between household members. (Regular work is in italics.)

Table 2.1 *Gendered Tasks*

Location	Men's work	Women's work	Children's work
In and around the house:	Manufacturing objects for sale *Watering and feeding animals* *Looking after children* Chopping wood	*Cooking,* *Tidying sweeping,* *Washing clothes* *Washing pots,* Assisting in production Feeding pigs	*Looking after children* *Sweeping house* *Feeding pigs* *Washing pans* *Washing clothes*
Outdoors and out of hamlet:	*Providing firewood* Herding cattle (only three family households) Working in garden *Tending horses* Constructing houses Making clay bricks Farm labour Gathering mushrooms Wage labour (occasional) Business (occasional) Services for peasants	*Fetching water* *Collecting firewood* Working in garden *Bartering/begging in villages* Making clay bricks Gathering wild food *Scavenging in town* Sorcery, fortune telling Farm labour Herding cattle *Services for villagers*	*Running errands* *Fetching water* Collecting and chopping firewood Gathering wild food Begging in town Scavenging Herding cattle

The gender division of tasks in the household cut across divisions concerning age, but was consistent with divisions of space and time. Women and men were occupied in different places, and women worked for many more hours every day and had less leisure time than men. Implications of gender divisions will be discussed in the next chapter.

Children in the Household

The Rom idea of childhood is different from the general idea of childhood in Romanian society. Children's position in the hamlet community corresponds to some degree with Philippe Aries's idea of children in a society without the awareness of childhood (Ariés, 1996: 125). Rom children are not protected from any aspects of adult life – they share the plights and tasks of their elders from an early age. They are given no special training or education, and no special food, toys or clothes. Although the hamlet Roma in many ways treat their children as adults, expecting them to share most of the hardship and joys of adult life, they are not regarded as adults in the sense of morally responsible social beings; 'Romness' is seen to be a matter of physical and spiritual development. The sense of shame so important in the Roma's understanding of themselves, although inherent in the Rom child, is seen to develop according to the physical growth and development of the body (see also Okely, 1983). Without an evolved sense of shame, children are not responsible for their actions. As individual character is given at birth and as maturation is seen as a question of the unfolding of inherent traits, parents are not responsible for the character of their children and are not imagined to play a central role as agents in the formation of the child's personality (see also Gropper, 1975). The hamlet Roma raise their children to live the same or a similar life to their own, as Roma. The Rom belief in the innate properties of the person expresses and supports in my view the strong value the Roma place on personal autonomy, while the role of the caretakers in evoking or kindling the person's innate properties stresses the intersubjectivity, interaction and interdependency of individuals.

Work and Play

As illustrated, children contribute substantially to the subsistence of their family household. Children of both sexes start accompanying their mothers and sisters to town to scavenge and beg at about the age of five or six. Young girls generally beg close to grown women, while older girls may beg together and on their own. Boys generally spread out all over town in small groups, begging, doing odd jobs, washing car windscreens and shop windows, stealing etc. Many young girls also accompany their mothers when they beg and barter in the village. As the Roma get most of their subsistence from gaže, and women are the main providers, the girls must learn how to handle gaže in many contexts. Although children's work is not strictly gendered, the gender division of labour is infused in their habitus by participating in work from an early age. As children generally work together outside the control of adults, play is an integral part of their work. Thus they are left to solve problems in their own ways, developing creativity and self-reliance.

'School is a Gažo Thing'

Hamlet children did not attend school, and only a few adults in the hamlet were literate (see also Okely, 1983; Stewart, 1997). The NGO has built a school in the hamlet for the youngest children and Rom children are admitted to the village school, but their attendance in both is very sporadic. Hamlet Roma see no use for school for their children; they may go if they want, but will not be encouraged by their parents. School is not a *Romano*, but a *gažikano* thing from the Roma's point of view. Thus the discipline of the body, submission to a regime of place and time (expressed through schedules, enclosure and forced labour) special to the school and so important in preparing the child for the world of wage labour, is not part of the hamlet children's socialisation. Mind and body discipline are of course not separable, and the school regime of body discipline is paired with a power regime of knowledge that classifies knowledge and subjects in hierarchical ways (Bourdieu, 1990: 68–67). This process of classification aims to induce in the child both respect and longing for the knowledge he or she does not have and shame about personal defects and shortcomings as motivating factors. By evading school, Roma thus evade domination by this power regime that they see as *gažikanes* (non-Rom) and the stigma and self-hatred reported among ethnically stigmatised children in many minority contexts (Eidheim, 1977; Høgmo, 1986), but they also evade the possibility of competing for a social position in the majority society.

I do, however, suggest that the stigma attached to ţigani does influence the development of the child in several ways. In hospitals, where they are put in a special ward for ţigani only, in courtrooms and in jail and on their irregular visits to school, where they often are patronised and ridiculed, and in many other different contexts where they are at the mercy of the majority's power, it may be difficult to avoid the stigma altogether. Thus gaže evaluation and contempt is not altogether rejected. I suppose that such experiences foster some degree of personal uncertainty and a certain ambivalence about being ţigani and not gaže that causes frustration and aggression expressed as contempt both towards gaže and towards other Roma. This ambivalence is perhaps a necessary condition for 'understanding' the gaže community and for engaging in permanent and close economic interaction with the ambiguous 'other'.

The Moral Economy

Pooling or Sharing

Sharing is seen as a general moral value that defines the relationship between members of family households, familia and ideally between all kin and all Roma, in contrast to the relationship to gaže. The ideology of sharing is practised at its most complete between the members of a family household. Sharing is practised through informal visiting, through 'borrowing' money, food and items when necessary and by ritual meals (*pačiva*). Kurva did not only feed her own children, but her grandchildren and nephews as well when they were around and hungry. Sharing is talked about as a moral value that is central to self-understanding; it is talked of as a property of the relationship of the Roma as brothers and sisters (Stewart, 1997). Kurva told me that what she really disliked about people was stinginess. 'The Roma are not stingy', she said and that this separates them from gaže. The Roma, however, often complained about 'others' who were not willing to share and that not all Rom nowadays shared like they used to in the old days. All these complaints emphasise sharing as a central value of Rom culture (*romanimo*). Sharing, equality and honour are combined to constitute a central moral cluster in opposition to stinginess, inequality and shame.

The Political Ideology of Sharing

The idea that all Roma are 'brothers and sisters' means that all Roma are potential kin and part of a sharing relationship. Non-Roma are not marriageable and hence they will never enter into relationships of sharing with Roma. This idea of sharing very strongly evokes the notions of community and equality but, as we have seen, not everything is shared. Although the practice of sharing is restricted by the ideology of self-sufficient households, and although the Roma are ambiguous about the practice of sharing, they are in no doubt about what is the proper Rom way: romanes. The general act of sharing is referred to as *to give*: *te des*. As Joska's brother in-law argued to my husband: 'You are my brother and you are rich. You must give me money (*trubul te des man love)'*. By evoking kinship, sharing was presented as obligatory. The idea that all surpluses should be shared is also expressed in the rituals of pačiv and in the expectation of a share of meat when a relative slaughters a pig. Thus to slaughter a pig when no one else does means you will have very little to store (salt, dry). The hamlet Roma do not hold property rights over territories; every Rom has, in principle, equal access to most resources and this, paired with the ideology of sharing, ascertains the relatively even distribution of wealth and thus the relatively equal relations of power among hamlet Roma. This points to the notion and practice of sharing as a political ideology (Woodburn, 1998), and as emblematic of Rom collective identity. The Roma very clearly state that they do not save, they spend – in contrast to the gaže who save and are not generous. They describe with disgust how gaže even keep a record of what they give.

Sharing and Self-sufficiency – The Dual Model of Honour and Equality

In contrast to the closed households in the village, the openness of the Rom households is almost startling. There are no gates or locked doors in the hamlet, somebody is always at home, and visiting is a moral obligation between relatives. To an outsider it may be difficult to decide who belongs to the household and who does not, as people keep streaming in and out of each other's houses for no obvious reason. This streaming, which at first seemed spontaneous and unlimited, was, however, ordered and structured by kin relations and by notions of shame (*lažav*), and honour (*pačiv*). Just as visiting was talked about as 'showing respect', so was too much visiting seen as shameful. Whereas too much visiting and help raised questions about dependency, poverty and shame, too little visiting raised questions about enmity, claims to superiority and lack of respect. The ideal of sharing among Roma thus rests on a strong moral obligation of self-sufficiency. All tasks necessary for the viability of the family household are performed by its members, and resources are pooled according to the ideology of sharing. Leonardo Piasere discusses this same trait among the Xoraxané Gypsies of Yugoslavia who exploited new niches in Italy in the 1980s (Piasere, 1987: 129). Although related families worked together in many instances they emphasised that they only worked for their own domestic unit. A respectable woman is hardworking and fulfils her obligation as a provider, but as her household is a segment in a wider *familia*, support and co-operation may be expected. The respect she may expect is, however, based on her ability and willingness to work hard: Vulpe was a woman of about twentyfive years with seven children between the ages of one and ten. Her husband had been in jail for the last three years and Vulpe provided for her children by offering sex to men in town and then when they were drunk stealing their money. Sometimes she was away for days, working in different towns in the area. Her eldest son of eight years often accompanied her to town to protect her. Although she was responsible for her family household, her *familia*, who all lived in the hamlet, assisted her in different ways. Her youngest brother generally looked after her husband's horses, his young, childless wife usually cooked for the children when Vulpe was away, and her mother helped the eldest daughter look after the toddlers. In spite of this co-operation, Vulpe left for town almost every day and stayed until the last evening train in order to provide for her children. I sympathised with her hardship and told her to come to me for financial help when she had problems, but she never did. On the contrary she insisted on buying me cigarettes and coffee when we met in the village because I had given her children bread on some occasions.

A woman is expected to manage on her own, relatively independent of her husband. As most men spent some time in jail, most women had experienced such periods and knew they should not rely on others for daily subsistence. In spite of her somewhat dubious profession, Vulpe was a respected woman in the hamlet.

Sharing, visiting and co-operation mark the relationship between ideally self-sufficient and equal households. Family households are thus both open and bounded, they are both political and economic, emotional segments of a more or less corporate familia and self-sufficient political and economic entities uniting into familias for special political and economic purposes. The combination of interdependency and self-sufficiency of family households composing a familia expresses what Piasere calls 'productive autonomy' which makes possible the flexibility of the Rom mode of production:

> The productive autonomy enables each family to leave a kumpánja without damaging its own production or that of other members, and to join another where there are relatives or friends that will accept it (Piasere, 1987: 128).

Although productive autonomy is an ideal among hamlet Roma, in practical life it was, as we shall see, challenged with the arrival of the NGO gift.

'Carrying Ţigani on Our Backs' – Parasitism or Symbiosis?

The subsistence strategy that is dependent on the extraction of the surplus of the production of another population is often negatively termed parasitism. And the villagers often complained that they were 'carrying the ţigani on their backs'. The continuum of symbiosis and parasitism should, however, be examined in every empirical case of relations between Gypsies (and related groups) and their customers, and should be understood as changing in accordance with the economic and political situation of both groups. Their relative positions on this continuum are an indication of the relative power ratio between the groups. My claim, which will be discussed in Part Two of this book, is that villagers and Roma form a social figuration of asymmetric interdependency. The Roma in the present case had very few material goods that the peasants really needed; most of the goods and services they offered could be supplied by others. Achim refers in his historiography about groups of tigani in the seventeenth and eighteenth centuries that did not specialise in any specific art, but survived by a combination of begging, exchange, petty trade and wooden household products (Achim, 2004). This may have been the historical tradition of the hamlet group. The important exception is their workforce, which was exchanged for quite low wages. Their advantage was that they were available, mobile and many, so that the peasants generally could find someone when they needed work to be done. The Roma did not, however, constitute a stable work supply; they would turn down a request if they had better options. On the other hand, their economic dependency on peasants did oblige them to always be alert to peasants' needs. Every season had its specific opportunities for exchange with the peasants. The first mushrooms in springtime were desired by all; before the new crops could be harvested and after the last crop had been consumed everybody would be craving fresh greens. As soon as the beans started growing in spring, boys and men in the hamlet started cutting rods in the woods and their women walked from door to door in the village exchanging them for cash or kind. When the maize had been harvested in October, the Roma were let into the fields to pick up the leftovers for their horses. Their stigmatised position at the bottom of Romanian society as poor and uncivilised, forced and enabled them to exploit resources and perform tasks morally condemned by villagers. The hamlet Roma had to adapt economically to the peasants' changing needs and desires and exploit their alleged poverty, 'strangeness' and helplessness to establish economic exchange. In an economic sense, then, family households, although ideally self-sufficient, are almost entirely economically dependent on relations outside their hamlet and even the village. Unlike relations among Roma that are based on the logic of sharing, relations between Roma and gažo are based on an ideal of exchange and negative reciprocity (Sahlins, 1988); getting much for little – the opposite of interdependency, which is expressed as sharing between 'brothers' (Stewart, 1999).

Notes

1. From now on 'the hamlet' stands for this Rom village.
2. *Rom* and *Romni* are the *Romanes* terms for married man and woman, see vocabulary.
3. I use the emic term, because daughter-in-law does not cover the central characteristics of a *bori*. This will be discussed later in connection with marriage.
4. *Ştergar* is the Romanian word for the embroidered linen towels that have great symbolic significance in rural Transylvania. They are also used for covering baskets with gifts in ritual gift exchange in the village.
5. The Roma here use this Romanian term for religious pictures and for all sorts of pretty, bright pictures, photographs etc.
6. Both Romanians and Roma put red ribbons on their babies to protect them from the evil eye.
7. Herding is paid partly in cash and partly in food. The *bulibaša* household get about 1 mill. lei (about US$ 150 in 1996) a season, and one pound of meat and one pound of bread and milk every day. Every cattle-owner contributes this amount in turn (according to Joska).
8. A European NGO donates two trailers with clothes to the Roma of this hamlet every year, most of which are sold to villagers. This exchange is discussed in Part Two of this book.
9. Gypsy children are often barefoot in their shoes or boots even in mid-winter, and their clothes consist of all kinds of items put together to cover their body
10. *Romanes* is an adverb meaning the way of life and moral values of the Roma as well as the language. A capital R will be used to denote the language. *Romanes*

is also used frequently to cover the meaning of *romanimo*; Rom cosmology or culture.

11. It is not reasonable to see it as 'a house' in the Levi Straussian sense (1987) as the Rom family household lacks important traits discussed for the house as a type of political corporation. The perpetuation of the familia is not fixed to an estate, a physical building or a territory, but to the name of its most influential leader (a father).

12. In the Ceauşescu era, collective farms were worked with tractors and modern equipment. After the revolution when land was returned to former owners, no family had money to buy modern equipment and loans were not available so the peasants went back to the hoe and the horses and even oxen. Only some villagers have horses, and the others hire them for ploughing, sowing etc.

13. *Pačiv* is a ritual meal given in honour of someone, at betrothals, to seal business deals, at marriage ceremonies, at funerals, to settle disputes and on other occasions. Note that the word also means *honour* and that is what is achieved by such a meal for giver and receiver. This will be discussed further in chapter 5.

Chapter 3
Gender, Shame and Honour

Introduction

The Roma express what it means to be a woman by stating what women do. As Bakro emphasised: 'What should a man do without his wife, only women can raise our children and get food from gaže (*numa le Romnja žanen te xoxaven le gažen)*'. When we asked Joska's sister Mariora to describe her life she talked about her work and hardship:

> Well, Jorgole (addressing Lars Gjerde), in the morning I get up, I make a fire, I wake up the children and I start thinking what to give them to eat. I have many children, and they need a lot of food. But I have not much to give them, just a little. I put some grease in the frying pan to fry two potatoes to give them. Then I have to think where to go to find something to eat. I have nothing here so I go into the street to beg from the gaže to give them something to eat, poor children. Some give me a little, others give me nothing. I bring them (the children) potatoes, meat, bread, flour, a little milk. I walk with one child in my sling, poor thing. The children are hungry, worried and unhappy! When I come home I put the pot on the fire to cook and after that I have to wash clothes, to clean up, to wash the children. Some days we go to town to the rubbish bins to find bread for the pigs, and to find something to eat. Some people give us food that we would throw away ourselves. We go together, eighteen, twenty women, we go to and fro. Sometimes the police beat us and throw us off the train because we do not have money to buy tickets. Then we will not come home that day. We will have to stay at some station and come home the next morning, the children hungry and unhappy, poor children! About eleven o'clock I go to bed tired and 'broken' – poor me! Seven children! I have been walking with them two years in my arms (*duj bers andi brača*)! I have to walk around a lot with my gathering bag (*straica*), on my back and a child in my arms. That's the women's situation. They are more worried and unhappy than the men. Look at the little one! Wherever I go I take him with me in my arms! Always a child in my arms! When we have money we can bring home

something to eat and when we do not have money we do not eat. When we receive the family allowance we have some money and also when M comes we will have a little money. Then we can put things in order. I am finished, may you be lucky. (*T'aves baxtalo*)!

Asked to tell us about her life, Mariora presented a depressing picture that revolves totally around her plights as a mother and a provider.[5] This expresses quite well the general idea that women's troubles are natural and given, tied to her role as mother and provider for her children. Women's tasks are given by their physical bodies marked by the symbolic properties generally expressed by notions of shame (lažav). The women told us that there is no work or task a woman may not perform, while there are several that a man cannot do. There are, however, several tasks that are considered inappropriate for men. Scavenging, begging and bartering, washing clothes, sweeping, fetching drinking water and cooking the daily meals are all work considered inappropriate for men. One woman explained to me why men do not go scavenging: 'The men do not shame themselves (*le Roma na keren penge lažav*)'. For men to perform these tasks is considered shameful. For women they are considered to be necessary for the viability of the household and thus not shameful. The women who made a living by stealing did, however, consider scavenging and begging to be shameful, and often told me how bad the women smelt when they came home from town. Raita, Kurva's sister, did not want me to come with her to town scavenging, but as she could not say this directly she used a lot of tricks to prevent me coming with her. Kurva did not go scavenging, saying it was too physically dirty (*melalo*). The more wealthy Roma from town despised scavengers and thus seemed to consider all Roma that scavenged for a living as uncivilized and shameful. Before concluding that women are considered more shameful than men, I need to look closer at the notion of shame among the hamlet Roma.

Femaleness and – Shame?

The Roma say they 'have shame': *si ame lažav*.[6] Having shame is expressed as a property of Rom as a people, and this is what most clearly makes them different from the peasants (and gaže in general). To have a sense of shame is to differentiate between proper behaviour and shameless behaviour and proper behaviour is to behave so as to avoid shame. 'Look', they said, 'Because we have shame our women are decently dressed'. It is the women that are the most explicit symbols of the Roma's inherent sense of shame. The headscarf, the ancle-long skirt and the apron worn by married women were presented as markers of the household's and hamlet's sense of shame and a measure of the respect it should expect. The length of women's dress was also one important feature in distinguishing different subcategories of Roma. Having a sense of shame is knowing that the body, especially the sexual aspect (the lower part) of the body, should be properly covered in public. Women's bodies are inherently more shameful than men's bodies and may shame both men and women if not culturally manipulated by clothes, facial expressions, gestures and rituals. Performed by women, tasks that were seen to shame men, as scavenging and begging, on the contrary confirmed femaleness as industriousness. They were necessary for subsistence, and performed well they brought prosperity and thus respect and even honour to the household. An industrious woman was a source of pride to her husband and her household; she was respected as long as she avoided shameless behaviour and, most important, observed the rituals of separation. Romnja, then, had a freedom of movement in the gaže world that rendered them out of the immediate control of men.

And men talked about women not only as difficult to control, but also as indispensable: 'Only women can raise our children and take food from gaže'. They give birth to and feed children and they fed the whole family household and its livestock. Women were in charge of cooking, and prepared food is embedded with strong positive values. The stove is the heart of any household and the cook is the one who converts whatever is scraped off the gaže surplus into livelihood for the whole household. Roma declare that the food they cook is much tastier and richer than the food cooked by gaže. Food is also the basic means of reciprocity and exchange between Roma. Ritual meals given in honour of some person or group are the proper way of settling disputes and closing agreements among Roma. As providers and cooks, women perform tasks that are vital to the household and community, not only in a material sense, but the household's degree of honour and respect is dependent on the prepared food it has to share, exchange and present to guests. Villagers pitied hamlet women who had to go scavenging for a living and regarded it as disgusting and shameless, work only fit for ţigani. This confirmed the notion of t‚igani as poor and different from villagers. Women's roles as providers, however, earned them respect, and scavenging for bread in town to feed their pigs was regarded as economically rational, although morally degrading, from a village point of view. Hamlet women's position in the village hierarchy therefore allowed them to exploit economic niches that are not open to men or to gaže. Their economic role as providers and their degraded position from a village point of view permitted them to breach social conventions in the Romanian world in general and profit economically. The notion of shame also models the division between Roma and gaže, conceptualised, by Roma, as a division between: 'the people that have a sense of shame and know how to avoid it and the people that don't know'. This division is crucial to the constitution of Rom identity just as it is crucial to the economic viability of the Roma (Gay y Blasco, 1999; Okely, 1983; Stewart, 1997; Sutherland, 1975). The viability of any Rom community depends on the crossing of these symbolic boundaries between male and female, Rom and gaže. And as we have seen, women are the principal border-crossers (see Okely, 1975). In contrast to the Gypsies in England and Hungary (Okely, 1975, Stewart, 1997), the hamlet Roma did not treat food or objects from gaže as polluted, nor did they ever talk of gaže as polluting or impure in general. Although hamlet Roma tried to deny their dependency on gaže, it was not easy. Whenever someone would complain about how nasty and stingy gaže were, Joska would correct them, saying something like: 'O really? And what should you do without gaže?' My interpretation is that it is gaže's ignorance of and indifference to the necessity of keeping the boundaries between aspects of maleness and femaleness that are shameless (bilažaveski). The Roma, as they see it themselves, know how to counteract the inherent danger of female powers and are thus morally superior to gaže

Shifting Selves – Mothers, Wives, Traders and Beggars

The role of women in the hamlet economy must be understood in relation to their local adaptation as well as to gender ideology among Roma in general. The variety of economic resources exploited by Roma and the symbolic boundary between Roma and gaže necessitate a variety of roles and types of behaviour that can best be understood by applying the notions of subject positions and shifting selves (Ewing, 1990; Moore, 1994). Moore emphasises that nowhere is there only one single female or male subject position, but a variety that are inscribed in the often contradictory discourses of gender and power relations (Moore, 1994: 63). There are of course more than two possible femininities among hamlet Romnja, my argument is, however, that their equally important tasks as mothers and providers may be seen as the axis along which these varieties are structured. Applying these ideas I suggest that the domestic and economic roles of women and men, although apparently governed by contradictory values, as Okely discusses for English travellers (Okely, 1975), should rather be treated as different social positions tied to different social contexts. In my material (as in Okely's) Gypsy men and women actively exploit and confirm non-Gypsy stereotypes for subsistence, and these stereotypes thus influence their behaviour in most exchanges.

Prudent Wives and Mothers

As a Romni a woman is subjected to several everyday rituals aiming at protecting the household from her polluting power as she is expected to show respect and deference towards her husband and his male kin. This expectation is especially strong towards young women, and decreases as women have several children and gain increased respect. As a wife, a woman will generally adhere to these values and will seek to fulfil these expectations by her self-presentation; such as the way she dresses and her general behaviour. Young hamlet women generally acted in a respectful manner towards their husbands and older male relatives and were generally withdrawn, leaving the scene to males in public.

Uncontrollable Scavengers

Hamlet women were also expected to be good providers, and as providers quite other qualities are needed. When women and children went to town scavenging, stealing and begging, as they explained themselves, frivolous demeanour was displayed. On these business trips they put on their bad clothes (dirty and torn), never or seldom paid for train tickets, smoked in non-smoking compartments and generally talked loudly, swore and shouted and expressed exactly the stereotype held by gaže of the wild and frivolous ţigani. There were, of course, differences in women's behaviour, but as they appeared as a band on these occasions, they were considered by gaže as such. Scavenging and begging was only done by Roma or Gypsy-like people and by explicitly expressing their difference, categorisation was maintained. Scavenging was regarded by most women in terms of some sort of freedom from the burdens of mothering and domestic tasks. Women often said they would go crazy if they could not escape the hamlet and their children regularly, and many said laughingly that they would not stop scavenging and stay at home even if they could.

Respectful and Humble Beggars

While scavenging and stealing were done in town among strangers, bartering and begging in the village demanded quite a different type of behaviour. Close co-existence with peasants not only necessitated adherence to local moral models, but most Romnja even shared these models to some degree. For exchange and barter the women appealed to the peasants' respect and pity for them as hardworking mothers and ill-treated wives. As ţigani men are considered drunkards and lazy good-for-nothings by peasants, the ţigan women are seen as cohering well to the village idea of motherhood as sacrifice (see Chapter 7). Both peasants and Roma are heavy drinkers, but stories about men drinking up every penny they earn were told only by Romnja, even those with sober men. Thus they evoked compassion and strengthened the village stereotype. In these contexts it was their shared plight and moral codes as women and mothers that were evoked. These relations even developed into friendship that was never publicly expressed, but disguised as barter relationships. But the swearing and uncontrollable scavenger was never far away, and if women were rejected or illtreated, this behaviour was effective in scaring off the offender. So behaviour that evoked sympathy, compassion, interest and fear, may be seen to maintain exchange relationships between peasants and Roma mainly through women.

Swearing, Frivolous Witches

Swearing with sexual connotations is common practice among the Roma in the hamlet, but it was mostly expressed by women and mostly towards children and youngsters. The general rule was that the older the woman the dirtier her swearing, but even young women and small girls possessed an arsenal of swearing that was exploited at need. Romanes also has a variety of idiomatic expressions with sexual meanings that are part of everyday language. To beg someone a favour in Romanes – to express the equivalent of 'please' – is commonly expressed by: 'I will eat your prick, or I will eat your cunt' (*xav čo kar, xav či miš*). Joskas wife is called Kurva. Kurva means prostitute both in Romanian, Hungarian and Romanes. The headman's wife was, however, in no way considered to be a prostitute; she was a respected woman with eleven children. 'Dirty' language was used both at home towards children and other adults and towards gaže when women appeared in groups in public places. As women grew older they generally took up healing, sorcery and fortune-telling as their livelihood. Magic formulas as well as swearing were important ingredients in this business, as were the peasants' expectations of the *ţiganca's* magical and dangerous powers. It was seen as both threatening and dangerous, but also powerful because it revealed knowledge and control of the evil forces (the devil).

Wives and Providers – Dependency and Autonomy

The women's many different tasks as providers together with their duties as wives and mothers presented them for a variety of social practices and discourses with very different and seemingly contradictory moral values. By obscene language and frivolous demeanour in interethnic contexts women expressed peasants' stereotypes about 'gypsiness' and, I will add, cultural autonomy. They confirmed the peasant's view of them as immoral and even promiscuous and they also expressed that they did not care. Swearing and obscene language was however also expressed in Romanes and directed towards fellow Roma. While women's swearing could be interpreted as the expression of difference and independence in interethnic contexts, it conveyed a parallel message toward Gypsy men. By sexualised speech, women expressed their unruliness and their opposition to the male moral order at the same time as they confirmed that they were more shameless than men. Although representing a breach of the moral model of shame, obscene language was, however, overruled by the general demeanour that defines romanimo: proper dress, correct public behaviour between men and women, and rules of separation. These are tacit models woven into the fabric of everyday life, and they convey a different message: *Gypsy women have a sense of shame, just like men, and may act to enhance it. As long as they dress properly, respect the rules of conduct and thus accept their subordination to men, they are respected and are therefore honourable even if they swear like whores.* As providers, women demanded and expressed the ideals of individuality, self-sufficiency and autonomy valued among Roma. As wives and mothers they adhered to the values of dependency and co-operation expected of all Roma and the subordination and consent to male leadership. Thus instead of seeing this as being exposed to contradictory values and expectations (Okely, 1975), I suggest seeing it as an example of shifting multiple selves taking up different subject positions, all confined to a dual and ambiguous cultural construct of values concerning male/female, Rom/gažo and dependency/ autonomy (Ewing, 1990; Moore, 1994).

Maleness and Honour?

Men are household leaders and represent the household in public. Every man is responsible for the respect and honour attached to his household and this also influences the respect of his familia. A proper man is honourable: *pačivalo*. Men are supposed to behave in a respectful manner, show dignity expressed by autonomy, strength of will and body, and to control themselves and their dependants.[7] All men are considered equal, but their own or their dependants' acts may enhance or diminish their honour and the respect they may receive from other men. Men prided themselves on being consumers of women's work, not on being providers. Some men even emphasised that drinking, sleeping and eating is what the good life is all about. But 'alas, being poor we have to work'. As we have seen, manual or wage labour did not enhance a man's honour or respect and was generally avoided by household heads. On the other hand, it was considered shameful for a man to let his wife and children go hungry and badly dressed, and men that performed manual labour talked scornfully about men who only drank and got 'paid' by their women. As households are expected to be self-sufficient, the men are responsible for the wellbeing of their family. That usually means that they have a hardworking wife, bora and children. Although not providers of daily subsistence, men were generally expected to procure money for houses, equipment and materials for women's skirts, and for rituals and other necessary expenditure. The only honourable way a man could make money was by some sort of trade: *biznica* (see also Voiculescu, 2002). To strike a good bargain is to have luck (*bax*): 'to get something for nothing' (See Stewart, 1997: 142). The hamlet Roma seemed to have this perspective: as long as gaže produce enough food for the Romnja to gather, why give up the good life? Kurva's brother Thulo expressed this philosophy in his way: 'Man has come to earth to enjoy himself (*o manuš avilo pi phuv te distrol pe)*'.

Honour and respect (*respeto*) is achieved in competition with other Roma, and sharing is a fundamental way of achieving respect. Respect is not achieved only by refraining from shameless behaviour; although not always possible, this is always expected of any Rom person. Respect is closely connected to the accumulation of wealth to share in a pačiv. A man's ability to share not only by giving ritual meals but also in everyday situations and to serve guests at lifecycle celebrations, is dependent on a hardworking wife and bori and a man's own luck – his ability to make money. Thus honour and respect, although the responsibility of men, are impossible without women, and shame, although originating from women's bodies, is also a criterion for the evaluation of male behaviour.

To avoid shameless activities men often find it safer to stay at home and let women and children do the dirty work in times when dirty work is the only work available. Not only should a Rom adhere to Rom moral values but to some extent the moral values of peasants and Romanians are also valid for him. Cheating on trains threatens the ideal of male dignity, because if caught it exposes him to ridicule by Romanians and Roma. Being caught red-handed shows lack of control and of luck. While women may swear, laugh and generally make a nuisance of themselves in public and thus always be visible and 'different', men are more discreet, controlled and respectful. The business exchanges men involve in with gaže are obtained in competition with others who can supply similar goods and services. Some degree of trust and respect is crucial for this kind of exchange. While women's success as providers is dependent on their ability to present themselves as either poor and pitiful or assertive and dangerous according to context, thus confirming and exploiting peasants' stereotypes of gypsiness, men's economic success is dependent on their ability to present themselves as cunning and trustworthy and thus to underplay the same stereotypes.

Drinking with Honour

Drinking is an act of great symbolic significance in Romania in general and also among Roma. Drinking is a male act; it is talked about as a necessity to establish friendship and brotherhood among men. Among Roma, drinking together is a proof of masculinity, strength, brotherhood, trust and equality. When the Roma boast about some strong and respected man they always talk about the amounts of spirits he can drink without getting drunk. Control is also crucial to masculinity, and although some degree of drunkenness seems to increase the feeling of brotherhood, men should know how to behave even when drunk. 'You do not stick your arm in the oven even if you are drunk (*na tos čo vas ando bov vi kana san mato*)', the Roma say, indicating that drunkenness does not free a man from responsibility. Ideally drinking together unites 'brothers'; in practice however it also separates them. Many men do not control themselves when they drink and serious fighting among 'brothers' almost always occurs between drunken men. This is one of the challenges at funerals, where men drink for three days, but where fighting is seen as interrupting the deceased's passage to heaven. I suggest that the disintegrating properties of alcohol make it a powerful way of proving maleness and brotherhood. An accepted way to balance the necessity to drink with the ability to maintain control is to make a vow in church to drink only a certain amount. Several hamlet men had given this vow, which is an agreement between the man and the priest in the presence of God. A usual amount agreed upon is around three cups of *rača* (plum brandy) and three bottles of beer a day. The values of autonomy, self-control and honour important for Rom masculinity is thus confirmed by drinking alcohol without losing control.

Husbands, Brothers, Businessmen and Workers

Like women, men's daily life engaged them in interaction with people in different social fields governed by different social practices and values. As household leaders they are expected to be in control and to be respected by their women and children, but as women are generally seen as uncontrollable this is a constant problem. This control implies having hardworking women and children that provide for the daily subsistence. Different stages in the household cycle and different economic situations among the gaže do, however, put different expectations on a man's participation in daily provision. When the couple is young, with young and incapable children, men may be obliged to assist their wives in providing subsistence if the household is to conform to the ideal of self-sufficiency. Under Ceauşescu, when all men without land were forced to work in government enterprises, all hamlet males were wage earners. As the male head of a family household, a man must be able to compete for respect, honour and equality, which means he must have something to share, and the more he has, the better his position. Dealing and business are, as Michael Stewart has shown in his study of horse-dealing and brotherhood among Roma in Hungary, coherent with the Roma's ideas of autonomy and luck as inherent traits of Rom maleness (Stewart, 1997: 17–26). Business transactions posit the Rom as an agent who, by his smartness and luck, can outwit gaže. Although the hamlet Roma did not generally have horses, any form of trade and business seems to adhere to values of autonomy, mastery and of superiority to gaže and seemed to enhance a man's self-respect as well as the respect of other Roma. Trade and business were not seen as exclusively male occupations – women were just as eager traders as men – but the special responsibility of males to enhance the respect and honour of the family household made them reluctant to take up any other occupations if they could avoid it. Manual labour, the production of tools and objects for the peasants, together with most types of wage labour, situates Roma at the mercy of gaže; dependent and inferior. This kind of work is contrary to the self-image of Roma and males as autonomous, equal and morally superior to peasants, and thus men try to avoid it (see also Stewart, 1997). When there was no other choice, when internal or external circumstances made it impossible to sustain a livelihood with respect and dignity without indulging in degrading occupations, men did such work, like women. And like women, men dealt with these seemingly contradictory roles by presenting different selves in different contexts, all, however, modelled on the same dualities of maleness/femaleness, Rom/gaže, and dependency/autonomy. Honour and respectability, although expected traits of Rom maleness, are therefore always on trial and has to be confirmed almost continually.

'How God has Made Things' – Complementarity and Ambiguity

The division of labour and the asymmetric power relationship between men and women expressed in terms of shame and honour were accepted by both sexes as 'how God has made (left) things (*gade mukhla les o Del)*'. But even though this was seen as the order of things, tasks were negotiated between wife and husband (see Gay y Blasco, 1999). Women often complained about their husbands leaving all the hard work to them and spending every penny in the bars. In particular tasks that are performed by both men and women, such as looking after children and feeding pigs, often caused disputes between spouses. Mature men did not order their wives around and wives did not accept being ordered around without protesting. Men's authority is legitimated on a common idea of their inherent honour as males, but the respect a man may deserve is just as much dependent on his wife. If she questions his authority and disrespects him, so will other men.

When men were drunk, in prison or at work, women performed men's tasks such as watering horses and getting firewood. When women were in town, men had to feed their children and fetch water if they had no able children around. Several men had experienced being alone with their children while their wives were in jail. Militaru, the only divorced single man in the hamlet, had to wash his own clothes, and Joska sometimes had to herd all day alone. Joska and Kurva's son Millionaru would sometimes refused to fetch firewood when Kurva wanted him to and she cursed him and asked someone else. Young women often asked their husbands to look after children, go shopping and so on when they had planned other things, and an argument could arise. During a pačiv given to a household head in the hamlet, the married daughter of that household was present with her husband. Their only child was sleeping alone at home and the husband kept on urging her to go and see to him. She answered angrily that he could go himself, but he never stopped. At last she went, sneering loudly through her teeth: 'How many rights do you have? (*so de drepturi si tu?*)'.

The Rom Couple – Ideal Unity of Separate Units

The couple is mutually dependent for honour and subsistence and the Roma see it as an interdependency of maleness and femaleness. The couple is thus a living example of the crossing of symbolic borders between maleness and femaleness and of the vital necessity of such border crossing. The couple forms a social relationship at the same time dangerous and vital that one would expect to be protected by ritual (Douglas, 1966). And as we shall see, the ritual separation of femaleness from maleness is crucial to the self-understanding of Roma as morally superior to gaže. This separation was expressed in the hamlet by a system of ritual separation that will be discussed more thoroughly in later chapters. But rituals of separation were also performed between spouses in everyday co-operation. Joska and Kurva referred with disgust and horror to the gažo youths who would kiss in front of their elders or in public places. Although Kurva and Joska spent most of their time together and seemed to enjoy each other's company, they never publically expressed affection in any physical way. Married couples that were still sexually active did not dance together in public, and married women should avoid passing in front of a sitting man. The symbolic border between spouses is also marked by speech. When men talked about their wives, and especially about something referring to the sexual relation between them, they expressed it like this: 'You know my wife (do excuse me) and I have six children'. Many men add 'excuse me' (*te jertis*) almost as a suffix to 'my wife': 'My wife, excuse me, went to town yesterday to visit her sister'. Women showed this discretion only when they spoke about something that was directly connected to female procreation, lower body parts or birth.

Even the young newly-weds living in the parents' household should express shame and respect by never touching or kissing in front of elders. The relationship between Kurva and Joska's son Teddi and his wife

Violetta was very different from their own, as the young people generally did not present themselves as a couple in public. Teddi spent his time with his friends while Violetta stayed in the house or at work or with her friends, and they only seldom went anywhere together. Kurva often scolded Teddi for spending too much time with his friends instead of with his children: 'Don't you have a wife and children?' she asked. Such scolding illustrated Teddi's position as a child in his mother's household and was probably part of the explanation for why he spent time with his friends (see Barth, 1971). Although the young could be boisterous and offensive in their age and gender groups, they were however both respectful and quiet in the presence of their elders. This is the general pattern among young couples. As couples grow older and have more children, the co-operation and complementarity of the Rom and Romni is more and more visible. Especially when the household's bori takes over most of the daily tasks of the Romni, she spends more and more time with her husband. Marriage is supposed to last a lifetime among the Roma, and although the first years of marriage are usually turbulent and may lead to break-ups, divorce is seldom later in life. Although Kurva, like most women, saw the relationship Rom/Romni as ideally asymmetrical, with the man as the family head, she referred to herself and Joska as friends that discussed important matters, worked together and decided together. In practical life, age seemed to change a structurally asymmetrical relationship between spouses into a more or less symmetrical one, the Rom still always representing his household in public. This complementarity of the Rom couple entails the ideas that producing children and subsistence brings honour, and producing honour and respect is materially rewarding. In the long, warm, summer afternoons mature couples spent hours dozing on rags and blankets outside their houses, chatting and looking at their playing children and grandchildren.

Notes

1. This expression means *in a sling*. Children are supposed to be carried for two years.
2. The name of the NGO that brings clothes to the hamlet Roma.
3. This expression always ends an account, a story etc.
4. This text was recorded and transcribed by Lars Gjerde, *Jorgole* in the text.
5. When asked to tell of her life as a woman into a tape recorder she gives the public version used in begging and barter. This does not mean that her life is not difficult but only that it is the only way she knows of talking about her life, in this general way, to gaže. The household is comparably well off, the children are not too numerous and they always have enough to eat.
6. 'Having shame' must be interpreted as having a sense of shame; being a moral person.
7. See Abu-Lughod (1986) about the Alwlad 'Ali.

Chapter 4
Amari Familia: Belonging Together

Introduction

One day in early spring, Joska told us that he and Kurva were going to celebrate a wedding between his fifteen years old son and the daughter of Joska´s sister Nuca who also lived in the hamlet. In fact, he stressed, it would not be a real wedding (*biav*), but only a small party (*kef*). Joska asked me to videotape the occasion. The 'wedding' was celebrated on a Sunday but was prepared for the day before. Kurva, her married and unmarried daughters in the hamlet and one of her sisters, together with Joska and Kurva´s brothers, prepared food and decorations. Food was prepared in huge quantities: cabbage rolls filled with rice and meat, chicken, the traditional Romanian celebration cake, and other foodstuffs. Local spirits and beer in abundance were bought and the schoolhouse[1] was decorated for the occasion. The small room was full of busy women and in the centre was Kurva, shouting nervous commands to everybody and scolding the children. 'Hey, Dana go and get the butter under the big bed in the other room, quickly! Can't you find it you stupid girl! Go and eat the Lord's prick! Hey, Lelenz get me some water, go quickly, do you hear me, go now or I'll beat your head off!'. There was an atmosphere of nervous and feverish excitement typical of women's preparations of big parties everywhere.

When we arrived in the hamlet the next day, music could be heard from many houses and people had started drinking and dancing. As we approached the bride's house with the video-camera together with Thulo, the accordion player, a group of male youths led by Phuro and Paris, Joska's and the bride's elder brothers, shouted that they 'went to fetch the groom'. Arm in arm with the young groom, the men entered the bride's house 'to take the bride home', accompanied by dancing and shouting male relatives and children. In the bride's house the bride was seated in a corner wearing a silk blouse, a long pleated flowery skirt (*coxa*), and apron (*ketrinsa*), but without the obligatory headscarf (*dikhlo*) of married women. All the other married women in the house wore headscarves as usual. Relatives on both sides pressed into the house exchanging greetings: 'For luck, I wish you many years my brother, may you be happy my sister, may you live, may God give you health and luck. (*T'aves baxtalo, but bers, muro phral, t'aves baxtalo muri phej, te trais, te del o Del bax taj sastimo*)'. These same phrases were repeated over and over again. A cassette player was playing Romanian Gypsy music, every adult was swinging around bottles of plum brandy and greeting each other, and children were shouting. As soon as the videocamera was turned on, every person in the tiny room started to dance and shout even louder. The bride was drawn onto the floor and danced with her eyes downcast, while the groom was seated most of the time on one of the beds looking uneasy and shy. The main door was open and youngsters kept pressing into the hall and the room in high spirits.

Outside people from the hamlet had gathered in the front yard of the house dancing, drinking and waiting for the couple to appear. Others sat scattered outside their houses drinking and talking; the party was in action. After some time, Paris came out into the courtyard with the groom, his new brother-in-law (*šjogoro*), on one arm, and the bride (his sister) on the other. The bride was accompanied by the bora of her household. Then Paris told me to pay attention and to record when he solemnly kissed first the groom, and then the bride. Then all the male members of the new *familia*, like Paris and his uncle Joska, now *xanamikuri*,[2] exchanged kisses in the same way. They started the procession towards the schoolhouse. The bride's mother Nuca and her brother Joska, together with other close relatives, were accompanied by more distant ones on both sides, singing and shouting. Thulo, the accordion player, with his brother Angel the violin player, made up the orchestra. Outside the schoolhouse, the procession stopped again, and again Paris kissed his sister and his new brother-in-law and danced solemnly with them. Paris was by now quite drunk and kissed the bride repeatedly, everybody roaring with laughter when the bride tried to avoid him or wipe her mouth.

In the schoolhouse a long table was set along three walls and the bride and groom were placed in the middle. Only married men were seated at the table with the exception of the bride, and Joska's elder brother's wife. The women were standing by the opposite wall and soon the floor was filled with people, mostly women, youngsters of both sexes and children. The bride and groom looked shy and uneasy, but were constantly dragged to their feet by the now very drunk Paris to dance and be kissed. Joska and Kurva, the groom's parents, and Nuca, the bride's mother, served the seated guests and danced together with the rest of the guests. As all people in the hamlet are related in some way, the wedding was open to anybody, but not everybody in the hamlet showed up.

After about two to three hours of dancing, eating and shouting, people started to leave. As the tables were cleared and the children started eating the leftovers, the bride's second eldest brother, Kalo, appeared in the doorway and came roaring into the room in tears, naked to his waist, shouting that he had been insulted and he wanted to fight. He was very drunk and one of the groom's uncles, also very drunk, accepted the challenge. Their wives, however, interfered and pulled the two men apart shouting and swearing and finally everybody withdrew and the 'little kef' was over. Some days later we asked Joska how his new bori had settled in and he replied half smiling: 'Why shouldn't she settle in well? It must be better here than where she came from (his sister's house). Anyway, if she doesn't like it she'd better go back!'

Amari Familia: The Meaning of Relatedness

Brotherhood: The Ideological Basis of Famila

I have opened this chapter by describing a wedding, as marriage is the basic institution in Rom social organisation as it is basic for the constitution of social identity. The marriage institution is crucial for my discussion of relatedness and the social meaning of familia among the Roma (see Williams, 1983). The term *relatedness* indicates that biological and natural relations are only one way of creating enduring bonds between people, and is well suited to explore how people create relatives in different local contexts (Carsten, 2000). The Roma constantly repeated: 'We are all relatives up here (*ame sam njamuri sa*)', and a young man proudly told me: 'We all come from four men'. These four men (two pairs of brothers) are the grandfathers of today's heads of family households. The hamlet Roma do not form traditional lineages or clans. Every grown-up individual traces descent only to his/her grandparents. Based on these shallow lineages is, however, an ideology of patrilineal descent as constituting relatedness of a special kind: that between brothers (Gay y Blasco, 1999; Stewart, 1997). Ideas of common patrilineal descent, expressed by the stress on males as household heads and as the founders of familii, by the core symbol of brotherhood and by a general virilocal residence pattern, form the model for creating relatedness in general. The affection and alliance between brothers and sisters and the bonds created by siblings are expected to last for life, as is the relation between sons and parents and to a certain extent also daughters and parents. Wives and daughters cross the boundaries of independent households, thus creating alliance but also rupture (Gropper, 1975: 86; Stewart, 1997: 65,67).

Relatives by marriage are called *comnati*, while relatives both through descent and through marriage are referred to as *njamuri*, this latter term may also refer to the Roma one knows and to whom one has some kind of relations, and in some contexts even to Roma in general.[3] There was, as we shall see, considerable tension expressed both in symbols and in practice between expectations of loyalty towards cognatic and affinal relatives. Even if the natal bilateral family is seen to share the same blood, marriage outside the close family strengthens loyalties to a great number of relatives and contributes to the flexible and expanding kin networks characteristic of Rom social organisation.

Familia as a Moral Category

'Our family (*amari familia*) are the only decent people up here ... .'; 'Do not talk to others, only to people in our family, the others are bad ...'; 'Our family does not steal, I shall die (if I lie) (*te merav me*), none of us has ever stolen as much as an apple, that is what our family is like'; 'That family is no good, they all fight and drink, keep away from them', etc.

Such statements and warnings followed us throughout the year in the hamlet. When we asked who the *we* and the *them* were, the answers were usually quite aloof: 'Oh you know, our family and the others', followed by names of households heads. All hamlet inhabitants are related in some way and they all have the same family name. In such circumstances kinship loses its meaning as a means of creating subgroups, and some extra criteria are needed to distinguish those special kin relations that are necessary to create more stable loyalty (Cohen, 1994: 110). As most hamlet Roma begged to be photographed whenever they saw a camera, I started taking 'family portraits', asking them to gather the members of their familia to be photographed. When they received the photos, I asked who was missing and who did not belong. In that way I gathered a photo archive of family households that I used to inquire about familia relations. By carefully tracing relations between family households through photos and by observing the behaviour of individuals and members of such units in ritual celebrations and situations of conflict, and by listening to gossip in the hamlet and among other Roma, a pattern emerged out of the apparent arbitrary relations that constitute a familia. What the hamlet Roma refer to as 'familia' is composed of:

a) a family household, usually a couple, their children and one or more married sons with bora and children. This core is gradually enlarged by

b) married sons with wives and children (at least some of them) and/or

c) in case of 'uxorilocal marriages' (the husband becomes a member of the wife's familia), a daughter and her husband and children: plus

d) any family household bilaterally related to any of these households in and outside the hamlet according to some relevant context.

This pattern is very much the same as Stewart (1997) described among the settled Roma in Hungary under socialist government and has been is described as the extended family among the American Kalderašşa (Sutherland, 1975). The pattern is both systematic and flexible. The notion of 'amari familia' is composed of a selected number of sisters and brothers with their spouses, with other close relatives, agnates and cognates, added onto it. Amari familia does not necessarily consist of bloodrelated persons nor does it necessarily consist of people in the hamlet, but may comprise familii in other hamlets as well. Most people in the hamlet do, however, consider themselves part of a familia there. Those that do not, complain about this fact and some try to define themselves as associates of one of the hamlet familia if possible.

As long as one of the parents is still alive, unmarried children and married sons usually belong to their familia. When the parents die, the sons split up into different family households. Some may perpetuate the familia of their natal household, while others may join other familii and often enter into competition with their brothers. Sisters with their husbands usually join their husband's familia or, generally in cases of uxorilocal marriages, one or more of their brothers' familia.

Real and Ordinary Weddings; Marriage Preferences

The wedding described in the opening of this chapter was the celebration of the marriage between the son and daughter of siblings, Joska and Nuca, who have both lived most of their lives in the hamlet. Joska did not refer to the wedding by the Romanes word biav, but called it a small party, kef. By this he was indicating that this was not a 'real wedding'. So what is a real wedding? To answer this question I will look at different features constituting a marriage. Like Roma in general, the hamlet Roma marry without any interference from the state or the church. From the Romanian point of view their marriages are illegal, and their children are only officially registered by birth. From the Rom point of view marriage institutionalises the only legitimate sexual relation between women and men. By marriage girls and boys are transformed to complete persons, to Rom. As discussed in Chapter 3 it is the married couple that constitutes the moral, economic and political core of the Rom familia. A divorced man can not receive guests; he can not give a pačiv without shaming himself by doing the necessary female tasks himself. Thus he is restricted from entering into the competition for honour and respect so important among men. An unmarried or divorced woman is socially a child: she does not have a public voice and usually lives with her father. Only after her sons (if she has any) marry, will they represent their mother's family household in public.

The only restrictions of marriage among the hamlet Roma are between members of the immediate family, between uncles and nieces, aunts and nephews and between Roma and gaže. These restrictions are, however, not expressed as rules, but as a self-evident question of morality and practicality. As the gaže 'have no shame' and do not speak Romanes, and as such mixed marriages are also rejected by gaže, they will not generally happen. As marriage to gaže does not create alliance, and thus kinship, it is not strategically interesting. When such marriages did occur they were the result of individual choice, but were not rejected if they were seen as prosperous for the family household or familia in general. The hamlet Roma preferred to marry Roma of their own subgroup, generally Roma to whom they were already related. Although most Roma told us that it was bad to marry too close, first- and second-cousin marriages were common, both between cross and parallel cousins (*vero/verišoara*) (Stewart, 1997; Sutherland, 1975; see also Williams, 1985). These were regarded as true Roma (*Roma čače*), people one knows and can trust because they already belong to one's kin network and speak Romanes properly.

Official Marriages, Ordinary Marriages and Individual Marriages

Although the Roma see biological kinship as the basis of constructing social groups, I will consider kinship as a practical construction (Bourdieu, 1990: 167). This emphasis on the practical and strategic aspects of kinship is important in order to understand relatedness among the hamlet the Roma. In his discussion of marriage as strategy among the Kabyle peasants Bourdieu (1986: 168) introduced the terms 'practical kin' and 'official' or 'representational kin'. *Practical kin* refers to relations created by ordinary marriages between close kin who live together. These marriages are often not publicly celebrated and are not seen as prestigious, parallel-cousin marriages being an example of such alliances. *Official kin*, on the other hand, is created by extra-ordinary marriages – exogamous cross-cousin marriages or even marriages to other tribes – and are celebrated by extravagant weddings: 'It is practical kin who make marriages; it is official kin who celebrate them' (Bourdieu, 1986: 34). While ordinary marriages strengthen relations already established by particular individual ties, the ideal marriages are the cross-cousin exogamous marriages, that express marriage as alliance and are the kind of marriages that bring honour and prestige to the family and preserve the institution of marriage (Bourdieu, 1990). This model offers an interpretation of the social and political meaning of different marriage practices and the notions of "real weddings" among the hamlet Roma. I will, however, add a third category to the model: individual marriages creating no relations (in the sense of alliance) apart from that between the spouses.

Extra-ordinary and Ordinary Arranged Marriages

The common way of talking about arranging a marriage was for the parents to say: 'I take a bori for my son (*Lav mange ek bori more şaveske*)'. This expresses marriage as an arrangement between the parents-in-law, and the bride and spouse as the result of this arrangement and not vice versa as is the modern Romanian (and Western) idea of marriage. Such an alliance is to be preceded by a ritual of proposal (*mangimo*), where the male head of a familia asks another familia head for his daughter in marriage for his son, and where they negotiate the alliance and most importantly the bride wealth.[4] When explaining what they meant by a 'real wedding' the Roma told us about the wedding arranged by Joska's and his male cousin in Cluj some years ago. They boasted that Joska had received US$ 500 in brideprice, and that the wedding had lasted for three days, as the groom's familia was very rich. This wedding was always referred to when the Roma talked about weddings in general and I take this marriage to be an example of the extra-ordinary marriage creating official kin and thus alliance outside the hamlet.

Although Joska and Kurva's kef was not referred to as a real wedding and no bride wealth was exchanged, it celebrated a negotiated arrangement between the two familii rather than between the groom and bride. By this marriage, relations between these two familii were strengthened and the bride's family household could be incorporated into what Joska saw as his familia. The marriage created new bonds of mutual rights and obligation between Joska's family household and that of his sisters by relating Joska's niece as bori and his nephew (the brides father was dead) as his xanamik. The alliance being treated as one between men does not mean that women are not also part of these new relations, but that stress is put on the relations that are formed between family households represented by men. Women have the last word in selecting a bori and have also a say in rejecting a proposal. Kurva and her sister emphasised the role of the Romni in these matters: 'no bori comes into a house without the wife's consent'.

Individual or Love Marriages

One woman explained:

> Before, we used to arrange great 'real weddings' (*biava čače*). Today the young just walk up and down for some time and then they are married, or the boy's parents ask for a bori, they have a little meal (*pačiv*) and the young move in together.

Many young people did choose their own partners moving into the man's parents' house when the woman became pregnant and were then considered a married couple without any public ritual. When I pointed out the discrepancy between 'real weddings' and actual weddings in the hamlet, the Roma seemed quite contradictory. Although most agreed about what a 'real wedding' was, there were many opinions about how marriages should be arranged. Some said that the young should marry on their own choice, and that parents should not demand bride wealth. Thulo and Varga claimed to be strongly against arranged marriages and argued that bride wealth is the same as selling your daughter, which is the Romanian view. They told us that it is uncivilized and that the young should make their own choice. Their only married daughter had 'walked up and down' with a young man in the hamlet. When she got pregnant she moved into his parents' house, but when the couple broke up after some months she moved back to her parents' with the baby. Thulo himself had married Varga in this same way after having broken up a marriage with Anabela, another woman in the hamlet. Thulo and Varga had, of course, an interest in defending this kind of love marriage. But even people who proclaimed that the young should choose their own spouses liked to tell us about other people's 'real weddings', and would boast about the amount of bride wealth paid.

Love or Strategy? Kin Obligations, Affection, and Marriage Preferences

The wedding Joska and Kurva arranged for their son was discussed for a long time and this discussion sheds light over the motivations and strategies behind the agreement of marriages. Already in the autumn of the previous year Joska and Kurva had started talking about taking a bori for their unmarried son of fifteen years. As the wedding never happened I started to ask people about it. Youngsters suggested that the bride did not want to marry as she already had a boyfriend. Women talked about the familii not agreeing on the matter. I asked the young girl's mother, Joska's widowed older sister, why the wedding was not arranged. She answered that she was not so happy about Joska's plans of taking her daughter as a bori as it was bad to marry close relatives, 'But what can I do, he is my brother and I cannot refuse'. I asked her what was preferable – to marry your daughter away in town or to marry her in the hamlet. She said it was best to marry your daughter to more distant kin, because marriage with close kin could cause serious problems among them. So the hamlet Roma had different opinions about how people should marry, whether the young should choose their own spouses or parents should arrange marriages. The disagreement and inconsistency was about the children's role in deciding marriage partners and about marriage as a strategic instrument rather than about what a marriage was or what a 'real wedding' was. In familii where love marriages prevailed, this solution was presented as a proper and good marriage, while those who had arranged marriages for their children were more vague about the matter when asked directly. They did, however, confirm their adherence to the custom of arranged marriages while at the same time consenting to the value of personal autonomy indirectly, by saying that they did not force their children into marriage. From the Romanian authorities' and the peasants' points of view, arranged marriages are uncivilized and they see bride wealth as proof of the cruelty of the țigani – 'they sell their daughters'. I suggest this opinion influenced the Roma's opinion of marriage and their self-presentation towards us as 'civilized Westerners'. I do not, however, see the prevalence of love marriages as an aspect of modernisation, but as an expression of the tension between the value placed on personal autonomy and that placed on parental authority. Along with a general ideal of personal autonomy, the will power and individuality of children is respected and balanced against the expectancy of respect towards elders and their will. As most family households have both children who have married individually and children who have married collectively, this balance is maintained.

Mixed Strategies?

I came to understand this as a general dilemma about marriage among hamlet Roma; to marry one's daughter in the hamlet can cause rupture between close relatives if things go wrong, but if it works out well it may strengthen the involved households politically. But to refuse when a brother or sister insists on such a marriage may cause conflict and rupture between siblings who are supposed to be allies. Most women I talked to insisted that it is better to marry outside the hamlet, preferably into a more affluent family and neighbourhood, while men tended to stress that they preferred to keep their daughters in the hamlet. Is it that women prefer to avoid the possible community ruptures that might evolve from hamlet endogamous marriages, while men prefer the possibility of strengthening their familia towards others in the hamlet through close kin relationships? As women work closely together when scavenging, exchange food and generally seem to form tighter co-operating groups than men do, such ruptures may be more damaging to their daily life than to the men. Men seemed more preoccupied with the strategic dilemma of either marrying one's daughter out of the hamlet and to expand one's potential cultural, social and material resources, or marrying her in the hamlet to strengthen and control the same resources in one's own family household and familia, in competition with other familii (see Bourdieu, 1990: 187 about the choice between fission and fusion).

But there were other considerations as well. Kurva explained to me that it was difficult to find spouses outside the hamlet because as she expressed it: 'The Roma here are too poor, dirty and they have no shame'.

She claimed that Roma elsewhere did not want to marry their daughters to the hamlet Roma, and that few Roma in other villagers wanted bora from the hamlet. Kurva herself had, however, both a daughter married out and a bori from a distant village, so her statement seemed to be about 'the others' and not about her own household. Most Roma in town who talked very badly about the hamlet Roma confirmed her statement. They described the hamlet Roma as bad and dirty drunkards and scavengers that they themselves would not wish for their children in marriage. This was, however, opposed by Roma in other hamlets in the district who told us that the relief gift from the West that had made the hamlet Roma rich and unwilling to share their fortune by marrying their daughters outside the hamlet. This implies that the new prosperity brought by the relief gift from abroad may have created a new strategic situation. By marrying all one's children in the hamlet to close kin, the economic resources could be concentrated and controlled (see also Sutherland, 1975: 217).

Limits to Strategy

Although interpreting marriage as strategy brings out the creative process of 'kinship making', in practical life, marriage and the making of kinship are also a result of individual affective bonds, of resistance to parental authority and of kinship morality. The moral models moulding the expectations of kin relations, together with affection, enmity and conflict, influence and often even destroy the conscious strategies people have, and leave them with practical solutions that are not optimal but must be handled anyway. Among the relatively poor hamlet Roma, who had little material and symbolic capital to compete for bora, arranged marriages played a less important practical role, but were not less significant as a cultural ideal that influenced social organisation. Hence every marriage was an issue of common interest and discussion in the hamlet.

Although men are responsible for arranging marriages, 'no bori comes into a house without the wife's consent'. Men may have strategies for increasing their own and their familia's respect and honour, but members of their own family household may have opposing interests. Wives may have interests or moral concerns that destroy men's strategies, as exemplified by women's preference for exogamous marriages for their daughters. When women have marriageable children, they are generally old from a Rom point of view and have acquired respect and influence that is used in important matters like their children's marriages. Daughters may destroy their parents' marriage strategies by shameless behaviour. Joska's daughter Kasablanka broke up a prestigious arranged marriage and destroyed her father's xanamik relationship. As the Roma say they do not force their children into marriage, the children's consent also influences a planned marriage. I assume that all these considerations play some role in the way the Roma think about marriage as they influence the strategies that lead to arranged marriages.

Abduction and elopement also come in the way of conscious strategy. Several Romnja from other hamlets told us they had been abducted by their husbands or their husbands' familii and married without their consent or the consent of their parents. Women in the hamlet warned me not to walk alone in the woods without my husband, as I could be abducted. The three instances I know of of abduction or possible abduction were of Kaštale women by Rom men, but abduction seemed to be a strategy employed both by individual men and by familii to 'take a bori' without paying brideprice, or to 'take a bori' from a family superior to them in social standing. I do not know how abductions are handled, but I suggest that some result in an agreement between the two familii, thus forming lasting mutual relations, while some lead to rupture and conflict.[5]

Divorce and Adultery

Adultery and divorce were two of the main causes of conflict in the hamlet and could lead to the rupture of all relations established at marriage. At least sixteen of the ninety-three adults over eighteen years old had been married twice and some thrice. Most of them had been married to people still living in the hamlet in new marriages. Most 'divorces' happened during the first years of marriage and before any children were born (with some exceptions that I know of). Everybody in the hamlet knew who had previously been married to whom and it was a theme for gossip, laughter and conflict. Accusations of adultery were one of the main causes for wife beating and for fights between men. Many Rom stated that whenever they got drunk they got preoccupied with the fear of their women being adulterous. As illustrated in the previous chapter, women are quite free to go wherever and whenever they wish. This and their often seemingly promiscuous behaviour in Romanian public arenas seem to pose a constant threat to the men's trust in their control of their wives and thus to their honour and authority as husbands and males.

The combination of different marriage practices and strategies, where individual love marriages appear to be the most common, does not, however, seem to destroy the value of marriage as alliance. The ideal and celebration of extra-ordinary weddings as expressions of 'real wedding' are shared by all, even if pragmatism and other considerations hinder them in arranging them for their own children. This combination of different practices in creating relatedness contributes to a flexible social practice that may be adaptable to changing social and economic circumstances.

Marriage and the Social Definition of Self

Descent and Marriage – Crossing Loyalties

Although I have argued that relations based on bilateral descent constitute the model of Rom relatedness, I will suggest that the tension between relations by descent and those by marriage should be understood in terms of duality, where loyalty to one's natal and to one's husband's household represent opposing poles. People make choices; position themselves between these two poles according to context. The necessity to balance one's affection and obligations towards agnates and affines presents every individual with multiple choices in everyday situations (Moore, 1994). Affection, kinship obligations and individual interests posit social persons in different positions in different contexts and make people present different aspects of self (Ewing, 1990). I will discuss some of these positions, the different expectations and obligations that are activated in different contexts and how they are handled.

Marriage generally does not create a new family household, as most young couple move in with the groom's parents and thus extend that household. All household members are thus involved in new relationships and as they acquire new social positions they change as social persons. The position of the bori most dramatically expresses the inherent tension of the new relations established by marriage and the vulnerability of such relations. Misolini, a disabled man who was supported by his wife Anabela, expressed this tension very strongly about his daughter-in-law: Anabela was telling us about their bori's family, that lived in the hamlet. Misolini got very angry and burst out that she no longer was a member of that familia, and she had better remember it, she was part of his familia now and belonged to no one else. The bori very hastily reassured him that of course, she was part of his his familia and no longer belonged to her father's. The young people had married for love and Misolini and his brother-in-law were on bad terms. The fact that his brother in-law was relatively wealthy and had been against the marriage was an insult to Misolini.

When a woman moves into her husband's household as bori, this expresses three changes in her social position: (1) she is transformed from young girl to woman: from *šei bari* to Romni, with rights and obligations towards a husband; (2) she is transformed from daughter to daughter-in-law: from šei to bori, with rights and obligations to her mother-in-law (*i sokra*), and to her father in law (*o sokro*); and (3) from being a member of her natal family household and familia, she and her children will now belong to those of her husband, but with rights and obligations towards both. The bori assists her mother-in-law with all necessary household tasks and takes orders from her and her father-in-law. The first bori in a family household is often treated as everybody's servant, but as more bora 'are taken', the work burden is eased. But every new bori especially one that is a result of an arranged marriage, is the pride of the family household, and hamlet men often asked us: 'Have you seen my beautiful new bori?', thus expressing the honour achieved by a good arrangement. The transformation of a daughter of one household into the wife and mother of another is a lifelong process and is perhaps only complete in her children. The position of bori may thus be seen as a liminal position between her agnatic and affinal relations. This liminality only ceases when her parents-in-law die or she heads a new, separate family household with bora of her own.

As a wife, a woman should accept her husband's authority in many matters and show him respect, but many young wives dispute this authority. The common practice of young wives returning temporarily to their natal households indicates that the mutual rights and duties of wives and husbands is an issue of disagreement and conflict. Women generally explained that they returned home if their husbands hit them and men generally said that their wives were bad and needed it. Joska's bori Violetta often went home to her mother and took her children with her when she had problems with her husband. On these occasions Kurva, her mother-in-law, was full of scorn towards both the girl and her familia; they were a bunch of good-for-nothings. Presidinte's (Joska's nephew) wife left him and their two eldest children and went to her mother's household in another hamlet whenever Presidinte was drinking too heavily. She spent almost as much time in her natal village as in her husband's. He then lived alone and had to look after the two older children of five and six and eat with his parents. Although he was not said to beat her, this was tolerated and several women told me about this with amusement, expressing their consent to such a strategy.

Going home of course means emphasising a woman's rights as a daughter over her duties as a wife and thus disrespecting her husband's (and her) household. Although her primary loyalty should be to her husband's familia, a bori is also expected to cultivate her relationship with her father's kin and thereby strengthen the alliance. But most women know that in a conflict situation, if she is maltreated, or her husband dies, goes to jail, or leaves her etc., her natal household and familia may be her only allies. This position, as a seal of the new alliance between family households, gives the bori a certain power not only to express her own interests when she is maltreated but to express other complaints as well: One late evening a young man knocked on our gate and asked us to drive him by car to a nearby village. He did not tell us why he wanted to go, but only spoke about his wife being there. We went with him and realised it was his wife's natal village and that she had probably run away to her mother because he had beaten her. When we arrived he sent for someone to fetch her, but she did not want to come. After a lot of arguing she came and he persuaded her to come home with him. Her mother was with her, and as the girl came into the car her mother told her not to come running home for small matters like this. If she was really beaten and treated badly she should come, but not for small matters. The mother in the case above reminded her daughter of the balance that she had to keep, between loyalty to her husband and loyalty to her parents, when she told her not to ask for support for 'small matters'. I discussed this episode with Vulpe, the husband's sister, the next day and she insisted that her brother had been right and that women deserve a beating now and then. When I protested, Vulpe said laughing: 'Perhaps not you, as you are a gaži, but we Romnja are very bad and deserve beating'. Vulpe's marriage is uxorilocal, she lives with her husband and her agnatic kin and was expressing herself as a good sister, supporting her brother's authority over the bori, echoing a general sentiment in the hamlet and thus supporting men's ideal authority over women. That does not mean that she, or any other woman, accepts her own husband's domination in all contexts. When a man drinks too much, for instance, and cannot perform his duties as household head he may lose respect and support from men and thus authority over his household.

Duality, Ambiguity and Shifting Selves

As emphasised, common descent, and, perhaps equally important, living together and sharing everything, seem to create the strongest affective and most morally obliging relationships between the hamlet Roma,[6] and we would expect ties between brothers and brothers and sisters to be more obliging than ties between spouses. This, however, is not always the case. As brothers are expected to head independent family households they may just as well be competitors and even enemies as allies. This ambiguity is especially significant between brothers living in uxorilocal affiliations. The man who for different reasons takes up uxorilocal residence is expected to change his loyalty and primary obligations from his own to his wife's natal family household. Stewart claims that this position is extremely shameful among the Harangos Roma (Stewart, 1997: 64). This man's social identity will probably always be somewhat dubious, but his children will be born members of his wife's familia and not of his. Although Joska's brothers-in-law were his allies in the hamlet and his relationship to his biological brother was fraught with conflict, the same brother played the role of his closest male kin during the described wedding while his brothers-in-law were not even seated at the wedding table. In that context descent was given priority over bilateral relations.

Although women are expected to shift their primary loyalty from their father's household to that of their husband, their brothers always consider themselves their sisters' protectors ready to support them if they are treated badly. We asked Kurva how she could accept that her brother Rabo beat his wife, Joska's niece, when he was drunk. She said that she and Joska had tried to stop him, but he did not listen to her. 'But she has brothers, you know', Joska commented, and he added[7] 'and one day they will have had enough and they will get him'. Kalo's challenge at his sister's wedding, described in the opening of this chapter, was, I suggest, a demonstration of the power of her brothers and a warning of what would happen if she should be badly treated and they thus insulted (see also Sutherland, 1975: 228). All these cases illustrate the tension between relations by descent and those by marriage, but they also illustrate how persons in different positions present different selves in different contexts. Even in her domestic position a women has many interests, concerns and obligations that allow her to express many selves – respectful and subordinated, but also assertive and independent, supporting male supremacy in one context and challenging it in the next, loyal to her husband and his household in one context and to her natal household in another. As Katherine Ewing has forcefully argued, this shifting does not make people experience inconsistency, ambivalence and conflict in general, but that 'individuals have a remarkable capacity to maintain an experience of wholeness in the face of radical contradictions, by keeping only one frame of reference in mind at any particular moment' (Ewing, 1990: 274). When I argue that the tension between agnatic and cognatic affiliation should be analysed as a duality, this is exactly because of people's ability to change frame of reference from one social situation to another thus handling what an outsider may see as inconsistency as aspects of wholeness – aspects that only in some contexts are brought together and act as dichotomies causing ambivalence and helplessness.

The Flexibility of the Rom Familia

To understand the composition of a familia, one must also understand the importance of affection and mutual sympathy, which both direct the formation of familii and follow from familia membership. Among all available brothers, brothers-in-law or cousins, some like each other and some do not, and this sympathy influences men's and women's choices of familia membership and support. But it also influences marriage arrangements – men and women want their daughter to marry into a pleasant and good familia as they want a bori from a nice familia. The moral habitus of the person is, however, seen to follow kin affiliation; a person is thus seen to constitute the relationships of which she is a part (Strathern, 1992a: 209), as revealed by the following example.

Joska was said to have married young and been 'adopted' into Kurva's familia, which was why 'he is nicer (*mai lašo*) than his brother Phuro', people said. Those of Kurva's brothers who were part of Joska's familia were said to be 'nice' and Joska spent much time with them. When Kurva explained why Joska and his brother Phuro were rivals, she said that Phuro's familia was bad (*beng*). Kurva's youngest brother was married to one of Phuro's daughters, and although he was liked by all Joska's familia his position was ambiguous. As a brother and a nice person, he 'should' belong to the Joska familia but his bad wife seemed to pose a problem to his membership. None of Joska's sisters in the hamlet were regarded as his familia. One was a widow by the brother of Phuro's wife, the other was married to one of Joska's paternal uncles, and although not familia, this sister's household was associated to Joska's familia while the first was not.

This created a rather complex situation: relations of descent and marriage were crossed by sympathy and by ideas of inherent badness and goodness of different families. A fragment of this situation is illustrated in Figure 4.1.

Only children of unwed parents are included in the in the fourth generation.

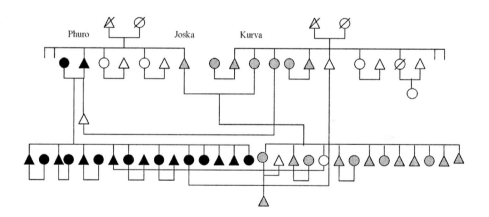

The grey indicates Joska and Kurva's familia, the black that of his brother Phuro. White indicates individuals with indeterminate familia relations.

Figure 4.1 Intermarriage of Joska's and Phuro's familii

Brotherhood: Love and Competition

Merging of households into larger units based on idioms of kinship such as a familia is a well known political strategy for the type of political organisation of Roma where there are no centralised power institutions above the household level (Evans-Pritchard, 1940). The ability to enforce one's will in competition with others is to a great extent dependent on the number of followers one can mobilise, and the familia forms an important political unit in this competition. Joska and Phuro provide an example of this competition between biological brothers in the same hamlet. This unresolved conflict and competition expressed itself through avoidance between members of their respective familii and through the constant gossip about the acts and general moral habitus of the other familia. But the tension sometimes exploded into minor fights between its members. The whole process of gossip, slander and eventual conflict reinforced enmity and made each familia seek the support from other familii in and outside the hamlet. Marriage was one strategy to seek such support. When Joska asked for his sister's daughter for one of his sons, I suggest this to be a strategy in this competition. She represented a household/familia with many sons and it was important for Joska to strengthen their obligation to their mother's brother's familia. Competition between brothers will be discussed in depth in chapter 5.

So, 'we-consciousness', expressed in terms of the bilaterally composed local familia, was constructed from a combination of: the feeling of belonging together on the basis of kinship; friendship; and political strategy. This was also based on face-to-face activity such as working, laughing and talking, and by the agreement of certain moral qualities. It was maintained by visiting, by sharing and co-operation, by common discourse and by ritual.

Translocal Community

Local Community: Everyday Social Exchange

Living close together reveals the shortcomings of kinship solidarity, but it also restrains individual and/collective greed. The social control in the hamlet is direct and fairly outspoken in contrast to the social control exerted towards distant kin. The hamlet Roma make this comparison and speak about other Roma in the hamlet as a bad and dirty lot, and their relatives living elsewhere as true, rich and good. As we have seen, the ideals of brotherhood, sharing and unity are only partly achieved in daily life. Strategies of avoidance, open conflicts and even fights are also part of everyday life and may create borders even between people who generally consider each other familia.

But the local familia is not the widest circle of Rom relatedness. Every familia is part of a kin network based on bilateral kin relations with familii in other hamlets that may be perceived of as closer and more binding than their relations to distant relatives in the hamlet. These translocal networks express the deterritorialised (Deleuze and Guattari, 1985) social organisation of Roma – a social organisation not dependent on sedentary habitation. With the local household and familia, translocal networks form political corporations reflecting the flexibility of Rom organisation as potentially sedentary and/or nomadic. From the government point of view, the hamlet appears as a corporate unit, relatively controllable and perceptible, with an appointed leader. The translocal networks, invisible to non-Roma, are, however, the decisive units for internal political processes and are crucial for the spatial flexibility of Roma. The hamlet and the translocal networks may be seen as different communities that are characterised by different symbolic features, boundaries and social practices (Cohen, 1985).

Funerals as Rituals for the Translocal Community

The boundaries marking the local Roma group as a community, separate from the village, are both symbolic and physical. These boundaries are based on kinship ties, ideas of common ancestry and language, and physical closeness, and are expressed by social practices such as begging and scavenging, by dress, by the physical structures of the hamlet and by the organisation of hamlet life. Translocal communities are not physically bounded, but rest on ideas of relations and belonging that the Roma talk of as spiritually closer, more enduring and involving more obligations than hamlet relations. These translocal boundaries are primarily expressed by ritual participation. Rom identity and social organisation rest on both these modes of community that should not be seen in opposition but as a duality of mutually dependent and reinforcing relations. Translocal communities are celebrated, created and confirmed primarily through the funeral ceremonies. Funerals bring men and women of different hamlets, but of the same or allied familii, together in different places for several days, drinking, weeping and thus safeguarding their dead relative's path to the world of the dead. Throughout winter, household heads travel from one funeral to another, sometimes with only days spent in the hamlet in between. I see these translocal networks of relatives as crucial for the continuation of Rom economic adaptation, social organisation and ideology. Death is the social event that threatens these communities, and funerals re-enact and confirm them.

Familia and Nacie: Kinship as Ethnicity

When the hamlet Roma say they are kin, this implies that they belong to the same nacie: the Vurdonara or Čurara. Nacie is a Rom word (Romanian: *naţio*) most commonly used about 'a people' with common language and traditions: an ethnic group. *Rasa* (*rasă* in Romanian) may be used in the same way but is used more seldom and often about categories of Roma without kinship ties who talk different dialects. The concepts of 'rasa' and 'nacie' are generally interchangeable and refer to groups of Roma related through kinship. Most of the Roma in the area call themselves Čurara and it is with other groups of Čurara that the hamlet Roma form translocal networks. It is also among the Čurara that they have enemies. Three elements classify what they perceive as different nacie or rasa of Roma: (1) the women's dress and hairstyle; (2) the men's occupation; and (3) the language (dialect) they speak (see Williams, 1983). The hamlet Roma say that they generally only marry Čurara in the area. Rasa is also also used about non-Roma like Hungarians, French etc. Some nacii/rasa are regarded as neither Rom nor gažo but a bit of both.

The quite rigid classification of subgroups of Roma used in literature about Roma written in Europe and the U.S.A. (e.g. Gropper, 1975; Sutherland, 1975; Williams, 1985), is not a feature of intergroup relations in Transylvania. Here I found the classification of subgroups or nacii/rasa to be an ongoing process with no apparent endproduct. Classifying and naming Roma appear to be very ad hoc and they often classified the same people differently in different situations (see also Voiculescu, 2002). Itinerant Roma who sold clothes, carpets and materials in the villages were sometimes referred to as *Bombakara* (from *bombak* – cotton) and sometimes as *Biznicara*. The Roma who produce tin guttering were sometimes called *Kelderara*, sometimes *Čuternara* (from gutter). Those known as *Lovara* in Europe and the U.S.A. were just as often called *Patronara* (from patron – owner). The people referred to as *Kaštale* by hamlet Roma and not regarded as real Roma (*Roma čače*), none the less called themselves Roma and there were several intermarriages between the groups. Classification is usually based on actual occupation, but sometimes also on living conditions. Joska told us that the Čuternara who called themselves Kelderara were really Čurara, like the hamlet Roma, who had learned the trade of the Kelderara (coppersmiths). All these occupational terms are a legacy from the feudal times, when ţigani were artisan slaves or serfs and classified according to the service they offered. The Roma often talked about an ongoing conflict with a local group of Čurara in a village at some distance from the hamlet. They described the relations between the groups as like a feud that burst into violence at certain times. In the last fight that was reported to have taken place some years before my fieldwork, the hamlet had split and Phuro's familia had sided with the 'enemy'. In this conflict, the hamlet is not a political corporation, as most familia have kin obligations outside the hamlet that may be stronger than those between hamlet dwellers. It is in relations and in conflicts with Roma from other nacii that the hamlet acts as a corporation: a community. In such conflicts, local kinship ties and belonging to the same nacie and the same hamlet create the necessary fusion against more distant relations. Perhaps most importantly – the hamlet is a community in relation to the peasant community of the village. In relations to gaže all Roma are kin or at least 'brothers' and of the same nacie, and thus at least conceptually closer related to one another than to any gaže. The pattern that emerges is not one of concentric circles of belonging and loyalty according to kinship, locality or nacie as in segmentary political organisation (Evans-Pritchard, 1940). A familia is not a clan; it is more complex and contextual and also expands the local hamlet, but it is always some conceptualisation of kinship that is the decisive factor for creating relatedness, belonging and community. However, the hamlet acts as one political corporation only in contexts when internal hamlet kinship ties are conceptualised as closer and more binding than those of their adversaries – in relation to other subgroups of Roma and to non-Roma. It is only in relation to Roma who are not related to any hamlet familii, and generally in conflicts with gaže, that the hamlet is one. This implies that groups of Roma that are seen as collective enemies to the hamlet are generally talked of as 'another nacie' as an explanation for the enmity.

No such conflicts or fights happened during my fieldwork, but the Kaštale were always talked about as 'other' by all hamlet Roma, even by the men married to Kaštale women. Conflicts with gaže were, however, a feature of everyday life in the hamlet. Not that those conflicts were expressed daily in relations with non-Roma, but relations with villagers and non-Roma in general were part of the daily discourse of 'us' and 'them'. The 'us' depended on the context, but in relation to villagers it was always 'us – the Roma' and often 'us – the hamlet' and only sometimes 'us – the Joska familia'. Ethnicity, as one feature of kinship, prescribes social loyalty. This loyalty is strengthened by the same type of collective loyalty expressed by villagers; they are all expected to side together against ţigani in any conflict. This conflation of kinship and ethnicity creates a strong emotional unity that draws one of the most efficient boundaries around the hamlet as a community.

Maintaining Relatedness

Visiting; Sharing Company, Food and Moral Community

Bourdieu (1986) claims that the making of kinship and relatedness is based upon continuous work of maintenance by different forms of economic and symbolic exchange. Visiting is an absolute obligation between close kin among the hamlet Roma, as among Roma in general (Stewart, 1997; Barth, 1955). To visit members of one's familia is considered a necessary expression of friendship and respect. Visiting is also an obligation between more distant kin such as brothers-in-law, xanamikuri and other allies. One might say that the familia consists of the people who walk in and out of each other's houses. Visits from a close member of one's familia does not require food or drink to be served, as visiting is primarily for sharing space and time chatting, gossiping, telling stories and jokes and supporting each other in times of trouble.

Besides visiting, borrowing and sharing material and symbolic objects contribute to the feeling and expression of 'we-consciousness' among members of a familia, almost as strong as that of a household. Food, clothes and money are expected to be shared among members of a familia (as discussed in Chapter 2), as are support, help and co-operation in tasks. When Kurva's brother Rabo slaughtered a pig, all the households of his familia were given a share. When Kurva lacked some condiment for supper she sent a child to a house in her familia. If Rita, Kurva's younger sister, was in town and her children were around when food was prepared in one of her sisters' or brothers' house, they were generally included in the meal. Everyday life together presupposes some sort of economic interdependency between hamlet households. The idiom of sharing, although an ideal, has a practical basis; it is certainly an assurance against economic catastrophe. No household will be left alone to let their children or members sicken or die of hunger as long as there is food in the hamlet, and everybody knows that.

Co-operation is also a way of sharing. When Joska and Kurva were preparing the kef, members of their familia helped out. Whenever Kurva's two brothers wanted us to drive to town with them to collect scrap metal for buckets, Joska was expected to come with us, although he never produced buckets himself. When the women go scavenging in town they tend to go with the women they define as their familia, but as this is a flexible notion they have a broad choice. Visiting, sharing and co-operation express and confirm relatedness created by kinship, marriage and affection. But, as we shall see, members of a familia also share symbolic substances.

True Words: Restructuring Moments

Whenever men were gathered together at rituals such as marriages, funerals or: pačiva, they drank alcohol in abundance and exchanged true words *'vorba čače'* (see also Stewart, 1997: 198).[8]

> May you have luck my brothers and sisters, my little uncle, my little grandfather! May God give you luck and health brothers, to our family and all our Gypsiness! (*T'aven baxtale mure phrala, mure pheja, muro kakoro, muro paporo. Te del tume o Del bax taj sastimo phrala, bax taj sastimo amari familiake, sa amari ciganiake!*).

These words and utterances, followed by kissing and handshakes, are repeated over and over again by men, and generally followed by drinking and cheering. Both men and women are generally gathered at weddings and funerals, but it is mostly men and older women that repeat the' true words'.[9] I suggest seeing this kind of speech as a kind of kinship discourse – as formal or ritualised speech that serves as social mantras, or as magic spells (Howell, 1986). The constant reassurance that 'our familia are decent people', 'we are not like the others', 'we never steal', 'we are to be trusted', etc. expresses and creates a symbolic 'sameness' or a common morality. This is linked both to belonging to a certain familia and to being Rom. Kinship solidarity is an ideal seldom achieved outside the familia or even the household. In real, everyday life, lack of support from kin, insults from close kinsmen, conflicts over women and children, theft and abuse are just as normal as harmony. 'True words' create restructuring moments (Stewart, 1997: 203) that express the central trait of Rom ideology and serve as instruments to evoke kinship morality and prevent conflict and rupture. Thus 'true words' expressing brother- and sisterhood, love and belonging counteract the possible dangers deriving from dual loyalties, competition and jealousy. This ritualised speech act does not gloss reality and it does not conceal the fact that everyday life among kinsmen is fraught with hate and conflict. It brings speakers and listeners together in an emotional state of love and unity and reinforces the belief that love and solidarity lie at the core of community life. So, drinking together and sharing 'true/pretty words' create the experience of being the same and wanting the same. It creates an atmosphere of forgiveness and community where the social perspective shifts from everyday individual trouble to collective principles and emotions.

Notes

1. This schoolhouse was built with money from the relief organisation, as has been mentioned earlier in this book, and is for Rom children up to 9 years old.

2. Two men exchanging children in marriage, see Romanes vocabulary.

3. The word is taken from the Romanian *neamuri*, which has approximately the same meaning; people related through blood and marriage; a people and a nation.

4. Among the Roma in Norway all marriages involve mangimo and bride wealth, and *biav* is celebrated. Marriage Tsiganes (Williams, 1984) is a detailed ethnography and discussion about the marriage ceremony among the Kalderas of Paris. The Rom 'real wedding' is very similar to the traditional Romanian weddings in Transylvania (see Kligman, 1988; Marian, 1995). See also Stewart (1997) about the mangimo among Hungarian Rom.

5. Elopement (*naşimo*), which is very common among Roma in Western Europe and America (Gay y Blasco, 1999; Gropper, 1975; Sutherland, 1975; Williams, 1984) was never mentioned among the hamlet Roma.

6. See Gay y Blasco about the Gitanos of Madrid (1999).

7. Thus almost quoting the Punjabi brothers in Veena Das's discussion about blood relatives in the Punjabi family (Das, 1998).

8. The hamlet Roma do not, however, 'sing their brotherhood' like the Roma of Harangos in Stewart's study.

9. Some men drink heavily in the village bars several times a week. These drinking parties are accompanied by the same 'pretty words' and utterances of love and togetherness, but they often end up in oral abuse, fighting and wife-beating.

Chapter 5
Competing for Equality

Introduction

Joska's oldest uncle in the hamlet, Fusuj, had been sent home from hospital to die among his family. Fusuj was sixty-five years old and had cancer. He was one of the elders and the father of four sons and four daughters, all married in the hamlet. His sons told us they wanted to give a *mesali*, a meal in his honour, and wanted us to videorecord it: 'to have something to remember him by when he is dead'. The date for this meal was not set, but it was to be held when the family had enough money to give a really nice mesali. Eventually the date was fixed for Christmas Eve. As the date became known in the hamlet, Joska's cousins, the sons of his other uncle Puca, told us they were having a mesali for their own parents and wanted us to film that event as well. And eventually most familii announced that they wanted to give a mesali 'for their old folks (*le phure*)'. It was always sons that wanted to give a mesali, although Fusuj's wife, Danka, was strongly engaged in the matter. On Christmas Eve we were to be brought from the village by Fusuj´s youngest son.

After a quiet evening spent with our Romanian family we walked through the pitch dark, frozen night up to the merry hamlet. Fusuj´s small hut was filled to capacity with his familia members and other kin. A long table, covered with all sorts of food and drink, filled the whole room. The walls were decorated with carpets, and the tape-recorder played popular Romanian Gypsy music (in Romanes). After some arranging and discussion where the eldest son was master of ceremonies, I was asked to start filming. Fusuj, very conscious about the event as a performance, turned to my husband and started to talk about the 'olden days': 'In the olden days Jorgole, we travelled through the villages with our children and our old folks'. He continued by telling a story, a typical Rom story about the poor Rom boy and the Emperor . After the story came to an end, music was turned on again and the guests started to dance. After a while,

Fusuj was encouraged to join in and accompanied by the joyful cries of everyone, he danced with his wife and his bora. When he sat down again and had calmed down, he started a speech of farewell to his family. He expressed his grief for having to leave them and his worry about their future without him: 'Look after one another and see to your business, raise your children, like I raised you'. When he burst into tears the whole party broke in to comfort him, his sons and bora, though, barely able to hold back their tears themselves. During the different phases of this mesali, men and women all the time lifted their glasses and bottles crying out: 'May God give you health and happiness, health and happiness, my brother, luck, luck my cousin, sister, my children… and so forth'.

We videotaped another mesali the same night and yet another later that year staged in much the same way as the two others, the most marked feature being their almost ritualised likeness in sequence and speech. As soon as the videos were copied and given to the different families, they were discussed and evaluated. Fusuj's mesali was found the most beautiful. I asked on what grounds they made this evaluation and the usual answer was that it contained dance, and true and beautiful speech (*vorbi šukar haj čače*), and that Fusuj had told a story (*paramiča*). This video was generally commented on as the most beautiful they had seen and everybody wanted me to film one just like it. This video's reputation went as far as to town, and Roma from other villages in the area begged me to film a mesali in their familia. A mesali given in honour of one's elders is regarded as pačiv – an exhibition of a family's honour – and enters into the hamlet competition of honour between familii.

Power: Domination and Resistance

Brotherhood, Competition and Integration

When I asked a young man how they resolved conflicts in the hamlet he explained:

> We all descend from four men: Joska's father, Kurva's father, Kalo's father and Fusuj's father. We are all kin, so we keep peace with each other. If an argument arises, which happens almost only when the men are drunk, it is settled. Because we are all kin we try to avoid disagreements and enmity. If an argument arises and it is not settled right away, the old men in the hamlet decide who is guilty. The guilty one is given some strokes with a whip, not too hard, and then the case is settled. Fights like that mostly happen between different nacii, but in the hamlet we are all one nacie. If enmity and conflict is not resolved, the guilty familia must move. This has happened many times in the hamlet.

This man presented an idealisation of hamlet relations, the same idealisation that is presented during celebrations where 'true words' are spoken. As has been emphasised throughout this book, although the Roma value equality, brotherhood and harmony, there none the less is an ongoing competition between hamlet family households and familii represented by adult males. So what is this competition about? This chapter aims to discuss that question.

The Roma see power/strength (*zor*), as an ability vested in persons that is dependent on many factors such as their personality, allies and physical condition. This is a general trait of tribal society, where relations of power and domination are maintained by personal strategy (Bourdieu, 1986: 183). Individuals are seen as competing with their own personal abilities and luck, *(bax)*, as their basic weapons, but they always represent a family household and familia. As Roma; brothers representing familii, individuals are regarded as moral equals in this competition. However, the Rom discourse on equality and autonomy of family heads disguises the structural relations of power, such as gender and age, as natural and given. It also disguises structural relations of power between Roma and the Romanian authorities as a question of personal abilities and moral properties. So although 'relations of domination can be set up and maintained only at the cost of strategies which must be endlessly renewed' (Bourdieu, 1986: 183), on a practical level, these strategies are structured. The symbolic order expressed in terms of shame as a property, unequally distributed between young and old, men and women, and Roma and gaže, represents a social structure based on the natural dominant position for mature males. So ideas of honour *(pačiv)* are the symbolic structures that legitimate male domination. Competition means that all strive for the same aim and that competition thus is itself a confirmation of the value of this aim (Simmel, 1955: 59). The ongoing competition among hamlet men for pačiv, and for zor, by means of material, cultural and social resources, based on the discourse of equality and autonomy, thus maintains and accentuates the dominant position of mature men. It is as mature men, men with respect and honour, that they are equals, and this is the condition and end of their competition.

But women and young people are not outside this competition. Although women and young people generally accept the symbolic order as natural and given, the ideal of equality is also theirs. Relations of power and domination structured by the symbolic order are not only maintained but also challenged by ideals of equality and independence. Women may support and even spur on their fathers, husbands, brothers and sons in their struggle for respect and honour, but they may also resist their domination and have plans and desires of their own, thus challenging male domination and influencing relations of power between men and between men and women. This supports Bourdieu's claim that relations of domination and power in tribal societies have to be endlessly renewed (Bourdieu, 1986), and I will add that in this process relations may be transformed in different contexts. Different family households may rise to influence and even exercise power over others in certain periods; women may have access to resources that strengthen their position both as a class and as individuals at different times and in different contexts. These changes may all influence the symbolic order of honour and brotherhood in different ways, but as long as honour and equality are central features of the competition between males, the symbolic order will be strengthened not weakened.

Sharing Resources and Competing for Honour

Competition for a common value, says Georg Simmel (1955: 58–59), may turn competitors against each other, but the value itself is abundant and in no way achieved by the competitors using their strength on each other. The competition for honour and respect is such a struggle and, as Simmel emphasises, the outcome of this competition is a confirmation of the value that all strive for and may even increase the value of the prize. The competition for honour and respect does not disrupt the hamlet as a community on the contrary it may strengthen the basic values that hold people together.

But the competition for honour is only one of many interests that preoccupy hamlet Roma, and some of these interests involve conflict where the use of power and violence may decide the outcome. Competition for cultural capital is dependent on, and interacts with the struggle for these other interests. These interests are foremost the access to material resources such as the gift of clothes from the foreign NGO; to territories and/or economic niches, such as as barter, begging clients etc.; but also the access to social resources such as the control of sons and daughters for marriage and support from allies and associates. By analysing conflicts involving some of these interests this chapter will discuss how the struggles for cultural, social and material capital are intermingled and how influence and power are the means and the outcome of these conflicts.

Wealth in the sense of money and objects is, however, not an instrument of influence and power per se: as honour/respect represents the main symbolic capital for power and influence, material capital must be 'purified' by ritual sharing in order to be converted into honour. Not that material capital (money, gold, horses, carpets) is in any way impure, but by not being shared such resources violate the ideas of brotherhood and equality and thus of community. The acquisitions of material capital and that of cultural capital are not necessarily interdependent, but generally interconnected. A man may have personal qualifications that deserve respect and influence, but if he does not engage in the competition for material wealth and thus has little to share, how can he reproduce and strengthen his influence? Respect and honour acquired by exploiting the code of romanimo is cultural capital that, together with material capital, is strategically converted into social capital: making profitable and wise alliances to strengthen one's position in competition and in case of confrontation or conflict. The question of influence and power is, however, a complex one: what is the nature of power in a society where equality is the ideal? What resources are exchanged in the competition for power and influence?

Accumulation of Wealth

The foraging economy of hamlet Roma keeps most family households with means for subsistence, and most families manage to accumulate money for doctors, weddings and funerals. Men may strike a lucky bargain, do some profitable business and accumulate some money that way. Families that have horses may earn money by hiring them to peasants for ploughing, and old women earn money by fortune-telling and magic. There are no absolute territorial rights attributed to different groups or familii of Roma (see also Piasere, 1987), but Roma from other hamlets do not beg or barter in the villages around the hamlet. Economic exchanges with peasants are generally based on the cultivation of personal clients and this can lead to competition between the women, but these economic activities are for daily subsistence. The surplus needed for cultural investments, such as arranging a pačiv, is only within reach of the mature heads of family households and familii in co-operation. Fusuj's pačiv was planned in September but held on Christmas Eve because the whole familia needed time to accumulate enough money for food and drink. Only after the clothes from the NGO were sold did the familia have enough money to arrange the pačiv.

The NGO gift represents the kind of lucky bargain that has been bestowed upon Roma and that makes it possible for those that can control it to accumulate wealth and power. Joska and Kurva's relation to this NGO is as follows. In the early 1990s a small European NGO, aimed at helping țigani in the area, made contact with a local Orthodox priest in order to find a group of poor țigani. Joska bulibaša was contacted through his good relations to this Orthodox priest and became contact person for the organisation. At the first meeting Joska and Kurva received members of the organisation in a royal manner. They kissed their hands and even shoes and invited them inside to eat and drink with them. When the trucks with clothes, oranges and bananas eventually arrived at the Rom hamlet the following autumn, a chaotic situation took place, all Roma fighting over the gifts. Due to close co-operation between Joska, Kurva and the leader of the organisation, the truck was eventually emptied without injury to anybody. Over the years this close co-operation between the NGO and Joska and Kurva has developed, and the process of handing out packages has become more and more smooth. The gift involves a lot of Romanian and Hungarian villagers as well. The NGO[1] has built up a network of 'helpers' among the villagers in order to clear the gift through the customs, to unload the truck and to distribute gifts to local hospitals, to the mayor's office and to other selected villagers.

Joska was not only trusted to write out and approve the lists of individuals in different family households to receive help in the hamlet, with his good relation to villagers, he was also part of the network of 'helpers' there. This gave Joska the authority to approve or reject lists and thus an advantage over the other hamlet Roma in the acquisition of clothes. Most hamlet Roma accepted that Joska was given this privilege, but many complained about the way he handled it. The clothes were mostly sold and bartered with peasants and represented a small fortune in Romanian terms. A normal family household was said to earn an average of the equivalent of US$150 in cash on this sale. Joska and Kurva and even his familia were, however, constantly being accused by other hamlet Roma of stealing their lists and their boxes, of setting up false lists for his allies outside the hamlet and so forth. This conflict accentuated the enmity between the Joska familia and their supporters, and his brother Phuro's familia and their supporters. It was a conflict that, as we shall see, seemed impossible to resolve because Joska was the only Rom trusted by the organisation. When the organisation after some years built a school for Roma children in the hamlet, it was placed next to Joska's house and Joska was given the key. Money for general development of the hamlet was put in a bank account with Joska and the leader of the organisation as the only ones to operate it. When the organisation wanted to make a well and install a water pump in the hamlet, all the equipment was controlled by Joska and an influential headmaster in the village school. When the organisation bought a house in the village, Joska was put in charge of cleaning, maintaining and even rebuilding the house. Only Joska and his wife had access to this house. Over the years Joska and Kurva have invested much money and effort in this relationship. They have given feasts for the whole visiting organisation in their house, they have kept the school locked and clean and have generally fought the other Roma to protect their relationship with the NGO. The influence they had on the organisation during our stay in the village and hamlet was formidable, a fact well known both by Roma and by peasants. The money and resources that flowed from the NGO passed through Joska and in some instances through certain villagers, and this of course gave Joska a certain degree of influence both in the hamlet and in the village. This influence together with Joska's good relationship with villagers was the basis for further co-operation with the mayor and other power holders in the village in 'swindling' the organisation for a substantial amount of money. So, to those in the village who might profit from the NGO, Joska was a necessary middleman to deal with. By thus cultivating his network of gaže, however, he endangered his relations to the Roma. This balance is the classic ambiguity of the middleman that renders him vulnerable and restricts his authority. To keep up good relations with the bulibaša is important for many villagers for many reasons apart from his position as a channel to the NGO. Many villagers consider good relations with the bulibaša as important for keeping peace with the ţigani in general, because they expect that the bulibaša has the authority to control his 'people'.

The hamlet Roma knew very well that Joska and his family exploited their position in the organisation (the NGO) to their own benefit. But they also realised that without him in that position they would probably get nothing. As long as they supported him, he would have the confidence of the organisation. If they turned against him everybody would lose. Joska on his part knew that whatever he managed to extract from the organisation he had to share with his fellow Roma to some extent. He is more their puppet than their master. The complicated webs of interests, Joska´s power to extract resources from the organisation, the powers of certain peasants to expose Joska, and his power to expose peasants, etc., together with the balance between the power of his fellow Roma to expose his deceit or simply just reject him as their bulibaša; they all circulated around Joska and Kurva as key actors. The NGO gift represented a new resource to the hamlet Roma that made it possible to accumulate wealth and transform it into competition for honour and equality.

The Joska familia was neither competing for power in the Romanian/Hungarian ethnic arena in the village, nor for formal political power in the village community. Like all Roma, Joska was trying to exploit the material and social resources of the gažo community to increase his cultural capital among Roma and strengthen his networks of potential supporters in case of open conflict. The commodity from outside, then, entered into the general flow of exchange, competition and struggle for all kinds of capital and was also important in strategic marriages. Joska's key position with the NGO made him an attractive ally in marriage arrangements. Joska and Kurva balanced their need to secure his position in the hamlet against his brother, with their need for allies in other hamlets. As all Roma in the area desired a share of the NGO gift, this conflict of interests increased internal enmity and the need for external allies. When Joska asked for his sister's daughter as bori (see Chapter 4) he strengthened his position in the hamlet. As his sister was the widow of Phuro's brother-in-law, her family (five married sons) was considered a supporter of the Phuro familia. The marriage changed this loyalty to Joska and his familia's benefit. Of course, Joska's position in the NGO also made this alliance profitable from his sister's point of view.

The Pačiv: Turning Money into Honour

The concept of 'lažav' (shame) was discussed in Chapter 2. Lažav is not confined to bodily or sexual behaviour but to all behaviour by men and women – to any breach of romanimo. The notion of pačiv (honour) is not to be understood as the opposite of lažav, as both properties are present in most persons but expressed in different contexts. Hamlet Roma seldom used the word lažav in conversation as it implicitly refers to all actions that respect and conform to romanimo (moral code of behaviour). They could use the term *pačivalo*, to refer to an honourable person, but they generally spoke of having respect (*respeto*). In daily conversation pačiv refers to the meal given in respect of someone. The meal that closes a successfully negotiated marriage is a pačiv. Given by the bride's family to the groom's it is an act of generosity and displays the giver's intention to share with his new ally or associate, an intention that of course is expected to be returned. A pačiv given in honour of an alliance or even to pay respect towards a competitor honours both the giver and the receiver, but it also provokes competition.

The pačiv that opened this chapter entered this cycle of competition for honour and respect. I did not understand this when I filmed the event, but it became obvious as rumours of the beauty of Fusuj's pačiv spread around the region. I do not know whether these kinds of pačiva, honouring one's elders restricted to the circle of close kin, had been held previous to our arrival. The camera made it possible to give a limited pačiv not involving distant kin and at the same time make it known outside the hamlet. In every pačiv I filmed, the presence of people outside the family household and familia was, however, necessary; if no affines were present, somebody was sent to fetch them and I was told to wait with the recording until they arrived. At Fusuj's pačiv the arrival of his xanamik (father of his bori) set the party off. However, the pačiv given for old or ill people also has another object. By honouring the old folks just before their death in this way, one contributes to their satisfaction with their life in this world and thereby eases their path to the other world after death.[2]

The pačiv is a multivocal ritual. It is a display of generosity towards a person one wishes to involve in a relationship of sharing, to confirm relationships. It is a display of the wealth and generosity of a family household and familia, and it is an invitation or an answer to competition. As a demonstration of what a family household or familia can present of material wealth and generosity, a pačiv is an instance of conspicuous consumption combining having and giving and converting material wealth into honour. The participants are likely to be people in power and the event is an instrument of status contest between them. The issue in such events is not, however, only a competition for status, but the disposition of central valuables is perhaps most significant. Arjun Appadurai notes:

'As in the kula,[3] so in such tournaments of value generally, strategic skill is culturally measured by the success with which actors attempt diversions or subversions of culturally conventionalised paths for the flows of things' (Appadurai, 1986: 21).

Seeing pačiva as tournaments of value opens some interesting paths. The value of equality and sharing among brothers excludes most items from commodisation, thus preventing the accumulation of wealth by commodity exchange between Roma. Wealth should be accumulated by transactions with gaže, but is only respected if it is shared among Roma. The Rom way of keeping one's wealth and transforming it to honour is by turning food, secular items of everyday sharing, into valuable objects. By presenting a pačiv with excesses of food and drink and accompanying it with 'pretty words', dancing and music, the central idiom of sharing is celebrated without too much cost. The giver presents the prosperity of his family household – an expression of the luck of its males, the hard work and respectability of its women, and the unity of its members. By displaying his wealth in a pačiv, the clever man may accumulate symbolic and social capital and still cohere to the value of equality, sharing and brotherhood. Most hamlet Roma were, as has been noted, too poor to arrange a big pačiv for guests from other hamlets, but by having their father's pačiv taped, Fusuj's sons overcame this problem as they distributed the videotape to Roma in the area and gained respect from many more and much more influential Roma than those in the hamlet. This is an example of the subversion of a modest hamlet pačiv into a wider cycle of competition, thus expanding the 'culturally conventionalised paths for the flow of things' (Appadurai, 1986: 21).

'Giving is Stupid, Not Giving is Bad': Balancing Respect, Sharing and Equality

Even generosity and sharing must be balanced. The hamlet Roma say: 'If you give you are stupid, if you don't give you are bad (*Kana des dilo san, kana na des beng san)*'. As long as wealth is shared there is little reason for bad feelings, but when it is not or it is shared insufficiently, angry feelings arise and equality is threatened. The competition for equality leads every man to look to his 'brother' and compare his honour, wealth or luck with his own. Joska was always accused of trying to acquire more of the NGO gifts than he was due. He was also being accused of presenting his familia as morally superior to other familia in the hamlet. Baro, the horseman, was accused of being rich and not wanting to share. But 'making oneself big', for instance by giving too great a pačiv, is seen as stupidity and possibly also as a threat to equality. The man that gives 'too much' is seen to be either lacking integrity or trying to dominate his equals. The balance between respect for another's individual prosperity, the obligation to share and the quest for equality is difficult to maintain.

Equal Brothers and Troublesome Women

The 'Murder' of Kurva's Sister

The Roma often referred to women as troublemakers and said that most problems between men derive from women. Men work to build up their reputation and respect but they rely on the co-operation of their women: wives, daughters and bora. Fights between women were not unusual and some had severe consequences. One day when we were out walking in the woods, we met a band of hamlet children collecting walnuts. We stopped and chatted. Kamelia, a girl of about ten pointed to a conspicuously dirty and ragged girl and told us she was her cousin and that she was an orphan because her mother had been killed by a woman in the hamlet. She complained that her cousin was ill treated by her maternal uncle and his wife with whom she now lived. 'I saw Kottori kill her mother', Kamelia triumphed. 'She had a long stick that she beat her with and after that she had to go to the hospital and there she died. And Varga (the orphan) is beaten every day by her uncle and has to do all the work.'

This story made a strong impression on me and I tried for a long time to find an explanation, to see it as a child's fantasy, as a misinterpretation or even as an invention to impress us. Little by little I came to understand that the main conflict that evolved around Joska's familia and that of his brother Phuro was connected to this fight. Phuro's wife, Kottori, was the one said to have killed the girl's mother. Later I came to understand that the dead mother was the sister of Kurva, Joska's wife. I also heard more and more hints of the death of this woman and of the cruelty of Kottori. An old woman who had recently left the hamlet told us that the dead woman had put 'evil words' on Phuro's familia before she died and that the familia was thus cursed forever. Later Kurva told me the whole story.

Her sister had lived in the hamlet with her husband and children, but then her husband had gone to Germany to find work. After some time her sister had started an affair and eventually moved in with another man in the hamlet. This man had been married to Kottori's daughter, but had left her. They (Kurva's sister and her lover) had a child together, but then the man went back to his wife. Kurva's sister was angry and one day she went to Kottori's house, where the couple lived, to get back an eiderdown cover she said was hers, and she and Kottori got into a fight. Kottori hit her over her chest and back with a broomstick so she fell and could not walk. Kurva took her to hospital, but her lungs were perforated by broken ribs and she died. The doctors wanted her to report the crime, but Kurva and Joska decided not to. It was impossible without having to leave the hamlet. The dead woman's husband later came back to the hamlet to collect his children. The wife's child with her lover was, however, left in the charge of Kurva's brother and his wife – another of Kottori's daughters.

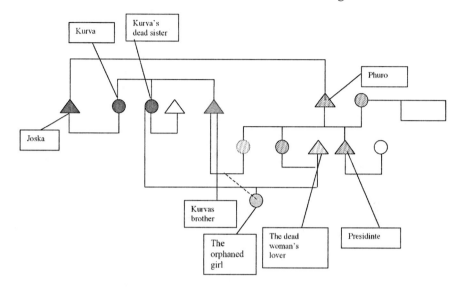

Figure 5. 1 *Marriage Relations between Kurva's and Kottori's Familii*

Figure 5. 1 illustrates how the two fighting familii are bound together by marriage. Only directly involved persons are included in the Figure, apart from Presidinte who appears in other chapters.

Kurva's sister's death had not been revenged in any way and the distress that was expressed by Kurva and certainly felt by her brothers and sisters in the hamlet endangered a whole range of relationships. Joska did not speak to his brother Phuro if he could help it, and avoided Phuro's many sons. Kurva's youngest brother was married to Phuro and Kottori's daughter, and they were the ones who housed (and allegedly maltreated) the dead woman's daughter. One of Joska's two sisters in the hamlet was the widow of Kottori's deceased brother, and her sons had obligations to their father's brother (married to Kottori). If Kurva and her brothers had accused Kottori of murder in public or reported the death to the police, this would have meant that one of the familia would have had to leave to settle elsewhere, thereby forcing every family household in the hamlet to make the choice of staying or leaving. In almost every family household some individual would have to reject either their natal family household or that of marriage. Moving away and establishing one's familia in another place is a common solution in cases of conflict, but for Joska this strategy would cost him and his familia their access to the NGO gift and thus a substantial part of their material and social capital. This was only one of several conflicts in the hamlet where what was seen as women's uncontrolled sexuality (sexual relations outside marriage) entered into and fuelled conflicts.

Kasablanka: Opposing Male Power?

Kasablanka is Joska and Kurva's second eldest daughter and was another example of conflicts caused by what was seen as uncontrolled sexuality. Kasablanka was the 'belle' of the hamlet and her parents' favourite and she was even considered beautiful among peasants. They admired her beauty and fair hair, and claimed she was more civilized than most ţiganci. But although in this respect the pride of the hamlet, she was considered shameless and a shame to her parents and familia in some respects. Kasablanka was in her early twenties and had 'been with many men' as the Roma express it. Her parents had married her off to some wealthy Rom far away (the real wedding) when she was about sixteen years old. She broke up the marriage and went back to her parents. Then, rumour said, she had an affair with a German and got pregnant. She gave birth to a boy who was placed in an orphanage and went back to her parents once again. When the boy was three years old Joska and Kurva took him home to their house. While I was in the village Kasablanka was living with her parents and the boy, but Joska and Kurva were his social parents as Kasablanka rejected him. Kasablanka then had a boyfriend from another Rom hamlet and one day we were told that she was marrying him. Joska and Kurva were angry with her for getting married without their knowing and said she would have been better off at home with them. The wedding was however quite cheerful and there was no trace of Joska and Kurva´s disapproval, but very few members of Joska's familia were present. When Kasablanka moved in with her new husband in his parents' home her child, now a boy of five, was left with Joska and Kurva. After a couple of months Kasablanka broke up her marriage and came back home again. Her parents were furious at first, but after a short while everything settled down.

Some months later Kasablanka was abducted by force from the train. None of her relatives tried to prevent it. Joska and Kurva, with a policeman they knew, went to the house where Kasablanka was held and beaten. She was released and her parents raised charges against the men. The gossip had it the men were her last husband's cousins and they had revenged her deceit. Later the same spring Kasablanka had an affair with a young man in the hamlet who had been married to Kurva's niece and had a child with her. She soon became pregnant and moved into his parents' house. Joska and Kurva were again furious and swore they would never talk to her again, but things settled down this time as well. However, no formal affinal relations were established between the two familii in the hamlet.

Kasablanka was both a pride and a shame to the Joska familia. As the beautiful and charming daughter of the hamlet bulibaša she had been an attractive marriage prospect, and as wealthy and influential Roma outside the hamlet had wanted her as bori, Joska could ask for a high bride wealth for her. When Kasablanka broke up the marriage, the shame cast on Joska was great. When she later was abducted, none of her female relatives were very angry. One woman told me they were pleased to get rid of her because she was a threat to all marriages. Although Kasablanka seemed to get more and more in the way for the strategic acquisition of moral capital of the Joska familia, their paternal affection for her seemed to overcome their political ambitions. But what was Kasablanka up to? Was she led by her emotions or may we interpret her actions as an expression of strategic choices? What may women like Kurva's sister and Kasablanka tell us about women's role in the competition for honour?

Male Domination – Female Resistance?

Jealousy and the loyalties of the different parties were the indirect causes of the death of Kurva's sister and of many of the conflicts in the hamlet. Misolino told us he used to beat his wife when he was younger because he was always afraid she might leave him for another man. Men and women hold Phuro's wife Kottori to be the evil source that has destroyed her sons as well – Phuro himself is never accused. In all the familii that are accused of being bad, it is the wife that is said to be the cause. Denka's wife is said to be the cause of the problems of their familia, as she beats her husband and is generally regarded as unpleasant. Stewart points to this practice of blaming women for conflicts as a way of preserving the moral ideal of brotherhood among the Harangos Roma (Stewart, 1997: 93). This understanding seems relevant to the hamlet Roma and is expressed in the general emphasis on troublesome women. The general presentation was that men build up their influence through cultural competition, alliances and wealth, but shameless woman may hinder or ruin this. But women's assets are not easily ignored. An industrious, beautiful and/or honourable woman may also be a man's strongest asset and as a wife she may become his only real partner in his political struggle. A boy becomes a man, Rom, through marriage (sexual relations) and it is as a Rom he is a political agent and may enter the competition for honour between equals. A divorced or widowed man should remarry, because a man cannot perform his social duties or receive visitors, and he cannot give pačiv without a woman.

But marriage is important in many other ways as well. Ideal maleness is achieved by acquiring wealth without effort, by making a profitable bargain, by fraud, chance or by others' work (see Stewart, 1997). In a society where all grown men are equals, men are dependent on women's, young people's and children's work to increase their family's wealth and honour. Thus men are dependent on women not only emotionally but also economically and politically. But this dependency makes them vulnerable, and controlling their women is a major preoccupation. This control is expressed by different strategies of domination towards daughters, bora and wives. We have seen examples of men's domination when it comes to women's dress and their observance of ritual separation. Men's control of women's sexuality by arranging marriages is another example. These control strategies are, however, generally authorised by women as adhering to romanimo.

Very few women I met did, however, accept unchallenged the general domination of their husbands, brothers or fathers. Their dual roles as providers and wives (daughters) teach them how to balance subordination with assertiveness and how to exploit male dependency to gain influence and resist general domination. Being part of a prosperous and influential family household and familia is as important for women as it is for men. Just like men, women are considered mature through marriage, but they acquire their public voice through men. To exercise power outside the family household a woman must gain influence over her husband. Men's obvious dependence on women is one of the strongest instruments for women's influence, but it is also the motivation for male domination. Women's room for manoeuvre lies exactly in the ambiguity of their roles. By being industrious and clever providers women gain honour for themselves by making it possible for their husbands and fathers to exercise their role as leaders. By avoiding shameless behaviour, they respect male supremacy in general as romanimo (the order of things), which brings luck and honour to males and females. But the assertiveness and relative shamelessness seen as inherent in women are expressed towards male Roma as well. Women do not only move freely and alone, out of the sight of men, they also openly negotiate their roles as mothers and wives. As long as women generally behave with shame, these negotiations do not seem to challenge the code of male supremacy. But some women do just that.

Challenging Male Dominance

Both Kasablanka and Kurva's sister challenged male supremacy, not necessarily by choosing their own sexual partners but by breaking out of marriage and 'having' many men. The five wives in the hamlet who earned money by fake prostitution, gave primacy to their role as providers over that of wives and may thus be seen to undermine the domination of husbands. Kasablanka's shamelessness is an expression of her wanting to decide for herself and 'live my own life' as she expressed it herself. She was very clear about wanting a modern life and to 'be treated like a Romanian lady (*Domnşioara*)', as she said. Being blonde and beautiful, she saw herself as special and she wanted to live a different life from the other hamlet women. By marrying several times on her own choice she forcefully demonstrated that neither her father nor any other male could control her and she thus opposed aspects of romanimo. These women did not dispute the gendered power relation legitimated by the notion of shame; they both adhered to the general code of behaviour towards husbands when it comes to dress and keeping the symbolic separation of male and female. They did, however, challenge the generalised exercise of dominance by men over their wives.

These cases show how emotion and strategy are intertwined in agency in many instances and how individual emotion may interfere with collective strategy in others. Kasablanka and the other 'bad' women serve to confirm men's idea about women as inherently shameless and uncontrollable, and I will suggest they confirm women's idea about men's dependency and impotency in controlling women. But of course by discussing and evaluating women's behaviour as shameless and in need of control, the dominant values are reinforced and symbolic domination persists. Symbolic superiority of men over women is legitimised through the moral code of romanimo, but this does not give men general a right to dominance. Their economic as well as emotional dependencies on women force them to balance domination against economic interests. Women, on their side, balance the power inherent in their role as providers with that of their role as wives, and may challenge men's efforts to control their mobility and thus male dominance. Respect, in the sense of honour and wealth in the Rom community, is only possible through the achievements of men and women in co-operation.

I suggest that women like Kasablanka and Kurva's sister should not be seen to resist the 'male force', but rather that their social practices were an expression of different interpretations of gender expectations and of cultural values in general. There are several, different, co-existing and sometimes conflicting cultural values and subjectivities that structure gender discourse, and although these discourses are hierarchically ordered this hierarchy is not absolute, undisputed or even static.

Conflict and Integration

Kinship and Conflict

Relatedness not only integrates people, it also separates them. The hamlet Roma are tied together with so many cross loyalties that when conflict does burst to the surface every family household is victimised. The bilateral kin relations characteristic of the hamlet community tie people together in contemporary networks rather than in historical lineages. Cross-kin loyalties based on descent and on marriage make people fear open conflict with possible loss of their loved ones and thus they may leave hate, enmity and fear unresolved. Such unresolved emotions may again endanger peaceful co-existence. This experience is echoed in many women's reluctance to marry their daughters in the hamlet because it causes too much trouble between and in familii. When cross-purposes, enmity and conflict evolve between close kin, many relationships are endangered and all will have to choose sides. The dramatic death of Kurva's sister is one example of a conflict that rested unresolved due to cross loyalties and economic interest. It is an example of how one specific interpersonal conflict that is not resolved continues to fuel hate and slander and thus the need for the adversaries to strengthen their familia against that of the other.

The Local Kris

The *kris*, the traditional Rom tribunal, is the only formal institution above family households and the most influential conflict-solving instrument that is generally acknowledged by all Roma. *Kris Romani* generally refers to an institution of conflict settlement that involves neutral arbiters, *krisatora*, usually from another group (nacie), than the people involved. Hamlet Roma said they did not practise kris anymore. They explained that all the old people were dead or had left for town, that no one respected the elders' decision, and that generally the hamlet Roma were a bad lot. Others said they had kris, but as the young were generally very bad these days and the bulibaša was without authority, kris decisions were not respected. Kris may mean many things in Romanes, as the word is used to denote any meeting of Roma and even meetings between Roma and gaže and between gaže.[4]

We were asked to film a mesali (a small pačiv) given by Phuro for his brother Joska. At first we interpreted it as an ordinary pačiv, honouring their parents, the same honouring meal that we had filmed many times in the hamlet. There were, however, certain features that set this event out as different from other pačiv we had observed. By looking at the tape later we realised that what we had thought was a general pačiv was connected to an incident in the ongoing conflict between Joska's and Phuor's two familii, that had happened several weeks ago. So why was it not referred to as a kris? My suggestion is that this conflict-settling pačiv led by the hamlet elders was seen as an internal conflict settling event, an instance of the local public institution with authority to settle hamlet matters, and thus not a kris Romani that involves more distant kin and arbiters. Although this local conflict settling institution is not supported by cohesive power, this system's legitimacy rests on a general consensus about the moral primacy of seniority and brotherhood. Furthermore, by not referring to it as a kris, the seriousness of the matter was played down to avoid stirring too much excitement in the hamlet (Stewart, 1997).

Conflict Avoidance

The ideal of equality and self-sufficiency prevents people from interfering in what they see as internal domestic matters. A man is his own master and nobody should tell him how to run his affairs. A husband may criticise his wife, but a woman should not interfere with the doings of another adult woman outside her family household. Mother and daughter live very near each other so that a woman may run to her mother when her husband beats her. The man's brothers and sisters generally disapprove of such behaviour, but they are hindered by conflicting moral values. The loyalty between siblings must be balanced against the mutual respect between males as autonomous family heads and the alliance between xanamikuri, thus interference may be costly and is avoided as long as possible. Men also avoid all sorts of direct challenges or disputes when they are sober, but engage in joking relationships; teasing each other in friendly ways. Especially the relationship between young men is characterised by joking insults that are to be received humorously. Such jokes seems to press the limits of a man's tolerance and thus to test his ability to control himself. It may also serve as a way of expressing the suppressed aggression that people may feel against each other and that must be controlled so as not to cause conflict. As long as the men were sober, they were able to control themselves and receive these joking insults in a proper manner. When they were drunk this control tended to weaken.

Women challenge each other much more directly than men do – 'everybody knows that women can not control their tongue', as one man said. Women from all the family households usually go to town scavenging together and constitute 'the hamlet women group' in most contexts. A conflict with women from other hamlets will generally tend to fuse hamlet women against the 'foreigners'. I suggest that women's reputation for bad language and lack of control and their closer co-operation and interdependency in daily matters takes the sting out of their openness. As men are far more preoccupied with their honour, they are more restricted in their expressions towards each other. This expression of gender division may serve to avoid open conflict by letting off steam for the whole family household through its women.

The Police

The police are generally not involved in conflicts between hamlet Roma, not even in the case of Kurva's sister when conflicts escalated to violence. I suggest that the cross loyalties created by marriage and descent made it impossible from the point of view of Joska and Kurva to bring the case to the Romanian court. Police intervention would have involved all hamlet inhabitants and put their dual loyalties to the test, with the possibility of ruining the hamlet as a community. Instead, the conflict between the two familii was turned into the ongoing competition for honour and respect. Although murder is an unacceptable solution between relatives, the shame inflicted on Joska's familia by the dead woman's adultery also weakened their prestige in and outside the hamlet and thus their chance of getting support from other Roma.

Violence is legitimate between members of a family household; husbands may beat their wives when they behave shamelessly, parents may beat their children, and older children may punish younger ones, but not without 'reason' and not 'too much'. Violence that was not regarded as reasonable was criticised and brothers were expected to look after their sisters. Between members of different families and between different hamlets or even groups of Roma, violence is a serious offence. Such events are generally solved by a kris and only reported to the police if it serves the involved parties. Joska reported the abduction of his daughter Kasablanka, to many Roma's disapproval. The perpetrators were, however, not related to the hamlet Roma and I do not believe they even were of the same nacie. Female relatives of the abductors that had been reported to the police revenged this by attacking hamlet women on the train on their way to town in the following weeks. The fact that Joska had friendly relations with the police officer suggests that he expected protection if the report had led to revenge, and that he thus felt safe. Apart from these considerations, Roma in general have no reason to trust the police; most Roma have been in jail for minor thefts and from their perspective the legal system functions by bribery rather than by the law.

Partition of The Hamlet

Partition is another way to handle unresolved enmity, but the price may be too high for all parties. The hamlet is a relatively new social structure among these Roma and it may also be a relatively temporary one. Until around 1950 the forefathers and some of the older Roma in the hamlet were nomadic. The village and Rom memory has it that the hamlet Roma used to settle down for the winter in hovels on the outskirts of the Hungarian part of the village, which the villagers destroyed every spring. When the Roma settled down in the 1950s, were made part of the Romanian proletariat and eventually built houses, the group seems to have consisted of four family households, all kin. The Roma say that twice as many Roma used to live in the hamlet 'before'. This seems to refer to before the arrival of the NGO, just after the revolution in 1989. These two events are closely linked and must have caused severe changes in the hamlet. If they were twice as many as today, they must have been around five hundred individuals to compete for the meagre resources of the village communities in the area. The advent of the NGO must have been seen as sent from heaven, but may have led to increased competition and conflict that only partition seems to have resolved. Most hamlet Roma became increasingly dependent on the NGO gift. The hamlet has been divided at least twice since the advent of the NGO and it seems that the remaining Roma try to hold on at almost any cost. Familii that either lost out in the power competition that preceded the partition or had kin and economic possibilities elsewhere moved out of the hamlet, thus losing access to the highly valued NGO gift. Some of these familii moved to areas in town or close to town and are prosperous today. They moved into hamlets already established by relatives or established new ones. All new settlements are, however, forming autonomous groups with relations to some of the familii in the hamlet. So, the NGO gift seems to have influenced demographic features of this area.

I do suggest, though, that conflict and the partition or flaking of the local group into new groups is an inherent trait of the social organisation and political economy of the Roma. The dependency on village economy also limits the number of Roma who can attach themselves to one village. The wage labour forced upon them by the Romanian state probably made possible a population density that could not be sustained once that economic source shut down. The competition for resources and the conflicts that arise from such competition have to be settled by co-operation or by force between the parties, as there is no system of centralised power to force cohesion on conflicting parties. Once conflict can no longer be avoided, one party must leave. The only way to restore honour once a party is defeated is to create independence from one's enemies by moving out, settling with other relatives or founding a new hamlet. The new hamlet may eventually create an alliance with the old one by marriage, or such ties may be perpetuated between some family households.

Although competition and conflict divide hamlet Roma in different family households and familii as adversaries in many contexts, the competition for honour and respect, the conflict settlements, the joking abuse, the gossip and the avoidance strategies keep hamlet Roma constantly preoccupied with each other and merge people together by common agreement or disagreement of what it means to be Rom. Although Joska hardly talked to his brother Phuro, his daughter was married to Phuro's son. The fact that they had grandchildren in common and were neighbours ensured that relationships were continued. Hamlet Roma cannot forget about each other or have no relationship; affection, obligations, strategy and hate bind them together. These integrative processes fuse the hamlet Roma against other groups and are put in motion when necessary.

Notes

1. This organisation relies on charity; used clothes, money and items are collected and redistributed. It also has had government support for building a school and digging a well in the hamlet.

2. See Chapter 7 about the death ritual.

3. Ritual gift exchange between the Trobriand Islanders described by Bronislaw K. Malinowski (1922).

4. Kris is practised among most groups of Roma in Europe and the U.S.A. In Norway krisatora are taken from France and Germany, and Norwegian Rom tell of kris meetings they attend all over Europe. For more about the kris Romani, see Williams (1985: 230) and (Gropper 1975: 81).

Chapter 6

Rom Leadership: Joska Bulibaša

Introduction

So how are we to understand the position of the bulibaša in a community of equal brothers? We have seen that the family household and the familia are central units in Rom organisation, and while the household is generally headed by the oldest male, the leadership of a familia is more problematic. The males in Joska's familia consisted of himself, some of his brothers and his wife's brothers, all heading different family households, but in spite of his position as bulibaša, Joska had no decision-making power towards his brothers or his brothers-in-law. His position as bulibaša, with good relations and trust in the gaže community, did, however, give his household access to certain resources that made him an attractive ally. His central position in the allocation and distribution of the NGO gift made him expect loyalty from those who benefited, but the strict code of equality did not give him authority to force his will through in any matter in the hamlet. Joska's domestic unit was perhaps the most influential in his familia, but that is not to imply that Joska was the leader. Joska's elder brother Phuro was, however, seen as the leader of his familia. As one of the oldest males in the hamlet, with a familia that consisted of sons, bora and sons-in-law, Phuro's position as head of his familia was given by his age and by his authority as father. Phuro and Kottori together took decisions concerning all their sons and bora as well as their in-living daughters and their husbands in matters that concerned their familia. Although their son Presidinte was a man of about thirty with a wife and five children, living in a separate domestic group, his father, Phuro, was seated at the table on his behalf to settle the conflict he had caused with Joska. This was a familia matter and Phuro and Kottori were his authorities. He accepted their decision to pay respect towards Joska as an obedient son and a good Rom. This is the authority of age that comes into play in matters of familia and most prominently between parents and children.

The hamlet Roma do not form stable patrilineal groups (*vici*), with formal leadership (Kaminski, 1987; Sutherland, 1975). As long as a father is capable and living, he will act as a leader of the households of his sons and daughters who belong to his familia. When he dies, brothers and sisters will split up into households with different heads to build new familii, or join together like Joska's familia without any legitimate leader. Internal leadership then lies in the hands of the leaders of family households.

Village Affairs – External Leadership

The Polish-Swedish anthropologist Ignazy-Marek Kaminski (1987) offers an extensive interpretation of power relations and leadership among the 'Polish' Roma in Sweden and Poland. By analysing what he terms internal and external leadership Kaminski argues that political changes and socio-economic pressure may turn external leadership into internal leadership. I will apply these insights to discuss the position of the bulibaša in the hamlet and the special Rom attitude to centralised leadership.

Kaminski described the position of the external leader (*voit*) among the Polish Roma as that of a mediator between the local and national majority authorities and the local Rom band or community (Kaminski, 1987: 342). The task of the voit was to collect taxes and other tributes and his position was exploited by the government representatives in their aim to control, repress, assimilate or exploit the Gypsies. The government needed a middleman with local authority to enforce these measures, and the Roma had to find ways to fulfil both the government's requests and their own interests. This was a vulnerable position and the man appointed was often a person with little internal respect. They had to find a person that could play the role of a representative and satisfy the government, but without internal authority to implement their policy. Should an internal leader become an external leader, political, economic and cultural independence was in danger. I argue that the role of the bulibaša among the Roma in Romania should be understood as that of an external leader, much as the voit among the 'Polish' Roma. As will be discussed further, and as is stressed by Kaminsky, internal leadership may be exploited to gain external leadership and vice versa. The position of bulibaša may give access to material and social resources that may in certain situations be converted to symbolic capital and to internal leadership.

Joska told us he had been chosen as bulibaša by the hamlet elders. He was the youngest son of his family, but he added with a smile, 'I was the smartest and I had been to school'. Joska was one of the few males in the hamlet who was literate. He also said that his father had been a bulibaša, but that was disputed among the Roma. Villagers referred to the bulibaša as the chief of the ţigani, using his gažo name. The hamlet Roma presented Joska as their bulibaša to outsiders, but he was never addressed as 'bulibaša' by his fellow Roma, but by his usual Rom name – Joska. Only gaže adressed him as 'bulibaša'. All strangers, however, were sent to his house and he was the one to speak on behalf of the hamlet in any conflict between Roma and peasants. Joska presented the hamlet's needs and desires to the village mayor, including their need for extra funds for Christmas, for social support funds in general and all their claims towards the Romanian state representatives in the village and county. But a closer look revealed that Joska did not have the authority to force his will through in any matter. As discussed, Joska's familia consisted almost entirely of his wife's kin and he was on bad terms with his only brother in the hamlet. I suggest that his somewhat ambiguous position as *žamutro*,[2] and the fact that he was literate and thereby his access to resources in the gaže world, together with his personal qualifications, made him the perfect mediator between the hamlet Roma and the gaže. His influence and potential power rested on his ability to channel resources from the gaže world to the group, and to ease conflicts between Roma and gaže. Even though it was difficult to see Joska's authority in practice, it was easy to see the expectations other Roma have of him as bulibaša. Whenever the hamlet Roma felt that their economic situation was unbearable, they urged the bulibaša to turn to the village mayor and ask for social benefits. This he often did, and on some occasions he managed to receive money 'for his people'. Every third month, the bulibaša walked around the hamlet collecting money for the electricity bill that was issued to the hamlet as a whole. He never received enough money and the electricity was cut off in the whole hamlet until someone paid the bill. This happened many times a year, but Joska still had no power to force anybody outside his own domestic group to pay. The solution was that some households, Joska's among them, paid for all.

Joska's position in relation to the NGO is a good example of his important function as mediator, and how this position could give him access to resources that were sought after both by peasants and by Roma. The NGO gift was probably the most valuable resource accessible to the Roma and its accessibility rested to a certain degree on the trust that the bulibaša could infuse in the NGO about his authority in the hamlet. To make him appear as a legitimate external leader, the hamlet Roma must present him as an internal leader – 'our bulibaša'. To his fellow Roma he was bulibaša the external leader, to the villagers he was the internal leader. Local power holders in the village, formal and informal, competed for control over all NGO resources in the area, but the NGO gift to the hamlet was the only one that forced them into co-operation with ţigani. As we shall see in Part II of this book, relations between peasants and Roma are based on cycles of exchange that rest on a minimum of trust between the parties. The bulibaša was an important aspect of this trust. He and his close family were generally treated with respect and sympathy by villagers who saw him as an internal leader. Nearly all villagers made an exception of the bulibaša and his family when speaking derogatorily of țigani. The bulibaša was considered a proper person (*om*) 'not like the rest'. Many peasants felt sorry for him having to control 'that gang of good-for-nothings'. Whenever we were driving our car in the region with Joska we had to stop to greet people, and he seemed to know people in all villages – Romanians, Hungarians and different groups of Roma.

Joska did not, however, only cultivate his relationships with hamlet Roma, the NGO and local power holders. He also cultivated relationships outside the local community, with both Roma and non-Roma, for different ends. A potential resource that Joska, on behalf of his domestic group, seemed to exploit for his own ends, was the control of the lists of names that the NGO used to distribute gifts. Rumour had it that Joska was selling 'lists' not only to make economic profit, but also to strengthen his network of allies outside the hamlet. When he was employed at the National Railway Company (as were many other Roma in the hamlet during the Ceaușescu period) Joska used his position to secure the Roma free fares to the nearby town and their own 'reserved' compartment. Joska explained to us that this favour was granted him because he was very much appreciated by the company. Peasants told us that the bulibaša paid the head of the station in town a small amount of money every year to let the hamlet women travel free. But there are many rumours. The fact is, however, that the women were only thrown off the train when the inspectors were from other parts of the country.

As an external leader, Joska bulibaša had a network of allies, supporters and clients both among Roma and among gaže, and this network could be exploited for personal (domestic unit) and collective (familia, hamlet) ends. When Kasablanka was abducted he could rely on this network of influence to co-operate with the police. The policeman in charge knew Joska as the bulibaša and took his problem seriously. It is likely that this local chief officer regularly received a portion of clothes in exchange for such favours. This influence was, of course, also developed and nurtured just as the hamlet women nurtured their exchange partners in the village. As it was crucial to the whole hamlet community, Joska's position as bulibaša, his external leadership, was never contested openly. The hamlet Roma knew that bad behaviour by individual Roma was to a certain degree tolerated in the village because of the bulibaša. So the bulibaša was made in some ways the peasants' 'ally' against the general uncivilised Roma, and that is exactly the most important feature of the external leader, not only in this village but in general. His ability to be accepted as '*Bulibaşa, şeful țiganilor* (chief of the țigani)' by villagers was the basis of his position in the hamlet. But it should be remembered that like all Roma, he exploited the resources of the gaže community to increase his wealth, influence and honour among Roma.

Converting External to Internal Leadership

Kaminski discusses the problems the Roma faced in keeping political and cultural autonomy when the externally appointed leader exploited his position to become an internal leader (Kaminski, 1987). One of the problems Kaminski saw in his material was the centralisation of power inherent in such a development. Internal leadership in a Polish Roma community was shared between many leaders of subgroups (*viči*), and the emergence of one leader was seen as a threat to this organisation (Kaminski, 1987). I suggest that the cultural code of equality and brotherhood between all Roma expressed by the competition for honour and the powerful idiom of sharing is a central structural element that works against any centralisation of power. When these values are threatened, so is the basis of every man's self-respect and dignity. Sharing is not only a moral ideal, but a man's practical insurance of belonging to a collective of brothers. Authority that is not based on biological criteria like age, gender and paternity threatens not only the order of things, but personhood itself and is generally challenged as illegitimate.

I do not know whether Joska was strategically seeking to exploit his influence as bulibaša to gain internal leadership in the hamlet, but I do know that he used his position to strengthen his influence both in his familia and more generally among Roma. Towards the end of our stay, for example, Joska and Kurva asked us to tell the leader of the NGO to register the school they had built in the hamlet as Joska's private property. When we asked how the other Roma would react to that Kurva burst out angrily: 'What should they say? We are the leaders up here anyway, we have all the trouble with receiving and feeding visitors from the organisation, the others do nothing'. In another instance, Thulo was complaining to Joska that the government had promised needy families social benefits on condition that they worked some days a week on government projects. Joska answered that he did not worry because as a bulibaša he would receive money without working. Thulo got very irritated and sneered: 'You a bulibaša? You are bulibaša in the loo, you are!'

These examples indicate that Joska did see his position as bulibaša as giving him the right to certain privileges, and that his wife also saw it in that way. But this was contested in the hamlet. The position of bulibaša as external leader left Joska in an ambiguous and vulnerable position among his fellow Roma. Having to cultivate relationships with gaže was by some interpreted as wanting to be a gažo, or even as preferring the company of gaže to that of Roma. The basis of Joska's influence was not in his ability to force but to persuade, and was always dependent on the respect the peasants had towards him, which rested on his ability to function as a mediator between the Rom community and the peasants and local authorities. His privileged position towards the NGO and the influence he exercised outside the hamlet were readily interpreted by the hamlet Roma as strategies to strengthen his own position and that of his familia in the hamlet towards other familii. His close contacts with powerful villagers rendered him vulnerable to accusations of betrayal, such as informing on the Roma's criminal activities. By reporting Kasablanka's abduction to the police, exploiting his contacts as bulibaša, he expressed trust towards the official judicial system and distrust of conflict-settling strategies among Roma. This did not pass without notice in the hamlet. Not one of Kasablanka's kinswomen had tried to stop the abduction. Her father being the bulibaša was not a good enough reason to interfere. Neither did I ever hear the Roma discuss the abduction as something that should be revenged. Joska and Kurva were left to solve the matter on their own. This was an explicit public rejection of any of his claims to internal authority.

Destroying Leadership

Even if Joska did not intend to make his way as an internal leader, I do suggest that his fellow Roma suspected him of trying. Every familia would support him as long as he used his position to increase the resources of their familia or those of the hamlet as a whole, but his claims to general authority and privilege were rejected. The balance between giving him enough support to make him function as a good mediator and not giving him enough support to legitimise his possible claim for internal leadership may be interpreted as both strategy and a gut reaction. The French sociologist Pierre Clastres discusses authority in stateless societies and asserts that the chief is there to serve society:

> 'It is society as such – the real locus of power – that exercises its authority over the chief. That is why it is impossible for the chief to reverse that relationship for his own ends, to put society in his service, to exercise what is termed power over the tribe: primitive society would never tolerate having a chief transform himself into a despot' (Clastres, 1977: 175).

Clastres goes on to argue that such a society keeps a close watch on the chief, limiting his possibilities to exploit his position. The political process of acephalous organisation based on kinship, equality and sharing is a process of competition for honour, wealth and influence that often leads to some sort of differentiation where some individual or corporation manages to gain more influence and more wealth than others (Clastres, 1977). When this is seen to threaten the value system of equality and power-sharing, a process of destroying the resources (symbolic and/or material) of legitimate leadership is set in motion. Eric R. Wolf discusses power and leadership in kinordered modes of production (Wolf, 1982). He asserts that chiefs that want to break the limitations of the kin order must lay hold of 'mechanisms that guarantee them independent power over resources'. 'This', says Wolf, requires 'new political instruments of domination ....' that may be applied directly on to 'brothers' or on the behalf of others. If this is not possible such ambitions will not be accepted, 'leaving them as chiefs only over the pumpkin' (Wolf, 1982: 99). The bulibaša is in a similar position among the hamlet Roma: every privilege he obtains that he does not share is taken as a sign of his rejection of romanimo, and undermines his authority. The authority of the bulibaša is in the hands of the community of family households and familia represented by males and is an instrument in the competition for resources among Roma. He is caught by the kinship order that makes him more prisoner than chief. I will conclude that I see this process of destroying leadership as an expression of resistance to the centralisation of power relations between men, and as an inherent trait of romanimo and the Rom habitus.

Big Men, Kings and Emperors – Minority and State

As suggested in the beginning of this chapter, Joska was chosen as bulibaša because of his personal attributes, as literate and good-looking, but most important because he was regarded to be harmless. Among most groups of Roma there are several so-called *'Roma bare'* (big men), who are established in a similar way as the Melanesian and South American 'big man' (Kaminski, 1987; Sutherland, 1975). In the hamlet all mature heads of domestic units could also be termed 'Roma bare' as an expression of respect. A Rom baro may also be the bulibaša of a local group of Roma, but generally he is not. Based on his position as leader of a family household, a Rom may, by controlling crucial resources, expand his influence and thus exercise power over his whole familia and even over several familii in many matters. But his position is dependent on his personal ability and will not be passed on to his successor (Stewart, 1997: 57). Even if a son or other male relative is appointed successor, he must compete for authority with other equal males. Nonetheless, the history of the Gypsies in Europe and the relations between Gypsies and gaže is full of Gypsy princes, kings, emperors and even queens. The Roma have at all times exploited the majority population's respect for centralised leadership, in order to gain respect and protect their relative cultural and political autonomy. When the Gypsies first presented themselves to the Western European kings and courts in the fifteenth century, they presented themselves as Egyptian nobility on pilgrimage, for instance as

'Lord Emaus of Egypt', and were at first warmly received all over Europe (see 'The Great Trick' in Fraser, 1995: 61). In Romania, most Romanians regarded the Emperor Čioba of Sibiu, who died in 1997, as an important Rom baro and as a powerful person. He was not only a very rich man he also owned a great international transport enterprise run by his familia and clients. He was also known as a benefactor and was said to have built schools and hospitals. When he died his funeral was shown on national television. The funeral procession passed through the flower-adorned streets of the medieval city of Sibiu and thousands of weeping Roma followed the coffin. After the funeral his son was officially (shown on national TV) crowned as his successor. The then Romanian president Emil Constantinescu sent an official telegram of condolence, and the TV reporters talked about him as a man of good deeds: '*Un om de treaba*'.

Nobody in the hamlet had told us about him and nobody seemed to know of his death before his funeral was on TV. There were no expressions of regret or of desire to join in the mourning either. When I asked them about their relations to Emperor Čioba they answered that he was their king, as he was king of all the Roma in Romania. I understood this answer to express their acceptance of him as one big man among others: as a Rom baro. Čioba may have been an external as well as an internal leader of his familia and possibly his local community in Sibiu, but he was not a leader of the Roma in any other sense. But to the gaže Čioba may have served as a consolation that even the uncivilised țigani can be ruled.

Notes

1. Vovoide in Romania, see Chapter 1 for the historical roots of this position. See also Stewart's discussion of the *vajda* (1997).

2. A son-in-law living with his wife's family household, a somewhat degrading position; a male bori.

Chapter 7

Romanimo: Towards a Rom Cosmology

Introduction

The Roma discourse on the property of shame as what makes them different from gaže is the most 'essentialist' representation of what I take to be a cosmological message, that of romanimo:[1] properties of true 'Romness'. This chapter will pull together what I see as core elements of the hamlet discourse on what it takes to be a true Rom as expressions of a Rom cosmology. 'Cosmology' in this sense is not to be understood as a coherent system of beliefs and practices. I would prefer to see Rom cosmology as an orientation in the world expressed by the symbolic representation of some core relationships. Central to the discourse of romanimo/romanes is the separation and even dichotomisation of some core relations in the Rom world: The relation between men and women, between life and death and between Rom and non-Rom. Although the core principles of romanimo are quite univocal, their interpretations both in the hamlet discourse and in social practice are contested and discussed, and are all the time accommodated to different contexts. In the absence of 'history' in the sense of one or more master myths about the past, of 'religion' in the sense of a coherent religious cosmology, and of fixed leadership in the sense of central power institutions, the notion of romanimo belongs to everybody and its meaning is dependent on the relation between individual interpretation, public discourse and the actual behaviour or case that evokes it. That it belongs to everybody does not, however, mean that anybody may have their interpretation publicly accepted. Romanimo is debated publicly in an explicit manner as a measure against which all behaviour is evaluated, but this debate is controlled and dominated by mature men and women. The interpretation of these principles and the implementation of the interpretations vary among groups of Roma and among individuals in any group, the agreement, however, being sufficient to establish common grounds: those among Roma.

Romanimo is not only subject to constant scrutiny, confrontation and influence by the Roma themselves; it is also influenced by the non-Roma they live among. Rom cosmology takes its shape in relation to Romanian Orthodox cosmology as it is interpreted and practised in the Transylvanian countryside.[2] As the Roma are constantly confronted by different cosmologies and by different interpretations of romanimo, consciousness and self-reflection mould their everyday practice and their cosmology. I thus see the relationship between the Rom cosmology as the hegemonic hamlet discourse and the religious cosmology of the village discourse as competing, sometimes conflicting, but also compatible. I prefer to regard hegemony as a relation of domination that is only partly achieved; there are in most contexts parallel, conflicting and competing hegemonic discourses that confront the subject's reflexivity (Gramsci, cited in Ewing, 1997: 22). I am talking of cosmology here as the publicly accepted version of a multivocal and dynamic worldview based on some specific orientations and relationships. The hegemonic Romanian village discourses and practices are both rejected and desired by the hamlet Roma as an expression of collective as well as personal identity, and may cause ambivalence and even conflict to individuals in many contexts. In others these cosmologies are compatible and in yet others only one is made relevant for action.

Although their expression varies, ideas of shame and symbolic impurity in relation to some sense of honour and symbolic purity, as expressed in rituals of separation of these elements, are traceable in all Rom populations everywhere and appear to be resistant to change (Okely, 1983; Stewart, 1997; Sutherland, 1975; Williams, 1985). Even if the Roma present these relations as dichotomies in general terms, they also talk about them and treat them as dualities, as oppositional principles that are not mutually exclusive but are combined in different ways in different contexts. This flexibility may be the decisive aspect of their permanence. I will discuss these issues by taking a closer look at the basic categories that are separated and the ideas and ritual work (Rudie, 1993) involved in this separation for the reproduction of romanimo and Rom society.

Separating Femaleness and Maleness

Shame and Honour as a System of Knowledge

Relations of shame and honour define the essence of Romanimo and by breaching the rules people risk being degraded in the eyes of fellow

Roma. Shame is a personal emotion that affects people's state of mind and expresses itself as bodily sensations patterned in cultural specific ways. Ideas of shame and honour are also societies' basic conceptual tools for the exercise of power and for coercion to social rules protecting a specific way of life (Elias, in Mennell and Goudsblom, 1998a: 19). To have shame it is not enough to know the difference between right and wrong. To have shame is expressed as a property of the Rom person, to be ashamed: *lašal pe*. Shame is embodied knowledge, and its essence is expressed by culturally defined bodily signs, such as downcast eyes and a blushing face and in a system of ritual work practised in everyday relations. Based on their inherent shame it is their knowledge about the sources of shame and the ritual work they employ to counteract shame that make the Roma, as they see it, morally superior to gaže. This implies that shame is reflected upon; as embodied knowledge it is both an emotionally and a morally loaded concept central to the hegemonic discourse of romanimo. In everyday situations shame is an expression of proper conduct and the emotional aspect is not questioned as long as the behaviour is seen as correct. Only when people violate ideas of shame by their behaviour may the question be raised; *is she (he) a proper Rom person, does she have shame?*

Mahrime: *The Essence of Romness*

In Western Europe and the U.S.A. the Romanes notion of *mahrime* has been treated as the essential concept in defining 'the real Rom'.[3] *Mahrime* is generally translated as 'ritual pollution' and used to denote a system of beliefs specific to most categories of Gypsies, but most elaborated among Roma. From my first day in the hamlet the idea of tracing signs of what I took to be 'the system of mahrime' became an obsession with me, as if the essence of 'Romness' was hidden in this practice. But when I tried to discuss the matter nobody in the hamlet seemed to have heard even the word before.

The hamlet is situated on a plain consisting of clay without concrete paving, and all winter and after heavy rains the whole area resembles a pigsty. Rubbish, old material, plastic bags, bits of iron etc. are tread down into the clay, paving the paths leading to the hamlet and between houses. The houses and huts are small and overcrowded, most floors consisting of packed earth, and there is very little possibility of keeping oneself, children and house clean in a hygienic sort of way. I found it interesting that there should exist an idea of symbolic purity among the Roma here, that did not influence their ideas of cleanliness in a material sense. However, most Roma seemed not to understand what we were talking about when we asked them what mahrime was all about. Thulo, one of Kurva's brothers, said it was something from a long time ago, but it was a bad thing and the Roma in the hamlet did not live by it. It was all about power competition (*politika*), he said, but he did not want to say more. After several months of fieldwork I was more or less sure that mahrime and ritual pollution were not important ideas in the moral order among these Roma.

Then halfway through my fieldwork something happened. The first to mention the concept was a Rom talking about the Romnja that earn their living by offering sex to drunk men in town and steal their money. He said angrily: '*Le žuvle mahril pe avri*', (lit. the women pollute themselves out (of the community)). He was, however, not willing to discuss it any further. The next was Thulo's wife, Varga, whom we had asked several times about this subject, but she always seemed to be confused about what we were talking about. The only thing she did say was that men's and women's clothes should be washed separately because dirt from women's clothes may '*kovlon leske injeri* (soften their (the men's) spirits)'. One evening we were gathered around a fire outside Joska's house. As she came along, I fetched the plastic bucket I used for peeling potatoes and offered it to her. She shrugged and said in an offended tone: '*Devla feril, na bešav pe ekh bradja* (God forbid, I do not sit on a bucket)'. I asked her why, but she only looked aloof when Joska explained: 'Our women do not sit on anything used for preparing food, we consider that a shame (*lažav*)'.

From then I was able to discuss matters of mahrime with Kurva and other women. Kurva said that before it had been forbidden to even touch any unprepared food or cooking utensils when they were menstruating (lit.: when you are ugly/bad (*cana san žungali*)), but today nobody bothered. She assured me, however, that women do still not cook when they menstruate. It means bad luck (without luck, *bibax*). The old women told me that women should not step over food, cooking utensils or anything connected with food, and avoid their skirt or apron touching anything connected with food. They also told me to keep the water bucket on a chair or a table so that nobody would step over it. As most food is prepared on the floor, these precautions seem hard to fulfil. The women emphasised, however, that it did not matter if food or cooking utensils fell on the ground as that dirt could be washed off.

Some time later we were visiting Anabela and Misolino, her husband. She works as a thief/prostitute and supports him as he is disabled. Misolino was drunk and talkative and when we asked them whether they knew about mahrime they both were eager to explain. Anabela explained that mahrime is not the same as *melalo* (dirty), but as the Romanian *spurcat*. *Spurcat* means 'impure' in a religious sense. So if one washes clothes in the same bucket as one prepares food, the bucket will be marhime and when a man eats the food he will become mahrime, which implies that he will not have luck. Misolino added that neither should a woman wash her headscarf in the tub she uses for food. Anabela explained that the headscarf is not mahrime as it covers the head, but it should not be done anyway because sweat will be mixed with food. The skirt and apron, however, are mahrime and will pollute food by contact. Misolino started telling us about some women in the hamlet that made their men mahrime by letting the blood from their... . He could not finish the sentence because of excuses, and then Anabela told him to keep quiet. She went on explaining that when washing clothes, men's clothes should be washed first, then women and children's. Everything that is connected with food, like napkins, tablecloths etc., must be washed before clothes. Then they both started talking about gaže, who do not separate these items, but wash everything in the same tub together and even use the same tub for food and clothes; 'But of course the gaže have no shame'.

The Dangerous Blood

I take this silence on the subject of mahrime to indicate its centrality and power among the hamlet Roma, but also ambiguity. Avoiding referring explicitly to it may be understood as a protective discretion, but it may also be explained in terms of the hamlet Roma's perceived shortcomings in adhering to the code (Stewart, 1997: 210). The explanations given to me suggest that menstruation and menstrual blood are connected to destruction, expressed by Anabela and Varga as 'taking away the luck and spirit of men'. Menstrual blood should be separated from contact, symbolically and materially, with men or anything belonging to males and even food in general. The idea that menstrual blood is destructive especially of men's power and luck, while the blood shed in childbirth is constructive, is widespread and found in different societies across the world (Abu-ughod, 1986; Counihan, 1999; Turner, 1967). This interpretation sheds light on the hamlet discourse on the dangerous relations between female substances, foremost menstrual blood, and maleness, or more accurately: men's prosperity. The idea that menstruation is dangerous to men of course has many meanings and possible interpretations. The hamlet discourse on this subject expresses, however, almost explicitly, that by menstruation women have the power to reject the male creative substances. I suggest this also may be seen as a rejection of maleness and possibly of men's power in general. Thus menstrual blood is equated to death, rejection of life, and is thus both powerful, dangerous and polluting, but not in its own right. It is primarily in combination with male life-giving power that menstruation is dangerous; in married women. Menstrual blood and other female bodily substances from unmarried or sexually inactive girls are not treated as dangerous or polluting. I see the idea of women as inherently 'bad' and less honourable than men as an expression of these ideas of menstruation as rejection of male creative powers. But not all blood is dangerous, because it is powerful it may also protect against danger. The colour red, signifying the power of blood, is used as a protective device in the hamlet. Red strings of wool are tied around infants' wrists and in the manes of horses to protect them from the evil eye, as is customary among villagers in general. The essential knowledge is that menstruation, seen as the destructive aspects of women's power, must be separated from the constructive aspects of men's power.

That Which is Separated

These are my interpretations; the Roma do not say more than I have already quoted. The fact that ideas of menstruation as polluting are old and widespread[4] suggests that they have developed under socio-economic circumstances when women seldom menstruated after marriage. Like most hamlet women today, women in earlier societies were generally pregnant most of their mature lives and several years of breastfeeding often prevented menstruation until the next pregnancy. Thus menstruation was probably an exception equated to abortion, not regular as among modern non-Gypsy women.

The notion of 'mahrime' is interpreted and practised differently among different groups of Roma according to their past and present social, cultural and political conditions and environment. Most scholars analysing Roma in Western societies have focused on the defilement aspect of mahrime, while my own position is that the separation aspect of mahrime has been underanalysed and should be given more analytical attention.[5] As we have seen, the hamlet Roma only very rarely refer to the concept explicitly, but when they do they generally speak of it in terms of separation: to 'mahrime' oneself out of the society, to separate clothes in washing, not to sit on buckets and so forth. The discourse on shame and shameful behaviour is thus an expression of the morally competent person, the true Rom, the person that knows how to separate the good from the bad. Mahrime, ritual defilement and separation are implicit elements of this discourse, notions too powerful to express explicitly (Stewart, 1997; Williams, 1985).[6] A woman's honour is dependent on her knowledge of the rules of separation, but it is balanced against her roles as nurturer and provider. Although asymmetric, the mutual dependency between men and women in the cosmological order is openly expressed in daily life. By keeping these rules of separation, men and women may interact rather freely, and women avoid being shameless and thus avoid shaming men.

Gender Politics

As Thulo said: 'Mahrime is a bad thing: it is about politics'. Thus the sense of shame and knowledge about proper rituals of separations are not regarded as evenly distributed among the Roma. Just like Romanes the language, also romanimo the cosmology is disputed among different nacie, and every nacie tends to regard their own as morally superior. The fact that the most elaborate description of the rules of separation was given to me by Anabela, one of the Kaštale women in the hamlet who earns her living by fake prostitution, points at the political aspect of the discourse of shame and separation. Anabela's symbolic capital among the Roma is quite ambiguous. She is a Kaštale woman, married to a rather alcoholic, disabled Rom and has only one child, and I often heard the men tease her husband about how she earned her money. Her reputation for being clever and making a lot of money did however enhance her respect in the eyes of men. While other women evaded the subject of mahrime because it was experienced as embarrassing as they wanted to present themselves as 'modern', and possibly because it was of less personal importance to them, Anabela willingly talked about it and about how the rituals of separation were violated in the hamlet. By presenting her knowledge of and adherence to the principles of separation, she also presented her sense of shame and herself as a respectable Romni, even more respectable than 'certain others' in the hamlet. The subordination of women by men, naturalised by the cosmological order, is thus made relevant by men and women to enhance their social and cultural resources in the competition for honour. Thus the discourse of shame is a discourse of power not only between different familii in the hamlet, but foremost between different groups and nacie of Roma. By participating in this evaluative discourse, the Roma share the cosmology of ritual separation and accommodate it to their practical circumstances.

Separating the Dead from the Living

Dangerous Death

Death is a destructive power that is seen as a constant and inexplicable threat to life among the Roma (Stewart, 1993: 23). Funerals are the most elaborate and the most frequent rituals celebrated in the hamlet. Most funerals occur during winter and men (and to some extent, women) spend days, weeks and months of every winter participating in funerals all over the area. The obligation to participate in the funeral of one's local and translocal family members is an inherent trait of romanimo, and not participating is interpreted as an insult and a rejection of the Rom brotherhood.[7] A funeral lasts for three days, from the moment of death to when the corpse is buried by the Orthodox priest. During this period the death wake is arranged and this constitutes the most important social ritual of the funeral. The funeral, however, does not mean the absolute separation of the dead from the living; the Roma celebrate a ritual meal (*pomana*) for the dead after three months and after six months, and sometimes also after one year. In the first weeks after a burial, the whole hamlet was cast in a nervous fever and everybody talked about the dead walking. Food was set out for the dead and all houses put extra bright bulbs in their outdoor lamps. The Roma said that they believed that the dead wanted to stay with their living relatives and tried to get back into the houses. They also feared that any wrong done to them in life would be avenged after death, but that with proper and strong funeral rites this danger could be averted.

Death of Authority and the Celebration of Equality

In hierarchical societies with central power holders and ancestor worship, the death ritual has been interpreted as a reconfirmation of authority where the deceased is turned into an ancestor and authority is thus restored in another mode (Bloch and Parry, 1982). Among the equality-ridden Roma, the death of a household head also means the dissolution of authority. During the wake and funeral all the mourners are equals – brothers and sisters. The deceased's sons are thereafter not under the authority of anyone, but will establish their own households and familii in alliance or in competition. Among the Roma it is equality that is restored by the death of household heads. The dead have no influence over the living once they have found their way to heaven, where they belong. By burning or selling their personal belongings, by not mentioning their name any more, and by leaving their graves to be overgrown, the individuality of the deceased is made to disappear after a year and he/she belongs to a obscure category, 'our ancestors' (*amare phure*).[8] This strategy of forgetting the dead is simultaneously also about forgetting the past as relevant for the present and is important in the quest for the equality of individuals. Patrick Williams argues, in the case of the Manouches of France, that by erasing all trace of the deceased's personality, they pay respect to his individuality. The idea of *'ne pas mettre son pas dans les traces d'un autre, ou, comme pour l'evocation de passé, les mettre avec tant de soin que les traces n'en soient en aucune facon modifiées* (not to step into another's footprints, or, for rememberance of the past, to place your step with such care that the other's footprints will not be modified in any sense)' (Williams, 1993: 15, my translation), is a way of creating a silence that should not be misinterpreted as emptiness or oblivion. Williams argues that it should instead be understood as respecting the irreplaceability and uniqueness of every individual and the absolute coincidence of every generation: 'We are the Manouches, we are what the Manouches have always been' (Williams, 1993: 15, my translation). Thus respect towards the elders does not open up the past but timelessness, a notion I find evocative for my understanding of the idea of being Roma that is reconfirmed by funeral rites. By denying the dead any permanent influence on the living and by paying them respect, not by prolonging their earthly authority but by confirming their individuality as a brother among brothers, the true state of romanimo is confirmed (Stewart, 1997).[9] Authority is not dead altogether – every son and daughter will now compete for influence and authority and themselves become heads of households and familii – but death reveals that authority is ephemeral, like everything else in life.

Death and Oblivion

I have suggested that translocal networks that make up the familia and potential allies are perceived as some sort of 'ideal' relatives and that these relations are maintained by participation in lifecycle rituals – primarily funerals. I further claimed that funerals are the most important public events among the hamlet Roma as rituals that separate the dead from the living. The destructive powers of death, personified by the devil who resides under the ground, are ritually separated from the creative powers of life, personified by living humans. The influence of the dead over the living is controlled by performing the correct funeral rites, by not using the names of newly deceased people, by not tending their graves and by forgetting about them as individuals. They disappear into the realm of the faceless, nameless *'amare phure'*. The authority they held in life vanishes with them, and the living can go on as equals as brothers. This separation does, however, value life in this world and devalue the world of the dead, in sharp contrast with Orthodox cosmology, with its theology of salvation. There is no idea of sin, punishment or salvation in the religious beliefs of the hamlet Roma: it is by being fully committed to this world of human existence among one's fellow Roma that a person may expect honour and fulfilment.

The Dangerous Spirits of Below

Joska explained that the dead body belongs to the devil, and the devil resides 'below' – in the earth – while the deceased's soul rises to God in heaven. The hamlet Roma seem to see the graveyard and the earth in general as the domain of death, or at least as the dangerous aspect of death that may interfere with the living in the form of ghosts. The Roma believe in evil spirits; this is most explicitly expressed in their fear of the evil eye and of snakes. The snake[10] plays an important role in Rom consciousness and lore, representing the devil. The snake does not only figure in stories, but is also a threat in their daily activities. Although there are no poisonous snakes in this area, young girls told me about a huge, dangerous snake that lives by the stream where they fetch water every day. They said it was very old and it wanted to eat them. Some women told us about a woman in a nearby hamlet who had nursed a snake, not voluntarily – it had overpowered her. The image of snakes wanting to drink women's milk is a recurrent theme among Roma and Gypsies in many places, together with the image of women involuntarily giving birth to snakes (Gjerde, 1994: 65; Okely, 1983: 94).[11] The association of evil with a threat to fertility and the productive aspects of womanhood confirms my interpretation that the Roma see womanhood as infused with powers of both destruction and construction. In fairytales (*paramiči*), the most prominent representation of the underworld of the evil forces is the dragon. The hero is always a young Gypsy boy who, because of his inventiveness and courage, manages to kill the dragon and win the emperor's daughter. Apart from its prominent role as representing the Devil in Christianity, my argument is that the anomalous position of the snake in Rom belief poses a special threat to a system of symbolic separation such as romanimo (Douglas, 1966). I take the snake to represent the evil spirits of death that intrude on the living. The snake is a boundary crosser; it is attracted to women and it invades the most intimate parts; the female womb. It is tempting here to point to a parallel in the expression from the fables of Æsop: 'To nurture a snake at one's breast' meaning to house a traitor unknowingly. I will not push the argument further, only state that the nauseating fear that snakes evoke in Roma may well represent a culturally moulded sentiment towards the dangers of unseparated elements. But the horror the Roma express towards the dead and death in general is also an expression of the fragility of their society. The Rom society is made up of family affiliation and translocal networks, both solely confirmed by symbolic boundaries and sentiments of loyalty. The problem of controlling the destructive powers of death by separating it from the living community and rearranging relations and boundaries among the living thus may be seen to constitute the core of the Rom death ritual and possibly the core of ritual separation.

Separating the Roma and the Gaže

The Discourse on Difference

The Roma see Romanes, their language, as one of the main constituting traits of being Rom. This is expressed in the conflation of terms denoting language and way of life: *Romanes*. Together with women's dress and male occupation, language is the criterion for distinguishing categories of people in general. Although appearance and occupation are distinguishing criteria, there are no expressive signs apart from language that differentiate a Rom from a gažo. A Rom may look like a gažo, but if he speaks Romanes he is considered Rom.

Although language and cosmology seem almost fused in people's perceptions, a social environment that confronts the subject with several languages and several cosmologies that all claim equal authority in different contexts creates reflexivity and consciousness both about the connections between language and cosmology and between the hegemonic claims of different cosmologies. Living in a multicultural environment, the Roma, as other groups in this area engage in a continuous process of self-reflection on their language and cosmology. This process of reflexivity serves both as a confirmation of one's own group's supremacy and as a reflection on difference and the presence of 'the other': dangerous, morally inferior and always present.

Controlling Shame

The notion of 'shame' has been discussed from different perspectives in the previous chapters. To sum up these discussions, the notion among hamlet Roma should not be understood as a property of a social person, but as a collective property of the Roma. Children are generally reproached by the question: 'Don't you have shame?', as a way of guiding their actions. The corrective exclamation: '*Rom san!* – (you are a Rom)', is often added to such scolding. Only by becoming gaže may a Rom person become totally shameless. The Roma are pragmatic; one of the harsh conditions of life is that they have to perform a lot of tasks and make a lot of choices that are not respectable; some of them even shameful according to romanes: 'But, alas, what can we do? The children are hungry' is the usual explanation for such behaviour. Keeping a balance between what one should do and what one has to do implies having a sense of shame and always avoiding shaming oneself and others if possible. Like shame, the notion of 'honour' sums up 'a bundle of virtues' (Gilmore, 1987: 93) among which shame, brotherly sharing, autonomy, controlling one's domestic unit and familia, respecting one's elders and gaining social prestige are fundamental. Honour is seen as a potential of the Rom person that can be increased or violated by behaviour. Honour is not a male virtue, but males seem to be more preoccupied with social prestige and with respect than women, and thus more vulnerable to accusations of shame.

Language, Power and Hegemony

Relations of power and dominance are immanent in language. The many hierarchic terms in colloquial Romanian that distinguishing between women, men and children, and between superiors and inferiors, are not present in Romanes. Only gender is marked in direct address as in conjugations in general. The Roma use the terms 'brother' (*phral*) and 'sister' (*phei*) to express respect towards equals, and 'cousin' (*vero/verišoara*) towards more distant equals, while notions of respect outside the household relations are expressed by: 'uncle' (*kako*), and 'aunt' (*bibi*). A good bulibaša, say the hamlet Roma, should have a big head and speak well. Linguistics is always discussed and debated at length when hamlet Roma are gathered. *Čače vorba* (true words) may mean both morally correct speech and linguistically correct words. There are many possible words for most concepts and objects, and which one is 'true Romanes' and thus 'good/pretty' is a topic for much discussion, especially among men. Every nacie of Roma tends to claim its language as superior and whenever Roma from different nacie meet, the topic of language may arise. Either both groups underplay differences so as not to shame the other (that has an inferior language), or disputes about correct Romanes arise.

The general Romanian view is that Romanes is an argot, not a language. Very few villagers seem to acknowledge that țigani have a language at all, and villagers reacted with general bewilderment and dismay when we told them that Romanes is a totally different language from Romanian. Although the hamlet Roma learn Romanian from an early age, they tend to speak it their own way – another expression of their 'difference'. The villagers take this as a proof of what they see as the general stupidity and inferiority of the țigani and not as a conscious maintenance of boundaries. Villagers also see the țigani way of speaking as somewhat aggressive and explosive, as if the words are spat out of the speakers' mouths – a proof of their violent nature. The Roma, on their side, know that gaže cannot understand their language and this is not only convenient in most contexts, it is a mark of their independence and superiority as only they speak both languages. The hegemonic Romanian-language discourse does not seem to affect the identity of the hamlet Roma in such a way as to make them hide, undercommunicate or polish their language. On the contrary it seems to fertilise self-reflection and consciousness of language as expressions and instruments of autonomy.

However, this is not the whole story. A process of social, cultural and linguistic transformation, often termed assimilation, is a trait of the Roma population in Romania as elsewhere (Achim, 2004). This transformation is often deliberate through marriage with gaže, through conscious acts for social mobility, and through poverty and the lack of other options than those presented by state institutions. Individuals and families that for different reasons choose to try to become gaže will very quickly change their language by using more and more Romanian and/or Hungarian words and expressions. These individuals are, of course, vulnerable to the Romanian hegemonic discourse about țigani as they have, so to say, chosen the other side. Like shame, Romanes is best understood as a system of embodied knowledge, a hegemonic, 'ethnic' discourse that is used explicitly to create unity and compliance among hamlet Roma and draw boundaries between other groups and categories of people. Being an oral language (only some educated Roma know the written Romanes) that is not even regarded as a language by gaže it is perhaps the most effective technology of symbolic separation and of collective Rom identity.

Sharing = Being Rom

The discourse and practice of sharing, visiting and general sociability are like shame talked about as 'romanimo'; qualities of Rom personality. The idea of 'a nice person', *lašo manuš*, is likewise modelled on ideas about romanimo, but it also sums up what I would call 'sociability': an ability or readiness to involve oneself in social life as a form of play (Georg Simmel in Frisby and Featherstone, 1997: 120). Kurva told me that 'a nice person' is good-tempered, smiling and pleasant, not touchy and sullen or easily offended. A nice person easily forgets wrongs that are done towards her. I take this to be a statement about sociability in Simmel's sense and about willingness to share. Willingness to joke and laugh, to stand teasing and even joking accusations, is often underlined by Roma themselves as important. Joking abuse is a general trait of friendly interaction in the hamlet that I see as a mode of handling aggression in a controlled way. It may also be understood as a special expression of what Roma see as sociability and sharing in a very broad sense, as if pushing one another towards the limit of self-respect could prove one's willingness to compromise one's individuality for the collective good-humour.

Sociability is expressed as beauty of demeanour, but physical beauty is also valued by the Roma and I believe the Roma experience it as an act of sociability and sharing. To put effort into one's appearance, to wear bright colours, have properly plaited hair and other traits that the Roma consider beautiful are a way of showing respect and generosity towards one another.[12] A beautiful appearance may be seen as a gift that is offered the community as an adornment (Simmel in Frisby and Featherstone, 1997: 132). Young men prefer bright colours in shirts and even in trousers and are preoccupied with their moustache. Shiny red silk is very popular both among men and women and may be worn for everyday use. Of course this emphasis on beauty is also an expression of competition between households and familii and a way of displaying wealth, but I see it as an expression of romanes: offering beauty is an act of generosity and of sociability and thus it is a moral act. The Roma often say that the villagers are badly dressed and generally ugly and this seems to be considered a trait of the gaže[13] in contrast to the more beautiful Roma.

Expressivity – Tolerance of 'The Eye'

From the time Roma children are very small they are encouraged to dance and sing at public gatherings and they are used to being observed and watched by gaže wherever they appear. Some parents encourage their children to steal from gaže in order to train them to stand up to scolding and punishment without fear. Women's and children's dress also make them stand out from the average villager, generally in a stigmatised sense. I suggest that this visibility in public places, as a strategic demeanour when women go scavenging, develop 'the conscience of the eye' in Richard Sennet's sense (Sennet in Bauman, 1995: 137) and, I would add, a tolerance of 'the eye'. While a conscience of 'the' eye creates a self-consciousness of being different, a tolerance of other people's gaze creates self-confidence in public performance that the Roma see as traits of themselves. This is contrasted to what they often see as the dullness and introvert personality of the gažo.

Discourses on Difference and Lived Experience

Apart from the daily boundary maintenance by ritual and other practices of separation of romanes from *gažikanes*, hamlet Roma have also developed a repertoire of collective practices that are context-bound to ward off the dangers posed by gažo society. These are not rules, but collective practices to handle confrontations with formal authorities and with local power holders without losing control of their way of life. The hamlet Roma avoid sending their children to school, but they always verbally consent to the gažo effort to educate them. They do not go to church, but express their devoutness through funeral rites and by expressing their religious sentiment. They avoid wage labour that puts them in an inferior position towards gaže and prefer doing business on their own terms. The balance between economic dependency and cultural autonomy is thus a constant struggle. They need to get hold of a share of the wealth of gaže without being polluted by their cosmology.

However, the qualitative differences between cognitive categories and 'lived experience' in people's cultural boundaries (F. Barth in Cohen, 2000) should be emphasised. So far this book has highlighted the differences and boundary creation rituals of the hamlet Roma, rather than their practical adaptation and compliance to the ways of the gaže. The Roma did, however, tend to deny any 'real' difference between Roma and gaže when we discussed such differnecs in general terms. They said things like: 'We are all the same really, there is no real difference', 'we are all people', 'we all come from Adam and Eve' and so forth. This is also what they exemplified in their daily lives. A Rom couple living like peasants in the village presented themselves as Roma *gažikane* (non-Rom

Roma), a term that seemed perfectly appropriate to the hamlet Roma. When we asked Joska and Kurva about them they said: 'But they have no children, that's why they are almost gaže; we would be like that too if we did not have children'. Many Roma also expressed a desire to become gaže, or at least to live like gaže. Kurva's mother was said to have been a gaži, her daughter had a child with a gažo and it turned out that several family households in the hamlet have relations to Roma who were once gaže. Relatives of Thulo and his household living in a nearby village appeared to be in a process of upward mobility and cultural change. Their two children went to school, the wife spoke half Romanes and half Romanian and the husband owned a tractor and was contracted by peasants to plough their fields. This was never commented on or laughed at by their relatives or any other Rom. All Roma know that Rom may transform to gažo and gažo to Rom: this is not denied nor hushed up among Roma as it is among villagers. When the Roma say that Rom and gažo are really the same, I interpret this as an expression of seeing 'Romness' and 'gažoness' as variations of a common humanness and thus as poles on a continuum. Everyday experience and, I suggest, Rom cosmology inform a theory of classification that is both dualistic and dual according to context. That makes it possible to be either Rom or gažo in some contexts and more or less Rom and more or less gažo in others. This classification implies flexible boundaries that are negotiable, and allow for the social transformations of Rom to gažo and the other way round when necessary.

Separate to Unite – Dependency and Autonomy

At this point it should become clear that rituals of separation are not about separation for its own sake, but about separating aspects that must be reunited in a controlled way. Death and the dead must be separated from the living in order for the living to preserve the idea of a society of equal brothers, but all humans will eventually unite with their loved ones in heaven. Only by exchange between men and women and between family households may the Roma form communities. Only by economic exchange with gaže may Roma survive as Roma. I further see these oppositions as expressions of the dual relational principles of dependency and autonomy that are inherent in the Rom way of life and cosmology. The value of brotherhood, sharing and dependency is paired with an ideology of autonomy and individuality. The value of equality and autonomy between males is paired with the value of natural gender asymmetry and women's dependence on men. The value of belonging, unity and autonomy of the family household is paired with the value of alliance and dependence on cognatic relations. The value of cultural and political independence of gažo society is paired with the economic dependence on gažo economy. Being Rom in opposition to gažo, and being Rom and gažo as different but interrelated and interdependent social categories, are different aspects of the same perspectives of Rom cosmology. Although romanimo may be regarded as an expression of the ultimate value placed on being Rom, the transformation from Rom to gažo is not seen as biology, but as social convention. It is always an option and it is always possible to be both, according to context. The challenge of the Rom way of life lies in the duality of the Rom mode of subsistence, which, on the one hand, attaches them as dependents on gažo production and economy, and the Rom cosmology, which, on the other hand, creates difference from and boundaries against the gažo cultural and economic hegemony. This duality demands a flexible cosmology or orientation in the world, which allows for a variety of adaptations to the majority society without losing the collective sense of self and separateness that can ward off incorporation.

Notes

1. *Romanimo* is a noun form derived from *Rom*; *romanes* is the adverbial form.
2. These beliefs and practices are probably influenced by pre-Christian religious beliefs and ideas as well as earlier Roman Catholic and Islamic rule in this part of Romania.
3. For discussions of mahrime among Gypsies in Western Europe and the U.S.A. see Gropper, 1975; Miller, 1968; Okely, 1983; Sutherland, 1975; Williams, 1983.
4. These ideas are still important to the Romanian Orthodox Church and of course to most Islamic societies.
5. There are, however, also some linguistically interesting aspects of the concept of 'mahrime', that might shed light on the Rom rituals of separation. According to general linguistic interpretation, *mahrime* is derived from the Greek word *magarizo*, meaning dirt/make dirty: that is taken up in Romanes as ritual defilement. This interpretation has cemented the concept of 'mahrime' as defilement representing a system of pollution. This is the way it has been interpreted by linguists and anthropologists working with Rom in Western Europe and the U.S.A. and this is the way it seems to be interpreted among the Norwegian Rom. However, the concept implies an obligatory element of separation and my suggestion is that this element is decisive for the understanding of the social practice of mahrime among the hamlet Roma and possibly among the Roma in this area in general. The Turkish and Arabic word *haram* (to set apart, to separate), with the participial form *mahrama* (set apart), forbidden, points to another possible etymological interpretation of *mahrime*. The Turkish word *mahrem* has a similar meaning. I suggest that the belief and social practice of mahrime, expressed in terms of shame among the hamlet Roma, should be understood in terms of the Arabic/Turkish haram (to separate), rather

than in terms of the Greek *magarizo* (dirt/pollution). This suggestion is not weakened by the fact that the Romanian territory has been influenced by Islamic thought and the Turkish language for centuries and that the Roma also, before they entered Romania, were probably Muslims or at least lived under Islamic rule (Beck, 1989; Achim, 2004). This claim needs linguistic investigation, the point I wish to make is that the idea of mahrime is interpreted and practised differently among different groups of Roma according to their past and present social, cultural and political conditions and environment.

6. Personal conversation with Patrick Williams.

7. For an exstensive analysis of the death ritual among the Harango Roma in Hungary see Stewart (1993).

8. Meaning both living, old relatives and ancestors in different contexts.

9. According to Stewart (1993) the death ritual is in some respects different among the Roma of Harango than among the hamlet Roma. I suggest these differences at least partly are due to different mortuary rites among the Roman Catholics and Romanian Orthodox.

10. Frogs are regarded as related to snakes and the Romanes word for 'devil', *beng* is the Hindi word for 'frog'.

11. I was told almost the same story by Roma in Norway in 1982.

12. Among villagers to be 'well arranged' (*bine aranjat*) expresses an appreciation of an orderly and attractive appearance. I take this to express something about sociability; one should not offend anyone by disorderly appearance. The Roma on their side offend village values by their dress, hair and disorderly appearance. Among themselves of course their appearance is an expression of Romanes and hence 'well arranged'.

13. The villagers, especially the old generation, are very sceptical of bright colours. They wear brown, black and grey. Bright colours are seen as Gypsy-like and thus unfit for Romanians.

Part II

Roma as Villagers

Introduction

The first part of this book was about the Rom world – not about a world exclusively Rom, because that does not exist; there are no spheres in the Rom world untouched by gaže. Rather, the first part presented the world from the Rom point of view. This second part follows the steep mud-track from the Rom hamlet on the hilltop down through the narrow, cement-covered track that leads between the houses of the outskirts of the village, over the railway line and into the church road that leads to the centre of the village, the market place and the Orthodox church. The church road is humorously called 'Gypsy road' (*stradă ţiganilor*) by villagers. This is the path the Roma walk every day into the village, but very seldom do villagers follow the path in reverse into the Rom hamlet. The symbolic border is drawn at the bottom of the hill where the mud-track begins towards the hamlet and the cement road towards the village. This is the point where villagers heading towards the pastures and the woods turn away from the path towards the hamlet and follow a path that bends around the hill and out of sight of the hamlet.

Leaving the Rom world is visualised very explicitly by leaving a physically undifferentiated environment and entering a strictly differentiated one. The hamlet is characterised by the cohabitation of animals and humans that at first sight seems chaotic. Dogs and small, half-naked children tumble along with huge pigs, while men and women sit outside their houses, watching or wandering about their tasks. The air is filled with the joyful screaming of children, the shouting of men and women and the barking of dogs, and this cacophony is accompanied by music from several transistor radios. Now and then the sound of thundering hooves drowns out all human sounds as the horses grazing nearby are chased through the hamlet by a band of barking dogs. Houses with doors flung open, messy yards, broken roofs and no fence or gate protecting the individual house or its inhabitants, the muddy tracks crossing the hamlet in all directions, literally paved with rubbish – all this gives the hamlet an appearance of carelessness, transience and anti-structure that is expressed by villagers in their depiction of Roma as nonhuman. Walking into the village, the environment becomes more and visibly differentiated, and ordered in a Romanian way. Small, neat houses lie on each side of the concrete road, surrounded by high walls and shut out from the street by tall, iron gates that prevent any eye peeping in from outside into the courtyard and the private space. Here dogs are inside the gate and tied up. The humans live at the front part of the houses and in the courtyard and the animals are at the back, all segregated into their own small areas. Only the geese roam freely in the streets. Children are at school, men at work, women at home or in the fields. The private space is separated from the public road, the animal domain from that of humans; the generations and sexes occupied with different tasks in different places. Just as the first part of this book was about the Rom world as it is lived in relation to the gažo world, so is this second part about aspects of the Romanian peasant world and about the actual interaction between Roma and villagers and the exchanges that tie them together in everyday contexts and in national discourses about Romanianness. Through the contrasted and interweaving cosmologies and daily interaction between Roma and villagers, the dependence and complementarity of these life-worlds will be traced. I will discuss how they are expressed and argue that they form a system of dependence, fear, even hatred and sometimes affection, where domination, submission and resistance take quite unexpected turns. It was by living and talking with Florica and her family that I came to understand the urgencies and preoccupations of everyday life in the village. Hence, I started my discussion of the hamlet with Joska's family household and I will start my discussion about the village with the household of Florica and Viorel.

Chapter 8

Village Life, Peasant Cosmology

Introduction

A Day in Florica and Viorel's Household

Every morning, in winter and summer, every seson, Florica gets up at six o'clock to milk her two goats and to feed the pigs and chicken. In spring, summer and autumn she then walks to her family's fields. She brings a bottle of water, a piece of lard, some onions and a piece of bread. Every morning the same exodus may be observed through the streets of the village: first the workers hurry through the village to the station to catch a train to work, then comes the first shepherd with the villagers' goats, followed by the second shepherd with the villagers' sheep, and lastly the third one walks slowly towards the green pastures with his flock of cow's. Florica and the other peasants leave at about the same time as the animals, their hoes on their shoulders. Florica usually walks alone or with one of her neighbours, mostly elderly women. Viorel, her husband, gets up shortly afterwards and starts his day as a repairman in the courtyard of their family house. Florica's parents built the house. As she was an only child, Viorel moved in with his in-laws after he and Florica married. Florica and Viorel are now in their late sixties/seventies and are both retired. Before the revolution, Florica worked at the village co-operative, while Viorel worked as a state-employed lorry driver. After the revolution and until her retirement four years ago, Florica worked in the village bakery; twelve-hour shifts, night and day, in addition to farm work. Now she works from dawn to sunset to supply the family with food. Viorel earns cash and goods besides his pension by repairing all sorts of things for his fellow villagers and even constructing simple instruments, crosses for funerals etc. and renovating flats. In spring and autumn he helps

Florica with the agricultural work, but always complains 'I don't like farming (*nu mi place agricultură*)'. They both feel trapped. They have been given back their parent's fields, but subsistence farming is a constant cause of concern, needing a lot of work and it barely keeps them from starving. Florica complains:

> 'Before, we had very few worries. We worked ten hours at the co-operative and earned enough money to buy what was necessary, we had free holidays at the Black Sea and free school for our children. Now we work ten to twelve hours a day on our land, and it gives very little because it is no good and we have to pay for ploughing, seeding, fertilising. We earn no money and wear ourselves out. … It is not worth it.'

In spite of this complaint, Florica always says she loves being in the fields with flowers, the birds and the fresh air, and she loves her little vegetable garden at the back of the house.

When the old folks are up, Aurora, their daughter, gets up and prepares her two children for school and her husband for his work. Her husband, Nicu, is from another village but lives with his in-laws just like Viorel did. He works at the railway company and leaves home every second or third day to stay for a week at work on the trains. His shirts must be ironed, his uniform brushed and his food prepared. The young family lives in the two main rooms of the house, while the grandparents live in the kitchen and a small adjacent room that Viorel just had finished. After seeing her children and husband off to school and work, Aurora cooks the family's daily meal, sweeps the floors of her rooms, goes shopping, or joins her mother in the fields. Tuesday is laundry day and this is Aurora's task. All the family's laundry is washed in the courtyard in an old (semi-automatic) washing machine. Water is drawn from the river that runs at the end of the garden behind the house. After washing, the clothes are carried down to the riverbed for rinsing. All village women do this in all weathers. All day long one can see women pulling small carts filled with laundry to and from the river. Every house has its own part of the riverbed for washing. All morning and most of the day one can hear the banging of the wooden paddles that women use to beat the dirt out of the clothes. The river is a public place, but mostly a female place. Even though some men spend time fishing, they do not wash clothes. But it is not a place for leisure and chatting; it is a place for working and for evaluating one another's work performance. After three months in the village, a woman I did not know stopped me in the street and told me how pleased she was to see me at the river washing like the other women.

Aurora's work is interrupted when the children, aged seven and eight, come back from school, as they need much attention and are never left on their own. The children have no tasks in the household or on the farm. They are expected to do well at school, to work hard with their homework to get good marks. A child's school achievements are public knowledge as they are read aloud at the public ceremony before summer holidays. Good marks are seen to be a sign of good mothering. Aurora spends most of the evening, often three to four hours, doing homework with her children, as do all mothers and some fathers in the village. Aurora complains that two children are really too much and I understand that complaint when I consider the amount of time she spends raising them according to village standards. Aurora and Nicu have planned to send their children to university, preferably to become lawyers, and that means sacrifice both for children and parents. Nicu has to earn enough money to save for their future education, and spends most of his time away from home. Aurora spends most of her time attending to and working with the children. But then, motherhood is generally talked about as a sacrifice in the village and sacrifice is considered a virtue. Florica says that ţigani produce children for their own pleasure, without thinking about the consequences, without caring for their education.

Between seven and eight o'clock, when the goats, cows and sheep come home from the pastures led by their herdsmen, the old women and some men come home from the fields. The rest of the family has had their meal when they were hungry, and Florica finally sits down to eat. In summer the children then have some free time to play in the street, while Florica often sits on a bench chatting with the neighbours. Before going to bed Florica has to prepare maize for the animals and feed them. By this time, after ten to twelve hours of work in the fields, she is so tired she can barely speak and goes to bed as soon as she can. In winter Aurora and Florica stay in the kitchen discussing the day's events, while Aurora´s husband watches TV in their part of the house, if he is home, and Viorel does the same in his part. Aurora then puts the children to bed and goes to sleep with them so as to be able to attend to their needs during night. She assures me they cannot go to sleep without her.

The Village Community

The Village as a Place

The village is a place in a different sense than the hamlet; it is very explicitly territorialised by walls, gates and fences separating the different private units from each other and from the public space, and by physical structures representing the political and religious authorities such as churches and official buildings. The physical boundaries between the village and its neighbouring villages are almost not visible to strangers, but it is symbolically bounded by name and as a political and administrative unit. Villagers express their love for and sense of belonging to the village and the area by constantly emphasising thebeauty, the clear fresh air, the beautiful clean river and the peacefulness, contrasted with the noisy and dirty towns. Old villagers still remember the land reform in the 1920s when earlier serfs and sharecroppers were allocated land to cultivate as free peasants. This lasted until in the 1950s when private ownership of land was taken from them, and most of them became agricultural workers on the local co-operative farm. Today most villagers have reclaimed the family land that was collectivised, and cultivate it once again on a family basis. I suggest that by cultivating the land, the villagers are in a different relationship with the area than are the Roma. Whereas Roma express their relationship to the area through their fellow Roma who inhabit it, peasants express this relationship by belonging not primarily to the people of the village, but to the landscape surrounding the village and to their private farm and land. Thus the landscape and geography of the village serve as identity-producing factors by evoking the moral values inherent in the Romanian idea of village life as authenticity (see Berge, 1997). I would add that the village represents a 'moral location' (Gupta and Ferguson, 1992) and should not be seen as a community encompassing inhabitants in any unified way. Although it is an agricultural village consisting mainly of peasants, teachers, civil servants and merchants make up the top levels of the social hierarchy. The village is further composed of people that define themselves as ethnic Hungarians, Slovaks and Roma, apart from Romanians, and who generally belong to different religious communities. Ethnic classification and boundaries divide not only social space, but also, to a certain degree, physical space, in the sense that the village is not one place but many. The family and the family farm appear as the only social units that bind people together in enduring loyalty, at least on an ideological level. The ideology of familism, analysed as a response to state control and permanent shortage under communism in general (Buchowski, 1996), is expressed in a general distrust towards anyone outside the range of relatives, towards representatives of local authorities and towards the state. As a basis for a later discussion of exchange between Roma and villagers, there follows a discussion of what I see to be constitutive discourses and social practices among villagers. This must not be misinterpreted, though, as any attempt to give a comprehensive picture of village life and cosmology.

Self-sufficiency, moderation and the ethos of labour are central aspects of peasant identity that are important for the evaluation of ţigani and other social categories. Likewise, ideas of cleanliness, purity and modernity are central to the village discourse and important criteria for social classification.The village discourse of civilizaţie position all categories of villagers according to a hierarchy of moral and biological traits which governs much of social practice. Lack of trust in social relations and fear of public space and strangers create a xenophobia that confirms 'otherness' as biologically given. Distrust, ideas of strangers and familism, all aspects of the ideal unity and solidarity of the domestic group as an emotional and political bulwark against a hostile society, are significant ideas in the formation of the village as a community.

Moderation and the Gender Order

Gospodărią

The household of the family farm (*gospodărią*) is the main unit of production and consumption and comprise people actually living together and pooling their resources. Most households are composed of three generations: one son or daughter with spouse and children in addition to the old couple and the property that belongs to them – land, houses and animals. The average village family, however, encompasses more than one household; married children living elsewhere, grandchildren belonging to different households and sometimes siblings of the household heads may be regarded part of one's family. Ethnically endogamous marriages are the rule in the village, but there is a strict taboo against first-cousin marriages. There are, nevertheless, many marriages between ethnic Hungarians and Romanians in the village and this appears to have been the reality for a long time. Florica told us that her grandmother had been Hungarian. The practice of uxorilocal residence, where a daughter brings her husband into her natal household, is common and should partly be understood in relation to the birth-rate and the inheritance rules. Families rarely have more than two children, who both inherit from their parents on equal terms. This makes two children of opposite sexes the ideal family composition as possessions will not be diminished and both sets of parents will have a child at home after their marriage and one that is free to settle with his in-laws or move out. And most families do have two children of opposite sexes. Although most families have one grown child who lives outside the natal household, these children keep their rights and obligations in the family farm. Many households were economically dependent on their children living elsewhere and exchange networks were crucial to the viability of many family farms. Family planning and two-child families have been prevalent in Romania since the First World War as a strategy to increase household viability (Verdery, 1983: 299).

Children in the Household

Children are, as already noted, not expected to participate in household or farm work: their responsibility is to work for a good education, one that may bring prosperity to the family. This is a rather interesting trait of peasant socialisation and points at the ambiguity of peasant ideology in the village. The burdens and contentment of peasant life, which honours the old generation, are not seen as suited for the young. 'The good peasant life' is something that children are learnt to respect, but avoid. This may partly be due to the fact that the future looks economically bleak for small peasants, and that education has long been regarded as the vehicle for social mobility in the hierarchical Romanian society (Verdery, 1983: 62). Children are disciplined for formal education from an early age. Parents and grandparents constantly scrutinised and corrected their grandchildren's comportment and actions, so that their physical movements were restricted and their appearance adjusted to fit village norms (see Stewart 1999). Thus village children, in contrast to hamlet children, were seldom free from parental and grandparental control. They were encouraged to adapt to a hierarchical society that depends on discipline of its lower subjects. They were trained to work hard for a reward later, and although they were expected to share this reward with their family, they were not trained for collective responsibility in the present. The reward, one might add, was far away as only few students are admitted to university.

Family and Kin

Relatives outside the family did not play a role in the daily life of Viorel and Florica. Obligations to relatives were often played down, and replaced by those to godparents; a relationship moulded and often based on kinship ties and neighbour relations. Godparents may play a significant role in a person and family's economic viability and political influence and are generally chosen among influential relatives. More distant relatives do, however, play a part in lifecycle rituals such as marriages, baptism and funerals, when kin are obliged to participate and exchange gifts. Although the ideal of the corporate family seemed to include parents and all children economically and emotionally as parts of the family farm, in practical life this was more complex. Post-marriage residence caused conflicts about inheritance and equal division between siblings, as well as split loyalties between parents and in-laws. Viorel was on bad terms both with his son Silvano and with his son-in-law Nicu. Silvano and his wife Maria, complained to us that his parents only cared about their daughter who lived with them and her children, and that Silvano did not receive his share of his family's resources. Viorel complained that Silvano refused to work properly and that he never helped him with the crops or with his repair jobs. So the united family that by industry and content feeds its members by their own production on their own land is the ideal peasant family that is not always experienced in daily life. This ideology also implies mutual and enduring dependency; parents are expected to support their children as long as necessary and children to look after their parents in old age.

Moderation and the Ethos of Manual Labour

According to Viorel, the only real work is that which produces a tangible product, such as food or objects. He sneered at his son-in-law who worked as a civil servant. He did not regard that as work for a man. Viorel stated firmly that one of the problems about Jews was that they did not work. When we asked him what they did for a living, Viorel answered contemptuously that they did '*bizniță*'. Business (*bizniță*) is almost synonymous with crime in colloquial Romanian, although most villagers try to venture into some sort of dealing to add to their meagre pensions or salaries. Bizniță is what Jews and țigani are seen as doing, and is not regarded honest and honourable work. The general Romanian contempt towards business may be an expression of communist ideology and of fear for the future as presented by the market liberalisation in Romania. Jews are generally blamed for Westernisation and urbanity; țigani are blamed for Romania's problems with the market (Verdery, 1996: 98). But market economy was experienced ambiguously by the peasants, and was also associated with modernisation, democracy and the end of communist rule. In spite of its alleged immorality, Viorel himself, his son-in-law and his son, along with most villagers I talked to, had tried to establish different kinds of small-scale business that had failed (see Konstantinov and Thuen, 1998).

Florica was occupied with one basic task: producing, conserving and preparing food for her family on a daily basis and for the winter. To be fed by the family farm expresses unity, and every Romanian, even in towns, will insist that food (water, wine, spirits) from their own family land is the best in the world. Making jam, pickling vegetables, drying herbs and keeping a full pantry, which had almost stopped under Ceauașescu, had once more become necessary both in the village and in town, and was talked about in terms of honour (*cinste*). A study of the heavily polluted industrial town of Copșa Mica discusses how the home-grown products from people's small gardens played a crucial role in people coping with their industrially polluted environment. The cluster of values related to family/home/belonging was thought to seep into the home-grown food and render it morally superior and thus resistant to pollution (Berge, 2000).

But ideas and ideals of individual initiative associated with democracy and modernity were also part of village discourse, most clearly expressed by young people. Viorel and Florica's daughter and son adhered to the ideal of self-sufficiency expressed by their elders, while they themselves were great spenders. The old couple's thrift enabled the young to spend their own earnings on consumer goods and ceremonial gifts. Brand new TV sets, video players and cameras, modern clothes and house equipment are objects of desire that express one's break with the village tradition of moderation and one's adherence to democracy, modernity and consumerism, which are seen as interchangeable values. This discrepancy between the old and young generations was a source of conflict as the old saw the outcome of their hard work and meagre savings spent on luxury goods they themselves rejected as immoral. Viorel, like other elderly villagers, expressed worry about the young generation and believed that 'the Ceauşescu time' had spoiled them completely: 'That was when they learned to receive without giving anything back: everything was supplied by the state'.

As a moral evaluation and a pragmatic assessment of the present turbulent times, villagers often said: 'Now we have democracy and everybody can do as he likes'. In the village cosmology ţigani were, by definition, associated with business, barter, theft and begging, not with work. As expressed in a much-cited proverb: 'ţigani always stay in the shadow and still they eat' (they get something for nothing).[1] The ţigani were also seen to violate the ethos of self-sufficiency as they violated the ethos of moderation in all its senses by their conspicuous consumption. Romanians denied by opacity their own dependence on ţigani services, thus strengthening their own ideals of contentment and self-sufficiency. However, what is seen as thrift by villagers is seen as greediness and stinginess by the Roma, to whom extravagance and spending are expressions of sociability: 'We are Roma. We don't save like the gaže, we always eat (consume) everything at once'.

Moderation and the Morality of Money

Carefulness and moderation permeate the life of the elderly couple. Viorel and Florica may have been extreme in this respect. Everything produced outside the home was regarded as potentially dangerous, contaminated and immoral. This went generally for all foodstuffs, but was considered valid for artefacts as well. Viorel boasted that he did not really have to buy anything; he could make everything he needed himself – and that was exactly what he did. One bright spring morning Florica wanted to paint the front gate, as all villagers do in spring, and told Viorel she would buy a paintbrush. Viorel refused and told her that was unnecessary and that he would make one himself. So he grabbed a pair of scissors, walked into the courtyard of a neighbour asked if he could cut off a piece of the horse's tail. Then he attached it to a stick, trimmed it and gave it to Florica.

According to village ethics, money gets its moral significance from the way it is earned. Honest work produces honest money.[2] Money is not in itself seen as evil – on the contrary it is highly valued and most families had bank savings in case of hard times. Money is seen as magic[3] and should be used with great care and only when there are no other options. But moderation and self-sufficiency are only respected when they are balanced with hospitality. Romanians in the village see hospitality as a trait of their national character that they contrast to that of Hungarians and Germans (Berge, 2000; Verdery, 1983). The village was often presented by town people as the incarnation of Romanian virtues, among them hospitality. Hospitality was most explicitly expressed by the way one received and treated guests. The ideal of sharing one's bed and table with guests points to what the Romanians themselves see as the inherent 'warmth', 'liveliness' and 'spontaneity' of Romanians (virtues that the Roma ascribe to themselves in contrast to peasants).

The Gender Order: An Industrious Woman and a Respected Man

Every morning Florica greeted me with these words: 'Good morning madam, have you got up? You are hardworking! (*Bună dimineaţă Doamnă, V-aţi trăsit ? Harnică sînteţi!*)' As I generally got up about three hours later than she did, I never knew how to interpret this greeting. A woman is foremost expected to be hardworking (*harnică*). She may be pretty, she may be intelligent, but it is her degree of industriousness that makes her a respectable woman. So the industrious woman who provides for her family by producing the family's food and sacrifices her individual desires and health for that of her children and husband is the proper Romanian village woman.

Villagers see the social roles of men and women as grounded in nature and thus good and unchangeable: men are strong and wise, natural leaders, while women are weak and helpless, natural dependants.[4] Both Viorel and Florica agreed that he was the family head; being male he was the wisest of the two, he was stronger than Florica and should always be respected. Florica constantly told me that women are weaker than men, especially physically, because they bear and give birth to children, and she always made sure that I kept warm and dry and was not tired: 'because women so easily get ill'. Gender inequality is very explicitly expressed in Orthodox ideology and practice in general. Women do not attend church services when they menstruate, and should be purified six weeks after giving birth in a special ritual, so that they may to be allowed into church again. Women stand at the back of the church while men are seated at the front. Married women cover their hair as an expression of humiliation and respect towards God, but also towards males and covillagers in general.[5] Florica only very rarely removed her headscarf and when she did, she hurredly put it on when villagers approached: 'If I don't they will say: look at Florica without her headscarf, she feels grand now!'.

The socialist government established equal possibilities for education and work for both sexes, but the ideology of gender inequality has been perpetuated and even strengthened in several ways (Baban and David, 1997; Kligman, 1994). Women were expected to take on the same work and education as men, but their role as mothers and housewives was not eased. As among the Roma, women were and are still generally blamed for problems and cruelty both locally and on a national level. It was thus a general statement that the problem about Ceauşescu was not really himself but his wife, Elena, who carried out all the mischief of his policy while he was responsible for the good achievements. Verdery claims that the political discourse in postsocialist states perpetuates this ideology by forefronting women's nurturing and emotional roles as 'their natural' roles, which were distorted under communism by opportunities for wage labour and education for women (Verdery, 1991: 80).

Village men are hardworking like their women, but a proper man was referred to as honest and honourable: cinstit and *om de treabă* (rather than harnic). Like Florica, Viorel said that men are stronger and have better heads than women and are therefore the natural leaders of households (see Pecican, 1997). The discourse of the male as provider and leader was, however, blurred by the practical interdependence of women and men in everyday life. Although Viorel and Nicu brought cash into the household and thus secured the family economically, this was only possible because Florica and to some extent, Aurora's produced the food for daily subsistence. Viorel saved most of his income for future uncertainties – he never spent a *leu* (Romanian penny) on himself or Florica – while Nicu used his money for what Florica saw as luxury. But in sharp contrast to gender relations among hamlet Roma, I never heard Florica or Aurora oppose their husbands' decisions or reproach their actions. The point is not that the women did not oppose their men, only that they confirmed the ideal male authority rather than negotiate or challenge it in public, as hamlet women do.

Suffering and Sacrifice

Enduring and suffering were expressed as an important aspect of women's industriousness and as a destiny and thus a plight. The female ideal of sacrifice and motherhood found in many catholic environments (Melhus, 1990) structured the rhetoric on children and mothering in this Romanian village in quite ambivalent ways, thus forming enduring ties. Having children was expressed as a burden and a responsibility and was often referred to in terms of moderation; one should only have as many children as one can feed and educate well. Mothers complained about the hardship of bearing and raising children and most women held that having more than two was impossible or at least irresponsible. Breastfeeding was avoided; young women said they had no milk because bearing the child had drained them. Under the Ceauşescu regime motherhood was presented as a national plight, and bearing many children for the nation was portrayed as a deed of heroism and thus sacrifice. Abortion was banned until after the fourth child, but it in spite of this it did not decrease much. After the revolution, abortion was again permitted and fertility is constantly decreasing (Baban and David, 1997). Village women often reproached ţiganci for irresponsible 'breeding' as they did not adhere to this idea of motherhood as a heavy plight. With their large families of dirty, uncontrollable children in rags they very vividly invert the village moral model: controlled fertility, hard work and self-sufficiency as the path to a good life. But some villagers reluctantly admitted that ţigan children seemed to be stronger and healthier than their own children, thus incorporating some ţigani women in a community of 'good mothers'.

Suffering is sometimes seen as a central ideal and value in Central Europe (Raduly, 1997) and hence also an aspect of masculinity. Ovidiu Pecican (1997) holds that sacrifice and the image of the martyr is one (of more) enduring models for maleness in Romania. Men often portray themselves as the personage of endless injustice, always the victims of circumstances outside themselves. Pecican supports his suggestion by referring to the leading themes in folk ballads and the historical and literary heroes of Romanian lore (Pecican, 1997). In the village this national rhetoric was especially cherished when men were drinking. In spite of the ideas of masculinity and control, alcoholism was very visible in the village and most families were somehow marked by their males' uncontrolled abuse of alcohol. Abuse of alcohol and heavy drinking were general accusations towards male ţigani, but villagers could not avoid seeing the communality of this problem. One of the few places peasants and ţigani socialised was in the village bars, and this could lead to friendship but certainly also to violence. Both hamlet and peasant women therefore saw alcohol as a threat to the unity of the family and to peaceful relationships between Roma and peasants; women's common predicament.

Villagers would often point to endurance and sacrifice as a trait of the Romanian historical experience that explained the Romanian's relation to ţigani and other groups. 'Look,' villagers would say, 'we Romanians are very tolerant. We carry the ţigani on our shoulders, but it is a heavy weight'. The image of endurance, tolerance and sacrifice was also expressed in terms of 'to bow one's head so that it should not be cut off' and 'to kiss the hand one cannot bite', characteristics the villagers gave themselves. The notion of endurance is strengthened by those of moderation and thrift, values that are confronted by what the villagers see as the irresponsible spending, drinking and generally unrestrained fulfilment of desire of ţigani.

Purity, Cleanliness and Modernity

Purity and Cleanliness

Florica had placed the Orthodox calendar in three different places in the house, as if always to be reminded of its demands. The calendar shows the great Orthodox feasts, the numerous holidays of saints and the periods of fasts. The Orthodox calendar imprints a yearly cyclical rhythm on peasant life, which resembles the rhythm of the day – the going and coming of people and animals between the village and the pastures and town. By means of the Orthodox calendar, religious morality is infused in everyday work and in the agricultural cycle that dominates peasant life. The priest's sermon is always about pragmatic problems of everyday life in the village that are interpreted by the daily text. Thus the sermon confirms the fusion of the profanity of everyday life with the sacred life of Christ. Hard work, the sanctity of motherhood, obedience and respect to elders, thrift and fasting to strengthen the willpower and resist the Devil – all these are religious aspects of everyday life. According to the village priest, the Orthodox Church does not concern itself with the exterior; it is the purity of the soul that matters. Purity of mind and body is important; women may not enter church when they menstruate, and fasting constitutes corporal modesty in general, i.e. sexual abstinence as well as bodily and mental purity – the avoidance of sin and evil.[6]

Ritual purity has its parallel in cleanliness. Washing clothes is a hard and important task in the village especially during winter when the temperature falls to more than ten degrees below zero and the river is ice cold. As few families have a washing machine; the river is the communal washing place. In spite of the hard work, children and women are always very clean and neat, and cleanliness (*a fi curat*) is talked about as a virtue, especially among the young. Florica assured us that the river has a special purifying property that makes it well suited not only for clothes but for all sorts of washing. Villagers throw all their rubbish into the river and talk about it as the village purifier (it cleans: *face curat*).

In many contexts purity and cleanliness are conflated. Thus the ţigani are not only seen as dirty, but in a sense they personify everything immoral and impure: 'They have no religion, they do not respect holidays, they do not go to church and they steal, swear and misbehave in general. They don't even marry, just have children with whoever they choose and they are dirty'. The idea of ritual purity by separation, so important to the Roma, is not known to the villagers. And although the Romnja wash their clothes in ponds of rainwater on the plain, physical cleanliness is not considered very important. While physical cleanliness appeared to be a moral trait and a sign of modernity for young women in the village, the old seemed to stick to religious piety and purity for their moral habitus and were much less preoccupied with physical cleanliness.

Bine Aranjat: *Appearance and Control*

The expression *bine aranjat* which may be translated as 'well groomed/arranged', was often expressed in appreciation of a woman. Romanian women said that Hungarian women were particularly *bine aranjate*, and some village women also merited this evaluation. A well groomed person looks ordered, disciplined and pleasant – face nicely made-up, clothes not disturbing moral norms and hair nicely set are seen as expressions of respect and social grace towards fellow villagers. Thus this may be interpreted as the social aspect of cleanliness and purity, respecting the moral ideals through clothes and comportment.

The village ideal of cleanliness as body discipline, order and pleasantness was explicitly inverted by ţiganci. In their dirty, colourful, torn clothes, long and often uncombed hair, open shirts showing their breasts etc., they not only opposed village standards but they even seemed to demonstrate their opposition by their comportment, thus not respecting fellow villagers. I suggest this is seen as an expression of the 'wildness' and lack of civilization alleged to ţiganci. By always being well groomed in public, by avoiding colourful clothes and by not 'having milk' to feed their babies, the villagers signified the difference between the wild and the civilized.

Hierarchy, Power and Civilizaţie

The Political Economy of the Village

The formal political leadership in the village was constituted by the locally elected mayor and the county council, served by the municipal administration. Both Hungarian and Romanian villagers were represented in the political leadership. All administrative positions (non-political) in the village, from the chief of police and the medical doctor to the headmaster (secondary school) and deputy headmaster all the way down to the pharmacist, constituted informal positions of influence in the power hierarchy of the village. The resources channelled to the mayor's office through the formal political channels were meagre and not sufficient to take care of the general welfare of villagers. As private and public economy was bad, there was a general competition for all economic resources. Those in high positions, holding public office, were generally able to monopolise public resources for their own ends and tried to gain control over other available resources by means of their official positions. As resources from relief organisations were not formally channelled through the political system, competition for these resources involved a wide range of villagers. This competition for resources permeated all relations in the village. Doctors increasingly expected gifts and even cash for their services; teachers were offered money by parents either to take in children who had not passed their exams or to give their children better marks. Many company employees also sold company materials for their own benefit. Romanians say humorously that it is not the wages that count when you decide on a particular job but how much you can steal at work.

Cunoştinţă: *Social Relations as Political Resource*

To obtain commodities and services controlled by certain groups or individuals ordinary villagers needed networks of acquaintances (*cunoscuţi*). Such networks have been important for a long time in Romania, but villagers told vivid stories of how they were a matter of life and death during the last hard decade of the Ceauşescu regime. The patron/client relationship of godparents and godchildren, often a relationship of great emotional value, could also give access to material resources and social prestige. Most villagers tried in similar ways to create networks of prestigious and influential and/or wealthy people and some succeeded. My husband and myself were regarded as influential people whom villagers were eager to include in their personal or family networks. We were invited visit to all sorts of people in the village and to several weddings by villagers we did not know, and often asked to be godparents. This interest was, of course, not purely economically motivated, as friendship and hospitality were just as important in most instances, but at some point we were generally expected to exercise our alleged influence, money or resources in exchange.

Village Etiquette

The mayor, the doctor, the secondary school teachers and the chief of police, and even the young pharmacist all hold privileged positions that make them part of the village elite. When entering a shop, these people were usually served immediately, even when there was a queue of customers. The peasants are at the bottom of this hierarchy and the peasants are mainly Romanians (ţigani are outside it). This ranking was expressed in a hierarchy of courteous greetings. *Sărut mână*, (lit. I kiss your hand) was the customary greeting for men towards women (and often also practised physically), and for children towards adults in general. Florica greeted everyone *cu pregătire* (lit. with education) in this way, a general practice throughout the village. The three forms of address: *dumneavoastră* (outside the family), *dumneata* (between spouses and towards parents) and *tu* (between children, friends) likewise expressed the hierarchy of gender, age and social position. This village hierarchy constitutes a sharp contrast to the equality- ridden Roma whom, although they generally conform to parts of this etiquette towards villagers, are regarded as disgustingly impolite by them.

Ethnicity, Civilizaţie and Biological Determinism

The village is divided into three quarters – Romanian, Hungarian and Rom (the hamlet). The boundary between the Romanian village and the Rom hamlet is interesting because there seems to be a transitory zone between people who are regarded as real villagers and families with more ambiguous relations to other villagers. The two first houses were inhabited by families of mixed Rom–Romanian ancestry. Some of these families lived like peasants, spoke only Romanian, and in all ways tried to hide their ţigani origin. One Rom couple, however, who presented themselves as Roma gažikane (lit. non-Gypsy Gypsies) looked like Romanians, earned their living by selling bags and scarves at the village markets and spoke Romanian and Romanes as suited them best. They showed no shame in speaking Romanes in public and always chatted with hamlet Roma when they met them in the village.

The idea of civilizaţie as a certain refinement in social manners and in appearance (*a fi bine aranjat*) and a certain degree of modernity is important to villagers as a distinction for evaluating ethnic categories. The village discourse of civilizaţie is hegemonic but multivocal; it is interpreted with some variation by villagers of all social classes and ethnic categories. Aurora was quite clear in her classification: Hungarians are more civilized than Romanians; they are cleaner, keep a better house, cook better food and are more conscious of their looks and generally more trustworthy. Germany and Scandinavia are referred to as the most civilized countries with the most civilized people. Ţigani are at the bottom of this ethnic hierarchy as they are uncivilized, dirty and generally immoral. Although Hungarians in the village were generally poor, they still seemed to hold much of the symbolic capital from their imperial epoch, expressed in their relatively high position in the ladder of civilizaţie. Thus civilizaţie has a double meaning: it is not only about order, social and bodily control, level of education and modernity, but it also contains ideas of foreignness.[7] But 'civilizaţie' also implies self-constraint, stinginess, a cold heart, and lack of hospitality and spontaneity, all vices that are regarded as non-Romanian. Romanians are considered much better peasants than Hungarians; and warmer, more hospitable and more emotional than Germans. The general idea that Hungarians, Romanians and ţigani are different sorts of people is strong. In daily discourse these differences were expressed in proverbs like: *'fiecare după dorul său,* (everyone must follow his heart)', and *'ăsta e soiul* (such is the breed)'. Difference was expressed as an external order of things. The idea of a naţie as common blood and of strong bonds between a naţie and soil (place of origin, as though ancestors have grown out of the soil like beans) is prevalent. Thus interethnic relations are talked of in terms of biological determinism (Haukanes, 1996). Viorel and Florica could not imagine such a being as a Romanian ţigani: either you are Romanian or you are a ţigan. She classified the Roma gaẑikane, who lived like Romanians and looked like Romanians, as ţigani because their parents had been ţigani. Even the children of the mixed Rom-Romanian couples in the village were regarded as ţigani. Only when all remembrance of any ţigan ancestry has vanished is a person conceived of as Romanian.[8] As this is possible only by moving away from one's village of origin, usually into town, villagers do not see the transformation and as they do not like it, they do not want to imagine it. The village cosmology of civilizaţie differs in significant ways from the cosmology of the hamlet Roma, who express ambiguity and duality in their ethnic cosmology. The Roma accept the possibility of transition and of being both gaẑo and Rom; Roma gaẑikane.

Distrust, Strangers and Familism

Trust is a Scarce Resource

Trust is a scarce resource in this situation, and the lack of trust challenges all relations in the village and evokes anger and fear. Several analyses of postsocialist societies point to the lack of trust in social relations as the outcome of centuries of a repressive and controlling state (Buchowski, 1996; Spülbeck, 1996). The last forty years of communist governance seem to have cemented this lack of trust by setting up a system of social control, such as *Securitate,*the secret police in Romania, that turned neighbours and even family members against each other as informants. Buchowski points to what he terms 'amoral familism' as one trait of this social lack of trust (Buchowski, 1996). A fundamental distrust of 'the other' as a threat to oneself and one's family was a general structuring feature of village relations. This was expressed and handled by the discourse of civilisaţie, and by a network of exchange relations where trust was tried out and confirmed or rejected. These networks did not, however, make people feel safe in general. When the boundaries between private and public, bad and good people were crossed in unexpected ways, it stirred anxiety and fear and revealed relations of domination and power that were masked by the institutionalised patterns of interaction. Ţigani are the notorious strangers in Romania, but they are not the only ones. Villagers saw every ethnic category other than themselves as strangers, inherently different and distrustful.

The fear I observed in Viorel´s eyes and in his voice after a bargain with five hamlet 'brothers' in his courtyard told me something about this complexity. Joska's oldest uncle in the hamlet had died and his four sons went to ask Viorel, the village mechanic, to make a cross for the next day's funeral. Viorel told us how four grown men (all from the hamlet) had entered his courtyard and in their shouting manner had told him they needed a cross for the next day. Male ţigani were usually not let into the courtyard of Romanian houses and certainly not four at a time. Viorel had told them he had much work to do and would need more time. He complained that he had felt quite abused and irritated and that 'they hadn't even brought the iron that was needed to make a cross, and just expected me to take care of everything'. The ţigani had got very upset and insisted they needed the cross the next day. Viorel explained that he had felt forced to do as they wanted, as he was all alone in the court. The next day they came back for the cross, even before the paint had had time to dry. When Viorel asked for money the oldest son said they had none, they would pay the next week. This made Viorel even angrier because he had put aside other urgent tasks to finish the cross. He insisted that he wanted the money. The ţigani started a row until one of them managed to calm down his brothers and they reluctantly paid.

When Viorel told us about this event he was very upset and talked angrily about the episode for the rest of the day. I should emphasise that these Roma were all young and had lived in the hamlet all their life. Viorel must have seen them since they were small boys, but it was obvious that their demeanour had frightened and humiliated him at the same time. The fact that they were ţigani overruled the fact that this was a cross for their father's funeral, a man of Viorel's age, whom he must have known. I would say that Viorel had not only been frightened, but he had felt powerless, and that such fear and experience of powerlessness is one of a variety of feelings that dominate all sides of social relations between villagers and ţigani. This episode illustrates the lack of trust between people who have lived together for the best part of their lives, but it also illustrates the lack of respect and submission the Roma may show towards villagers, and their apparent self-confidence in spite of their social position in the village.

Familism: 'Don't You Have a Home of Your Own?'

The boundaries between private and public space in the village are quite rigid. All houses are surrounded by high walls and all courtyards by tall iron gates that are always kept shut or even locked day and night. This gives the village a rather hostile air like a place under curfew. Once inside a courtyard however the warmth and friendliness of the peasants are overwhelming. In the warm season, when villagers sit outside their houses chatting in the warm dusk, this friendliness seeps out into the streets and changes the face of the village. Still, when the children ran out into the street to play Florica said: 'Stay at home, what are you doing out there?' And when a child came crying back home she scolded her: 'What are you doing out in the streets, I told you it's dangerous, don't you have a home of your own?' The street is strictly public and hence unsafe and dangerous, it is where strangers (*străini*), drunk țigani and villagers, fast cars, horse wagons and other dangers may occur. Only the house and courtyard are private, safe and friendly.

One afternoon, a woman living in the same street was heard swearing and jabbering in the street outside their house. She was obviously angry with someone and let the whole street know. Viorel cried out an answer over the locked gate and Florica and Aurora at once begged him to stop. 'The street is free' they said, 'Everybody may do or say what they wish without interference. One may only interfere in one's own courtyard or in one's own home. Leave her alone and let her jabber, if she is silly you don't have to be silly as well, just ignore her, that's the way she is.' And Florica added: '*Fiecare în cuibul său (everyone should look after their own business)*' (lit.: everyone his own nest). Viorel did not agree, stating that one had the right to speak up and that she should be stopped, but he did not continue. The notion of the street as open, unregulated space thus prevailed.

Villagers and Strangers

Next-door neighbours did walk in and out of each others' courtyards during the daytime, but more distant ones always knocked at the front gate before entering. The gate was generally closed and often locked and guarded by an angry dog, because, as Florica told us in a hushed voic 'the village is full of strangers'. The notion of 'străini', has a special meaning in Romanian history and folklore and even marrying someone from another village was regarded as wrong in many places.[9] There is a strong sentiment about the notion of 'nație' in Romanian history that is moulded on ideas about the family and the village in opposition to the threatening stranger (Verdery, 1996). The fear of strangers, the enmity and competition for resources and the code of hospitality make it important to 'handle inaccessibility'; to avoid people without stirring enmity (Haugen, 1978). Villagers often explained the lack of trust by the problem of țigani 'who steal everything' and by democracy 'that makes everybody follow their own fancy'. But when Viorel cursed his neighbour for not returning the tools he borrowed and when he warned us to be careful and never go out after dark and never ever to pay for something that was not received, the lack of trust was about more than țigani.

Amoral Familism?

The notion of familism or family-centrism implies that the nuclear and extended family act as a unit with strong emotional ties among members, that focus material interests and limit members' social contacts and interests outside the family (Buchowski, 1996: 85). The notion of 'amoral familism' refers to a type of social organisation based on family ideology where the family forms an economic, emotional and political unit as a protection against 'society' and where there is little solidarity or loyalty to people or groups outside this range. Amoral familism is thus based on ethical dualism, which implies rigid separation of loyalty inside the kin circle from that exercised towards outsiders. This again may imply double standards between private and state property (Buchowski, 1996). In the village the combination of familism, the value of self-sufficiency together with the dichotomy between the private and public spheres, the family and the society, express and create dualistic ideas about 'us' and 'other', and may be seen as expressions of amoral familism.

Trust and Reciprocity: Exchange in the Village

Trust: Reciprocity and Strangers

In spite of the expressed distrust, villagers form systems and cycles of exchange that involve not only Romanians, but also Hungarians and even țigani. These systems and cycles may well be seen as an expression of a public sphere, of 'civil society' that limits the effect of amoral familism (Hann 1996: 14). The phrase *cycle of exchange* refers to movements of services and objects between specific agents while *systems* denotes relatively stable exchange of certain goods and/or services (Lan, 1989: 208).

To be willing to exchange is a mark of trust; of showing trust and of being trustworthy. This is especially expressive in systems of delayed exchange that artisans like Viorel often carried out with their customers. The other party must, however, be known as a relatively decent person (om or om cinstit) or as relatively predictable to be regarded as a suitable partner for delayed exchange. Țigani, like strangers in general, are often requested to pay immediately and in cash as they were not trusted to pay later or to reciprocate in other ways. When the hamlet brothers demanded a cross for their father's grave and wanted to pay later, Viorel refused. By refusing to establish a barter relation of delayed exchange with them he expressed his distrust and rejection of them as proper villagers. The rest of this chapter will present the cycle of exchange between villagers containing several systems of exchange.

Sharing in the Family

Self-sufficiency and sharing resources are perhaps the most salient expression of familism as opposed to the hazard and unpredictability of the new 'market society'. Agricultural work among peasants was in most instances performed by household or family members who also were the consumers of these products. The ideas that home-grown food is superior to any other and that people should only eat what they produce themselves are also an expression of mistrust towards everything foreign to the family, the region and to Romania. Although the consumption of luxury food and items was desired by the young generation, the value attached to the production and sharing of food in the family was not overruled by ideas of modernity, but rather combined with these ideas and, to a certain extent, the one made the other possible.

Reciprocal Exchange between Villagers

Agricultural work is labour-intensive. Most peasants have no machinery, very few have horses and, as most peasants are elderly and often women, there is always need for an extra hand.[10] When extra hands were needed in the fields, neighbours 'helped one another out' on a reciprocal basis. Florica always exchanged work with a neighbour living down the street when her daughter or husband had other things to do. But this is only one example of the systems of exchange that were practised in the village. Most services rendered were not paid in cash, but returned either by another service or by foodstuffs. Viorel gave an example of how the system worked: he once repaired the water heater of a man in another village. This man was a furrier. When Viorel had finished his work he did not ask for money as he knew very well that he needed a new fur hat for winter and that Florica wanted a new one as well. This arrangement involved the two men in a relationship of delayed exchange, where a service received prompted a favour in return.

Cinste: Tournaments of Honour

Villagers were also engaged in different systems of what I will term 'gift exchange'. Such gifts were basically exchanged between villagers of the same ethnic group and religion, occasionally between Romanians and

Hungarians, but not between villagers and Roma. Ţigani, however, received alms, a special system of gift exchange in the ţigan/villager cycle that will be discussed in the next section. Cinste, the ritual gift, expresses, like the Rom pačiv, the mutual obligations binding related villagers together and expressing the relative social standing of the hosts.[11] Weddings were elaborate rituals in the village that activated exchange systems, as did baptisms and funerals. These systems of gift exchange involved villagers related by kinship, generally by the same religious faith and hence by ethnicity. The wedding meals were prepared a week in advance by relatives bringing the obligatory gift: cinste baskets, their contents meticulously written down by the hostess.[12]

Florica was invited to the wedding of her son's goddaughter but did not want to go. She did, however, prepare her household's contribution: a live chicken, twelve eggs, a pound of flour, a pound of sugar, a pound of lard etc. This was all packed into the cinste basket and the basket was covered with the embroidered cloth. She walked to the house where the wedding was being prepared and helped the other women with the preparations. The house was in a village about thirty minutes' walk away. All the women bringing gifts were assembled in the courtyard and more women arrived all the time with their baskets covered with embroidered cloths. The groom's mother wrote down the name of every woman that brought cinste and the contents of each basket. All families keep such books, but the system rests on a moral obligation of honour; the honour of giving, of receiving and of returning the gift. The number of cinste women turning up at one's child's wedding and the amount of food received would determine the splendour of the wedding party. After elaborate official and religious rituals that may last for three days, the wedding party is celebrated, even that often lasting for several days. The wedding culminates in a public announcement of the wedding gifts to the bride and groom. Every gift, predominantly cash, is formally announced by the master of ceremonies and written down in a book of debts, like the cinste contribution.

At this particular wedding between two families of modest economic means from the village, with two hundred invited guests, the wedding gifts alone represented about four annual salaries, or about US$1,500. A good monthly salary was around US$30 in 1996. The book-keeping assures that the gifts are repaid: the food (cinste) for the same at another occasion and the wedding gift for another wedding gift or in other ways. Florica's daughter and son-in-law, Aurora and Nicu, both Pentecostals, described with contempt what they saw as the competitive aspect of wedding gifts as: 'To make oneself king for a day (*Să se făcă rege pentru o zi*)'. In their view this competition forced or at least pressed everybody to give more money that they could afford. This view was confirmed when we soon came to understand that the amount of money (and sometimes things) given at weddings was known all over the village the next day and eagerly disputed, the giver's prestige and honour being matched to his gift and the outcome of this comparison evaluated. This supports the interpretation of cinste gifts and marriages as 'tournaments of honour', parallel to the Rom paciv.

Although ţigani were never invited to village weddings, the hostess or some of the 'cinste women' often told their special ţiganca about the wedding and allowed them to pick up the remains the next morning. In this way different cycles of exchange involving different social groups were interlinked. It was the ţiganci who made sure that the amount of the wedding gifts and the splendour or misery of the wedding were known all through the village and even beyond in a very short time.

Exchange and Reproduction of Hierarchy – Religious Gifts, Ciubuc and Mita˘

Most services in the village are exchanged in a reciprocal manner. However, the Orthodox priest (and I presume the other priests as well) was generally paid in cash for his particular religious services, such as prayers for deceased or even for living family members, read aloud in church; blessings for the house and the livestock; funeral sermons; baptisms; weddings; and even special rituals of purification performed in peoples private homes. But the priest also received gifts such as money and services from villagers.[13] Although health treatment was free, doctors expected to get small gifts or amounts of money from their patients. The villagers referred to these special payments as *ciubuc* or *mită* and they all seemed to have a fixed price. The problem, since the revolution, seemed to be that the ciubuc, which used to be a small sum of money or a small voluntary gift, today may amount to a huge and semi-fixed sum. Another problem was that many people knew that the ciubuc of the socialist era is considered as a bribe in democratic societies, and some officials even felt offended and rejected it. The practice was not only confusing to me, it also causes confusion to villagers and to Romanians in general.

Market Exchange

Market day was the weekly event in the village and most villagers and Roma were there in the course of the morning. The roads leading to the village were crowded with carts pulled by slow black or golden oxen or by quick horses and cars packed with peasants from all over the district who had come to the village market to sell and to buy. The weekly market offered local vegetables, food and dairy products, clothes, electrical items, furniture etc. and livestock. Only a few villagers sold their products at the market and they were mostly Hungarian, such as the village potters, one of the shop owners, and some older women selling sunflower seeds. The market was the only public sphere where all ethnic and social categories of the village mixed and exchanged freely.

But most of the exchange between villagers and ţigani went on inside courtyards and kitchens, hidden from the public eye. Reciprocity governs these relations that simultaneously are economic and social; negotiating and creating both difference and community. Rom and peasant cosmology are in many aspects divergent and even oppositional. I suggest, however, that the common value ascribed to the family, the shared experience of womanhood and women's roles as providers and mothers, together with the desire and necessity for economic exchange, create moral and practical grounds for common evaluation and for the flow of exchange between villagers and Roma. This exchange will be the theme of the next chapter.

Notes

1. This expresses the idea that ţigani do not toil the land in the burning sun like the peasants to produce their daily bread, but still they eat as well as peasants. It is a very accurate expression of how the peasants see ţigani in general: as cheats.

2. See Verdery about *bani nemunciţi* – (unearned money) as bad and wrong. ibid:184.

3. See Verdery's discussion about people's reactions and conceptualisation of Caritas in postsocialist Romania (1996: 169).

4. See also Feischmidt, Magyari-Vinze and Zentai, 1997; Klingman, 1994; Verdery, 1996, on gender ideology in postcommunist states.

5. In reality young married women have generally abandoned the headscarf for daily use.

6. The Orthodox Church does not accept celibacy, marriage and procreation are seen to fulfill the will of God. Nor does the Orthodox Church accept purgatory. In the Orthodox faith only heaven and hell exist. Neither does the Orthodox Church accept the Pope in Rome as a mediator between man and God. Man is seen as free under the protection of God (the village priest).

7. See Elias (2000) about the relation between *zivilization* and *kultur* in German tradition.

8. I do not claim this to be a trait of the Romanian way of thinking; the same ideas govern the Norwegian relationship between immigrants and Norwegians.

9. See the Romanian ethnologist S. F. Marian (1995).

10. There were many elderly widows in the hamlet, those that had husbands often farmed the family land as men often had other occupations.

11. *Cinste* is also the name of the gift presented in the locally made basket with food, covered by a traditional embroidered cloth (*şterg*) that women bring for the preparation of life-cycle rituals.

12. For a description and analysis of Transylavanian Orthodox weddings see Kligman, (1988).

13. Several of the elderly women worked on the priest's fields without being paid.

Chapter 9

Exchange and Power

Introduction

Every morning after the exodus of villagers to work and of livestock to the pastures, hamlet women appear in the village streets accompanied by children and sometimes by their husbands. They stop outside a gate, knock or softly cry out the name of the woman in charge of the household and are swiftly let into the courtyard, while the men wait outside. After a while they are let out again and proceed to their next visit. When they return to the hamlet in the early afternoon their bags are generally full of bread, potatoes and other foodstuffs.

In a society based on ideally self-sufficient subsistence farming and ethnic endogamy, governed by a weak state, exchange is what creates community and makes it visible (Strathern, 1992b). The scarcity of money, the notion of self-sufficiency and the relative absence of supra-village solidarity create a situation where barter and gift-exchange keep the village together as a moral community. Exchange should be seen to constitute a system of interests that involves villagers of all social and ethnic categories in relatively stable interpersonal relations between the organisation of family and state (Buchowski, 1996; Hann, 1996; White, 1996). Groups or persons that do not enter into exchange or refuse to reciprocate threaten the community and are thus deemed immoral. Romanians accuse Hungarians of being stingy and țigani of stealing, while Hungarians say that Romanians cheat and țigani steal. Roma for their part, accuse all gaže of being stingy and not sharing their wealth with them. All accusations are about their role in the system of exchange, where all groups accuse each other of not reciprocating in a proper manner. Thus the morality of reciprocity is steadily confirmed.

The village, then, is perhaps best understood as comprising different but interrelated communities bounded by ethnicity, class and religious affiliation. Villagers themselves are aware of this and often complain about the lack of 'unity' among them. I hold this to be a statement about the expectation of some sort of solidarity among villagers that does not function 'as it should'. Systems and cycles of exchange simultaneously compensate for the lack of central political authority and in some respects they challenge state control. Different cycles of exchange are governed by different cultural models that constitute and express different social relationships, different cosmologies and different power relations. The most interesting of these is the exchange between villagers and Roma because it constitutes the only field where the alleged difference between the groups must be overcome by creating some kind of common grounds. But what kind of relations and what kind of community are constituted and expressed by exchange?

The focus of this chapter is to discuss everyday relations of exchange that involve seemingly unequal and even incompatible social categories such as Roma and villagers guided by different cosmologies. The inequality between Roma and peasants on structural and organisational levels, is challenged, transformed and even partially inverted in interpersonal barter relationships. The organisational domination of villagers is expressed by their social position as Romanian and Hungarian; majority populations representing the political hegemony of the Romanian state. As such they control the material resources necessary for Rom subsistence and relate to the Roma as a stigmatised minority of dependants. The structural domination is expressed by the position of Roma as beggars in village cosmology and by the ethnic discourse of civilisaţie. I argue that by monopolising certain resources that the peasants desire and by exploiting their own position as 'stigmatised others' the Roma transform the peasants, ideally their patrons, into their clients in face-to-face relations.

This process is not to be analysed as one of domination and resistance (Scott, 1990), but as an ongoing process of negotiation of dependency and autonomy between two modes of existence and systems of power; the Roma as the 'nomadic mode' and the Romanians as the 'state mode' (Deleuze and Guattari, 1985). I have argued that Roma are totally dependent on villagers for their subsistence, while villagers are basically dependent on the land, on their co-villagers and on the state. Even if the villagers deny any dependence on tigani services or objects the systems of exchange challenge this notion as ideology. The economic and political inequality between Roma and villagers is not changed, however, by barter: this asymmetry is crucial for the working of the systems of exchange between the parties. The challenge of the Rom mode of subsistence is to overcome or blur this inequality and to present themselves as indispensable, necessary, desirable or at least tolerable to the peasants through the 'objects' they can offer. Barter relations are based on experience of mutual and equal desire for each other's objects, thus creating 'symbolic equality' (Humphrey and Hugh-Jones, 1992). By equal desire for each other's objects parties have, at least there and then, equal meaning for each other. As things and objects are articulations of cosmologies, the different cosmologies of Roma and villagers are represented and to some extent also exchanged in barter (Humphrey and Hugh-Jones, 1992: 8). As we shall see both Roma and villagers try to avoid this by keeping the relationship 'economic': Roma do this as a strategy to avoid the social and cultural dominance of village cosmology that is difficult to ward off in friendship; villagers to preserve themselves as independent and civilized by not fraternising with țigani. This introduction suggests treating all forms of exchange as instrumental and that it is principally the lapse of time between a 'gift' and a counter-gift that gives gifts an air of generosity and lack of calculation (Bourdieu, 1986; Bourdieu, 1990). Even though the power implications of the systems of exchange are only partially foreseen by individuals, I will argue that the mutual desire of each group to maintain the dependency of the other is a central focus of the exchange.

The previous chapters discussed cycles of exchange between hamlet Roma and between villagers; this chapter is about systems of exchange in the cycle between Roma and villagers. I will start this discussion by taking a closer look at the everyday exchanges that I myself experienced and sometimes took part in. My use of the different forms of the terms Rom and țigani in different contexts may be a bit confusing here, but I maintain that it is useful in highlighting the different perspectives that inform exchange.

Systems of Exchange between Roma and Villagers

The Pure Gift: Door Opener to Peasant Houses

About three times a week we heard a soft knock on the front gate of our village house and there was Varga often with her youngest daughter. They sat down very humbly in the kitchen and asked about our how we where and so forth. We chatted for a while and usually served Varga a cup of coffee, but she showed no sign of leaving. If we did not offer her anything by ourselves, she generally asked for some money that she needed for some special occasion, usually to buy medicine for her husband or some of her children, or just to buy bread. When she received what she asked for, she left, if not she stayed, often until we gave in and gave her what she wanted. She was on her daily rounds begging and bartering like the women that introduced this chapter. After a while we learnt to make use of these visits. Because she came alone and wanted something from us, we could ask her for things we wanted that only she could offer. So we asked her about events and relations in the hamlet and in the village that we could not ask people about directly. Some of this information was important for our understanding of the hamlet, the village, and relations between Roma and villagers.

Most hamlet women beg and barter in the village, and even though they seldom admit it; most villagers know most hamlet women and many are more or less always involved in some system of barter with some of them. The hamlet women primarily visit households where they have good relations and this makes it difficult for the peasants to refuse to give alms. Villagers characterise begging and stealing as the main occupation of ţigani. Alms go from villagers, and gaže in general, to ţigani and never the other way around.[1] Villagers see alms as 'pure gifts' that are not reciprocated, but are essential to belief systems based on notions of salvation (Parry, 1986). From an analytical perspective, this idea relates the poor and the more affluent into one moral community where the wealthy have the duty to give and the poor the obligation to receive on behalf of God, thereby easing the way to heaven for both. The ideology of the religious alms implies the rejection of social interdependence; it is by not being reciprocated that alms may lead to salvation. Thus any expected return must be secret or evaluated as something else (Parry 1986: 467–68). Even when alms are motivated by empathy and sentiments of intersubjectivity, they none the less rest on the idea of unilateral dependency; of giving, not exchanging. Exchanges between Roma and villagers are, however, so diverse and interlinked that it seems difficult for villagers to maintain the idea of alms as 'a pure gift' or even as a gift at all, although they do try.

Begging and Asymmetry: Alms for the Wretched ţigani

One aspect of the village ethnic discourse is expressed in terms of the peasants as the nurturers of the hamlet ţigani (and ţigani in general) as: 'The burden we Romanians must bear'. The alms given to ţigani are always food; home-grown and prepared at home, the product at the heart of peasant community that expresses the labour and devotion of the peasant in turning raw nature into a product of culture. Of course, food is the only surplus of the peasants' economy, and they underline that by giving alms of food to ţigani they ensure that the children will be fed. In the ethnic discourse of the village, begging may be seen as a basic idiom expressing the structural and organisational domination of ţigani by peasants and Romanians in general. Begging defines the relationship as one of unilateral dependency and defines ţigani as beggars with all its negative connotations. This emphasis on ţigani as dependants is, I suggest, crucial to the village ethnic relationship because it serves as a moral legitimisation of all other relations between villagers and Roma for both groups. The fact that the Roma continue to beg and the villagers continue to give alms in spite of the increasing poverty of peasants and the increasing relative 'wealth' of Roma, indicates that both parties wish to express their relationship in terms of unilateral dependency; that of ţigani on villagers. Thus the Roma confirm the peasant stereotype of them as childish spenders who can not plan ahead and always need the villagers to support them. We shall see that the Roma's apparent consent to the peasants' stereotypes of them as dependent and inferior is exploited for successful barter.

Begging is Asking for a Due Share

This consent to peasant stereotypes is, however, best understood as a necessary cultural strategy for the Roma mode of subsistence. Although the gažo is not part of the Rom sharing community, Thulo explained begging like this to us: 'Of course they (*gaže*) should share with us; we are poor and landless while they are rich'. This was a reasoning we often heard when the Roma felt they had to legitimise their economic activities. The reference to begging as sharing offers a different perspective of the village hierarchy by positioning villagers and Roma as inherently 'brothers'. By rhetorically turning it into a relation of sharing, they invoke the Rom ideology of altruism that implies that when they have something to share they will – even with gaže. Everybody knows that they will not, but that is also the case among brothers in general as some are not good sharers. This way of rhetorically including the gaže in a common sharing community can be seen as a parallel to the peasants' idea of the religious alms that evoke a religious community where Roma and villagers are all God's children.

But begging is foremost surrounded by a certain ambiguity that is expressed in many ways. The phrase Roma often used about begging: '*I lie to the gaže (te xoxavav le gažen)*', implyes that the gaže are double-crossed by the sly ţigan. This is exactly the negative reciprocity of which the villagers accuse the ţigani. The expression 'to lie to gaže' contradicts the idea of sharing and very explicitly places Roma and gaže as 'strangers' to each other. To lie to gaže, to tell stories about poverty, drunk men, hungry children and so forth to persuade the gaže to give, turns the Romni into the agent of the relation and the gaži into her victim. It also negates the Rom material dependency on gaže: '*it's all just a lie*'. From this perspective begging adheres to the Rom ideal of getting something for nothing, the ideal economic relationship between Roma and gaže. These different perspectives on begging, however, do not include seeing begging as reciprocal exchange. On the contrary, by seeing it as sharing or cheating, the Roma counteract the village emphasis on exchange as reciprocity. In this way the hamlet Roma also blur the material dependency that marks their mode of subsistence and relationship to peasants.

Begging in town implies a different relationship as giver and receiver are strangers to each other. Here some sort of empathy or religious piety may be the donor's primary motive, and the ideology of 'the pure gift' is more easily confirmed. The gratefulness of the receiver and the 'good conscience' of the giver is the only condition of the gift. If neither of those objectives is achieved, one does not give alms to strangers without being forced and then it is not regarded as alms but as theft. The difference between the ţigani cursing the stingy villager, and the town beggar cursing the stranger that refuses him, is that the latter does not form a relationship of any consequence.

Alms, Gossip and Slander

Begging, and the begging relationship as the basic legitimate relationship between Roma and villagers, disguises peasants' dependency on Roma and thus the power Roma may exercise in exchange relationships. It is as beggars that Romnja are let into the houses and kitchens of the peasants – to beg, but also to chat, barter and perform magic. By presenting the relationship as one of begging, secrets and (from a peasant point of view) uncivilised and improper objects and services may also be exchanged. As peasants are restricted in their movements and hence generally have little information about events outside the village, the ţigani are important messengers and may control, hold back and invent information. Information is exchanged for favours and for food and is thus a resource that Roma to a certain degree control, this control giving them a certain negotiating power in begging as well as in barter.

A week after our arrival in the village we were invited to a Romanian wedding. When the wedding gifts were collected and publicly announced, our gift was mistakenly presented as US$500 instead of 50, but then quickly corrected. At ten o'clock the next morning (the wedding had finished at six o'clock in the morning) we met a hamlet Romni in the street who approvingly told us she knew we had given US$500 as a wedding gift. We corrected this information, but the village gossip did not accept this correction, resulting in a later financial expectancy.

This information gave villagers an estimation of our wealth and expectations of our influence and value as acquaintances. As strangers we were considered a material resource and became a source of information and gossip. Mixtures of information, exaggerations, gossip and pure inventions make ţigani interesting although distrustful messengers. This is, however, exactly what empowers them towards the villagers. Because of their reputation as liars, information and gossip are more easily passed on to them than to villagers, and should the gossip be proven to be a lie, it is the messenger, the ignorant ţiganca, who is blamed rather than her source.

Begging or Barter?

Villagers avoid hiring hands for agricultural work and even selling home-grown products. What is not consumed by the family is kept for barter, for gift exchange and for alms. Barter of food mainly goes on between villagers and țigani just as alms are mainly given to țigani. Food is sometimes bartered in exchange for items that the țigani produce such as brooms, buckets etc., mud bricks, whips, baskets and other handmade objects. Wild food from the forest and plains gathered by the țigani is exchanged with the villagers for produce or even cooked food. A bucket of mushrooms equals a bucket of potatoes, a sack of wild apples might be exchanged for a piece of meat or some flour. I observed hamlet children of the ages of three or four carrying buckets of potato peel (for the pigs) that they exchanged with villagers for sunflower seeds on their own initiative. The Roma only manufactured objects for barter when there was no other way of obtaining food, and they were not proud of it. The peasants did not readily talk of these exchanges, probably because they challenged the idea of the begging and stealing țigan and revealed that villagers actually want something the țigan has to offer. It also revealed that the țigani actually 'work' in the peasant sense of the word. When they did talk about it, it was always in a derogatory way, they emphasised the bad quality of their products and that they bought them out of pity, and sometimes they did. So both parties seemed to regard this petty barter as somewhat degrading. Both complained that they gave more than they received. When they exchanged anyway, I suggest they did so in order to cultivate the relationship or because they had no better choice.

The relationship between begging and barter was however revealed to me by chance. One day I was out gathering wild strawberries with hamlet children; we stopped to rest and they started to play. They were playing 'țigani and gaže'. The smallest boy enacted a village woman, a shopkeeper, and the oldest girls enacted grown Romnja. As the 'Romnja' entered 'the shop', the boy (village woman) was instructed to call out to her son: 'Hey, come here. There are some țiganci coming into the shop'. Then the 'țiganci' asked for milk for their children and said they had no money to pay for it. The 'village woman' very reluctantly gave them some milk and was instructed (by the girls) to complain: 'Oh you țigani, when you need something you know where to find me, but where were you when I needed help with my potatoes? You promised to come, remember?' The 'țiganci' then excused themselves saying their children had been ill etc.

This scene was played over and over again with slightly different ingredients, but the sense was always the same: the village woman requested something back, mostly work in exchange for her generosity. This is interesting because what seemed at first sight to be evaluated as alms; 'pure gifts', could from a different perspective be evaluated as one instance of a general relation of exchange between villagers and Roma, where at least the villager hoped for a more or less balanced repayment of the gift.

Secret, Dirty and Illegal Barter

Eventually I learned more about the intertwined and ambiguous nature of barter. An example was the peasants' traditional stoves, used for baking celebrational bread and cakes. These turned out to be accessible also to Romnja with good exchange relations. Kurva and several other hamlet women baked bread and cakes for Christmas, Easter and other celebrations. 'I have a woman in the village', she explained, 'I do her favours in exchange'. But it turned out that food also was bartered for fortune-telling, magic and/or services that were secret, shameful or illegal and never talked openly about either by villagers or by Roma. At one of her begging visits at our house Varga told us that she was buying lice medicine for some villagers too ashamed to reveal their embarrassment in the village pharmacy. This service was usually exchanged for food and probably perpetuates the village assertion that only ţigani have lice. It also made me reflect about other possible secrets or 'dirty' services Roma performed for villagers. Then in a secret conversation the last month of our stay Kurva told me that two of the alcoholics in the village used to summon her when their families had hidden their money to prevent them from drinking. They were so desperate that they offered cutlery and other family valuables very cheaply. Kurva bought them and sold them for a higher price to other gaže. But there was more.

All elderly hamlet women performed fortune-telling and magic, even though few talked about it openly. Palmistry was the most usual magic, but some also performed exorcism. Roma do not believe in this kind of magic and fortune-telling so clients were always gaže. One Hungarian woman told me how a ţiganca had entered the bakery where she worked and asked for bread and offered to tell the woman's fortune in exchange. The woman agreed to the bargain and she was told about her husband's forthcoming death and burial. She assured us that the ţiganca was very clever and that we should try her. The ţiganca happened to be Saroie, the Romni sorcerer who had previously revealed to us some of the secrets of her trade:

> Many gaže want me to come to their house to take away the evil that brings sickness and misfortune to their family. I go and I try to find out what is the matter. They tell me about their problems and misfortunes and I tell them to recite a verse (unintelligible) with me. Then I find a string from my pocket and I ask them how many problems they have and how hard they want them to go

away. I ask them how many notes they will give to get rid of their problems. Then I tie as many knobs on the thread as they have problems and recite another verse that they say after me. When I have got the money I sing over the thread and recite over it in my hand. When I open my hand, all the knots are gone and so are the problems. But this is an easy case. Sometimes I come to women with much money hidden in the house and with many problems. After a while they ask me if I believe the money is the cause of their problems, I tell them I believe the devil is in the money and that I have to take away the money to make the devil go away.[2]

These séances were secret and looked at with contempt by villagers who saw themselves as modern and civilized. I do not think men usually participated; they were intimate gatherings of women. These Romnja told me that they could cure impotency, frigidity and barrenness and even make women attractive to men. So family secrets obtained by fortune-telling and exorcism performed by elderly Romnja entered into the chain of exchange and increased the mutual trust and/or interdependency of Roma/peasant relations. When Varga secretly bought lice medicine for peasant women, and when Kurva secretly bought silver cutlery from a village alcoholic, I suggest that not only the service rendered but the trust invested in the secrecy was returned by food and even by money. This trust had to be met by the Roma, but also by villagers. I suppose women who had been exposed to magic powers by a ţiganca would hesitate to turn her down when she asked for some bread or lard in another context. As many villagers believe magical power is inherent in ţigani, this resource was more or less available to all Roma, and was exploited for barter.

Violence and Theft

Most of the barter between Roma and villagers was between women. But towards the end of my fieldwork more and more of the exchanges between hamlet men and villagers were revealed. At the end of our stay we had lent our camera to a young boy in the next village, which he did not give back. Our friends in the village suggested he had sold it or lost it and did not have the nerve to tell us. One day we were discussing this with Viorel, who suggested we should take a band of ţigani to the boy's house and beat him up or at least threaten to beat him up. This was a suggestion made in earnest. The hamlet Roma had just the same suggestion about how to solve the problem, when we told them. I suggest villagers and Roma do make arrangements like that in certain circumstances when the police may be of no help. We did not follow their advice and learnt of no specific instances where this actually happened, but their existence was impossible to ascertain, as they would have been kept a secret anyway.

The house equipment that some men fabricated was usually bartered by their wives, but hamlet men did occasionally have special goods to offer. One day, when I entered Florica's kitchen, Missolino was there with Aurora, discussing something he had laid out on the table. He quickly left when I arrived and I asked Aurora what he had been doing. She answered smilingly that he had some jewellery that he wanted to sell and she added: 'He used to have much more and nicer gold, but nowadays it is very poor'. Aurora's ten-years-old daughter added: 'Baro (one of the elderly patriarchs in the hamlet) has much more gold than Missolino'.

Many small instances like that indicated that the hamlet men, like the women, have their own merchandise, stolen or not, which cannot be sold in market exchange because of their dubious origin. They were sold or bartered for what the villagers were willing to give in exchange. Villagers used to say about țigani that 'their heart is not warm unless they steal (*nu au inimă caldă dakă nu fura)*'. A medical doctor and his educated friend with whom we discussed țigani insisted that all wealthy țigani had made their fortune by theft. So in many contexts the nomination 'țigani' means thief or criminal and has only a vague affiliation to the actual ethnic category (few villagers would, however, consider the țigani as an ethnic group). Most villagers could tell some story about some țigan stealing this or that in their garden, courtyard, field etc. The stories concerned mostly chicken, goose, corn, vegetables and so forth, agricultural products, but sometimes also clothes hung out to dry. But one evening Florica referred to some incident when somebody had pinched something and said with a naughty smile: 'You don't sleep well if you don't steal anything, isn't that so? (*nu doarme bine dacă nu a furat ceva, nu e aşa?)*'. So villagers not only bought goods they knew were stolen, they expressed quite openly that certain forms of theft were acceptable and even good. This appeared to be a general opinion; it was not theft in itself that was regarded as a crime by villagers or Roma, but the harm it caused to social relations. Villagers saw theft of private property in the neighbourhood or village as a serious breach of the ideal of reciprocity and trust, endangering social relations. On the other hand, theft of state property was not regarded as criminal by the average villager because this was regarded as people's property, stolen by the state. Criminal theft, then, was classified as what țigani take from Romanian villagers. The thefts țigani carried out in town and offered villagers in barter were accepted as 'everybody knows that țigani steal'; it was theft from 'strangers' and did not threaten community life. So villagers had țigani steal on their behalf.

Roma made another distinction. Theft is not a concept within a community of sharing brothers and sisters, and among Roma ideally theft is nonexistent. Theft from gaže was legitimate and they did not differentiate between private and state property; it is all gaže property. To Roma, gaže property is what state property is to Romanians – something that they are entitled to (a share of). Stealing gaže property does not violate Rom values or endanger relations between Roma.

The Relief Gift: Trade Barter and Begging

The most important system of exchange between Roma and villagers was however the trade and barter of clothes, received as a relief gift, which were exchanged with villagers for food, money and services. This was a 'new' resource that was reliable and plenty: two full containers of second-hand and new modern clothes collected in a West European country. Before the gift reached the Roma, the mayor, the police and other influential families receive their due. This distribution was generally carried out after dark and in secret, as Roma as well as villagers were envious and critical about it. When the trucks reached the hamlet, the clothes were divided between all the households, and when every family member had picked his or her share for personal use, most of the rest was sold and bartered right away in the street leading from the hamlet to the village church.[3] The villagers on their side were offered very cheap, modern, Western clothes. The mayor and others of the village elite were said (by the Roma) to sneak into the hamlet the same night that the clothes arrived to pick their first choice before the clothes were sold in the village. As long as there were clothes left in the hamlet one could meet villagers, mostly after dark, knocking on doors in the hamlet looking for clothes. The rest of the year almost no villager or gažo in general sat foot in the hamlet. In recent years, gaže have even came all the way from town in cars to buy or barter clothes with the ţigani.

The women were in charge of the trade/barter; they decided the price and what should be sold while the men often stood in the background. In the haggling over prices, the Roma were stubborn. They knew very well that they had prestigious objects to offer. Only the poorest families sold out at once: most women tried to keep back clothes, both for sale when the choice was smaller, and for barter the rest of the year. Money was the main medium of exchange in this street trade, but there were no fixed prices and every peace was haggled over. 'Exchange by private treaty' (Firth in Appadurai, 1986: 19), where the relationship between the parties is important for settling the price, was a prominent feature of this exchange. I asked the hamlet women why they did not take the clothes to town where they would get a better price. They responded that it was very uncertain and that they were afraid that the clothes would be stolen on the train and in town by other Roma, and they added: 'It is better to sell them here, the gaže are very happy to buy the clothes', thus expressing interdependence and reciprocity towards fellow villagers. This exchange was, however, linked to the general system of barter in the village and begun long before the clothes arrived. Many villagers already had some rights to these clothes in delayed exchange for services rendered and for objects and alms already given. The clothes that were not sold at once were bartered or sold during winter. Potatoes, lard and other foodstuffs are the main items of exchange together with money. But the Roma would also ask for food or services from villagers in exchange for a first choice of next year's cargo or for certain types of clothes, cheaper clothes etc. Clothes were never traded or bartered with other Roma from other hamlets, only with gaže.

Villagers expressed mixed feelings about the situation. Most people questioned the sanity of the organisation that gives clothes to țigani and not to 'good Romanians'. Others found it just that the poor țigani were helped that way, but they often added that Romanians were poor as well. I had several discussions about this subject and one woman summed up what I take to be a general opinion:

> Of course we Romanians deserve the clothes just as much as the țigani and they should perhaps have been given to us instead. But how should she (the leader of the organisation) manage to divide them between us? We would fight even worse than the țigani. The organisation is wise to give them to the țigani and when they sell them cheap to us we all get our share of the gift.

There was, however, some comfort in what villagers expressed as a 'civilizing' effect of these gifts. Aurora told me that the hamlet țigani had become more civilized since receiving clothes from the West. Just as these clothes are used by young villagers as distinctions, signalising modernity towards the older generation, they may also signalise the transformation of țigani into 'decent people'. The clothes may thus be interpreted as incarnated signs – objects that have the ability to transform personality (Appadurai, 1986: 39). In another context Aurora complained that on the other hand the țigani had become even more lazy now that they no longer were obliged to work, and that they drank up most of the money they earned from selling the clothes. This probably indicated that villagers had difficulties getting țigani to work for them, once they did not need the money. Thus the 'civilizing' effect from Western clothes only seems to transform the țigan in a very superficial way, and under the surface he remains himself and ambiguous in the eyes of villagers.

Intertwining Systems of Exchange

Cultivating the Peasants

I have suggested that begging opens up the peasants' doors and makes them available for the Roma. Analogous to the way peasants cultivate the land and their gardens for subsistence, I suggest that the Roma cultivate begging/barter relationships with peasants for different sorts of exchange. Begging, barter and trade or mixtures of these exchange systems are what create mutual dependency and trust. Apart from the valuables like stolen goods and the relief gift, most of the goods bartered are not in high demand and peasants would not exchange them, even for food, if they had a better choice. But the way different systems of exchange are intertwined makes the control of one resource an instrument of power in exchange for another. Because Roma have good, cheap clothes to offer and because they have the power to curse and cast spells, they are not rejected when they offer their generally poorly homemade articles such as buckets, whips and baskets. The villagers generally say they buy them out of pity (*de milă*), thus confirming the ideal dependency. My point is that the alleged dependency of Roma on peasants is contextually inverted by the relief gift. The Romnja told me that they do not barter clothes with peasants who refuse them food when they beg, thus expressing their power to dominate the begging relationship. When peasants give the țigani bread, vegetables and meat for goods they do not really want, one motive is to keep the relationship warm so as to barter for clothes when they arrive. The petty barter is thus a way of building trust, but it also creates a debt to peasants that the Roma have to repay when the clothes arrive, the repayment securing further barter when winter comes and food is scarce.

Transformations of Power and Domination

The way exchange systems are intertwined transforms the dependent relationship of Roma on villagers to one of relative domination of peasants by the Roma. The gift of clothes is the key to this transformation by allowing for a kind of specialisation that changes old relations. To the villagers, the clothes are a means in the ongoing process of personal civilization and modernisation. The notion of 'civilizaţie' is, as previously discussed, expressed in terms of a 'nice' and well groomed appearance and a polite and graceful demeanour. The Western clothes represent the village perception of Western Europe – regarded as the centre of civilization. By their alleged good quality, bright colours and modern style they seem to signify the good and happy life of capitalist society as presented on American television channels in all peasant houses. The Western clothes thus also serve as signifiers of the difference between tradition, socialism and the difficult past on the one hand, and modernity, market capitalism and a better future on the other. The control of these clothes enables the Roma to obtain food throughout the year from the pantries of their peasant networks, most of it in direct barter but, as already described, some of it as investments in the following year's gift.

This precious and legitimate resource thus transforms ţigani into valuable acquaintances who must be treated well.

Because of their position in the relief organisation, some Roma may also strengthen their social position vis-a-vis power holders in the village. By promising the village mayor the first choice in his family's part of the clothes, Joska bulibaša may ask for favours in exchange. He may, for instance, ask the mayor to grant the hamlet Roma social benefit money for Christmas and thereby strengthen his support in the hamlet. The influence Joska bulibaša exerts on the leader of the relief organisation also sets him in a key position in the competition for assignments to projects initiated by the organisation. Joska can recommend people in his own or his familia's barter network in the village and reject villagers he sees as competitors. This power, although confined to Joska and Kurva, expands to a certain extent to all Roma; by treating ţigani badly, certain villagers may be excluded from this competition. I do not claim that all villagers participate in this competition, but many do and those who had lost were eager to relate their misfortune. Our Romanian host had tried to get a contract to install water pipes and pumps in the Rom hamlet but had been outmanoeuvred by a relative with close relations both to Joska and to the leader of the organisation. His story was confirmed by our own observations and by other villagers. Although these transformations of power do not transform power relations in the organisation of the village community, they certainly challenge features of the structural power relations.

Trust and Unpredictability

The outcome of these exchanges may be a confirmation and thus a perpetuation of trust, but may also be distrust. Trust thus created is, however, vulnerable and always paired with unpredictability. The predictability consists of a combination of trust and distrust that creates a condition of uncertainty that may promise gain or failure. For villagers to barter with ţigani, or with any stranger for that matter, may turn out to one's advantage or disadvantage; one never knows. The possibility of some extra, advantageous exchange reinforces the relations of barter with ţigani. One should always keep the relationship warm in case of some future, prosperous barter. Ţigani, unpredictable as they are (this is their predictability) may stumble over some really valuable objects; their immorality and unpredictability allow them access to resources unknown or unavailable to peasants (such as the relief gift or stolen goods) and one should always be prepared for that instance. During the socialist period, ţigani were said to have monopolised the black market just as they were said to be the main dealers in petrol across the Donau which fuelled the war in Bosnia. Reality or fiction, what remains of these stories is the fact that villagers portrayed them as shrewd traders. I suggest, then, that the relationship created or expressed by barter works through dependency, ambiguity and uncertainty, rather than by trust in a traditional sense.

Magic: Creating Intimate Relationships

Magic power is an aspect of all exchanges between Roma and villagers, and it is perhaps here that the power of the Rom over villagers in face-to-face interaction is strongest, but also most secret and hidden. The example of a session of exorcism of evil spirits (Saroie) illustrates how secrets not shared with neighbours or kin (money hidden around the house) are told to the Rom sorcerer. Through their practice these women come to know many of the secrets in the village; about infidel wives, impotent men, frigid or sterile women, family conflicts and so forth (Kurva and Saroie's accounts). This, together with gossip that is passed on to Roma, is a resource that may be exploited in competition for material resources and to exercise power in barter relations. This capital of secret knowledge is, according to villagers, the essence of being ţigan, as inherent in the ţigan person. As the saying goes: 'A child kissed by a ţigan cannot catch the evil eye (*un copil sărut d'un ţigan nu va fi deochiat*)'. It is, however, also invested in ţigani by villagers.

If we see the gossip and secrets of peasant societies as investments that build up the symbolic power of the ţigan, how are we to understand this exchange? What may the villagers gain from their investments or, put more plainly, why do villagers choose to confide in ţigani, who are perceived as unreliable and dangerous? Concepts like investment and capital are not helpful in understanding the more subtle aspects of interpersonal relations, such as ambivalence, sympathy and the need for consolation. The woman who had her fortune read by Saroie and had seen her husband's forthcoming death did not really believe in such prophecies, but time had 'proved' that Saroie was right. I suggest that the general political uncertainties, the recent social and economic changes that in many ways challenge traditional village values, pose an everyday problem for villagers of how to act in the world, how to plan ahead and how to solve their human relations, that the hamlet women propose to deal with. The Orthodox priest, spiritual 'parent' of all villagers, can only meet this demand to a certain degree. He is male, highly educated and has a social position that is superior to that of the villagers. Hamlet women, in spite of their difference, share the villagers' lives of worries and uncertainties, and they understand the villagers' needs and preoccupations. This relationship, then, is perhaps the most intimate and 'social' of the exchanges between villagers and Roma, and although interpreted in purely economic terms by Roma, I suspect a certain degree of sympathy and even intersubjectivity to develop on both sides.

Although different in kind, the magic and other secret services performed by țigani also reveal the uncivilized side of the peasants, according to their own standards, such as their pagan beliefs, their 'moral deficiencies' and their involvement in criminal activity. Outside or at the margins of social order in the village, the țigan is both willing and capable of performing acts that no peasant may perform without risking his reputation or security. This dependency on illegal services from țigan renders the peasants vulnerable and, like gossip and sorcery, invests much symbolic power in the țigani. The threat and exercise of physical violence may be reported to the police; one may protect oneself in many ways and one may fight back. Belief in magic renders peasants far more vulnerable, as their best remedy against evil spirits is țigan magic, while the Roma only fear curses from other Roma.

The Fear of the Dispossessed: The 'Sliminess' of țigani

It is not only the fear of their magic power that interferes with willagers exchange relationships with Roma, but also the attraction that this alleged magic has to villagers. This attraction is never explicitly expressed by peasants or Romanians in general, but must be interpreted by the observer based on mosaics of discourses, stories and proverbs, practices and images among villagers as well as among Roma. The story that circulated after the revolution that Ceaușescu had been a țigan is only one expression of the ambivalent feelings expressed in the village. This image points of course to the stereotype of the bad and criminal țigan, but I believe it to be more complex. Ceaușescu was very much admired in the countryside as the man who modernised Romania and brought the ordinary peasant a good life. The idea that Romania's dictator may have been a țigan expresses a general sentiment about the ingenuity, uncontrollability and unpredictability of the țigan; the fantastic being who may transform himself into anything. This co-existence of black and white magic, the dangerous and the wonderful, is a well known theme in anthropology concerning marginal ethnic groups viewed by the dominant groups as primitive and close to nature. The idea of the țigan having some sort of ability that allows him to transgress boundaries between social and ethnic groups, between life and death and between humans and the devil, infuses him with the unpredictability and uncontrollability of the nonsocial being (see van de Port, 1998: 163).

I suggest that this unpredictability is the psychological bond that works on the imagination of villagers and both frightens and attracts them: the sentiment that there are no limits, that for the țigan everything seems possible. Zygmunt Baumann discusses the ambiguity of the 'strangers' by referring to Mary Douglas's discussion of purity and danger and Jean Paul Sartre's analysis of 'the slimy':

Only at the very moment when I believe that I possess it, behold by a curious reversal, it possesses me … . If an object which I hold in my hands is solid, I can let go when I please; its inertia symbolizes for me my total power … Yet here is the slimy reversing the terms; (my self) is suddenly *compromised*, I open my hands, I want to let go of the slimy and it sticks to me, it draws me, it sucks at me … I am no longer the master … The slime is like a liquid seen in a nightmare, where all its properties are animated by a sort of life and turn back against me … If I dive into the water, if I plunge into it, if I let myself sink in it, I experience no discomfort, for I do not have any fear whatsoever that I may dissolve in it; I remain a solid in its liquidity. If I sink in the slimy, I feel that I am going to be lost in it … To touch the slimy is to risk being dissolved in sliminess (Sartre in Bauman, 1997: 26).

Bauman sums up his argument by asserting that sliminess stands for the loss of freedom and that freedom is a power relation. The unpredictability of țigani paired with their ability to transform not only themselves but the relationships they enter into, is precisely the 'sliminess' that makes the villagers feel powerless and that frightens them. I am pushing the point somewhat here; I do not believe these fantasies are at the forefront in everyday relations, but they may be activated in situations of conflict and crisis. The magic power especially of women is an important aspect of their well known transformative ability, although not all villagers believe in it. The fear of being cursed is rational, because the Roma are great cursers. Violence between Roma and villagers only seldom occurs and there were no stories among the peasants about Roma ever attacking them. The fear of physical violence, also prominent among villagers, is, however, a result of the idea of the uncontrollable, nonsocial, 'slimy' traits of the țigan.This fear of the dispossessed (oppressed minorities) is also expressed in the Romanian belief and practice of the evil eye (*deochi*). The evil eye is generally active in unequal relationships and attacks the thing or person that represents inequality. The Romanians do not talk of the evil eye as an act of jealousy or envy, they say that the person that casts the evil eye is not aware of it and cannot help it. A beautiful child, a pretty horse or a nice new television set may all be targets of the evil eye. The precaution is never to look too directly or too long at anything that one wants or admires and that belongs to others, or to hide precious objects from the evil spirits that operate through people's eyes.

Although the hamlet Roma exploit the power that these beliefs give them in the competition for resources, they must always balance this power against the necessity of cultivating relationships for exchange. To curse a household is a dangerous matter that not only cuts off a relationship but may also endanger general relations between Roma and villagers. I suppose that serious curses are only used in cases of emergency and that the implicit threat works as power to cohere. Magical power, then, does not oppose, but confirms the ideal hierarchical relationship between peasants and Roma.

Challenging Village Cosmology

'Now We Have Democracy and Everybody May Do as he Chooses'

Although the magical capacity alleged to all Roma is an important resource for their bargaining power with gaže, it is the barter and trade of clothes that most of all challenges the power relations of village cosmology. The fact that it is the uncivilised, traditional ţigan, signifying the bad past, who furnishes peasants with the means to look civilized and modern renders both the clothes and the exchange itself ambiguous and creates disorder in the village cosmology. As properties of objects are seen to seep into their owner (Appadurai, 1986), many peasants pointed out to us that ţigani had become more civilized after having received the clothes. They were not only dressed in a more civilized manner, they also behaved in a more civilized way. Not only do the Western clothes transform Romanian peasants into modern, Western-European consumers, they even seem to bring civilization to ţigani. I suggest that this rhetoric of the civilizing effect also serves to legitimate the villagers' dependence on ţigani in this exchange. But this legitimisation is ambivalent, and the Roma's general rejection of village moral values and their 'immoral' way of life does not disappear. From another perspective, by selling most of the clothes, the ţiganci express a rejection of the value of modernisation and civilization, and thus confirm their uncivilized state. My assertion is that by desiring the ţigani's valuables in the public space of the village, villagers lend some legitimacy to the ţigani that challenges the ethnic hierarchy and allows the ţigan to be seen as a villager rather than as a stranger. The boundaries between ţigani and villagers is thus blurred and the position of ţigani below that of Romanians on the 'civilization ladder' may also be questioned. If the ţigan no longer is a poor beggar, then what is a Romanian in relation to a Hungarian? It is as uncivilised beggars and thieves that ţigani are inscribed in the cosmological order, and the clothes disturb this cosmology by portraying the ţigan as something else; as almost 'civilized'? The ambiguity of ţigani, bad and desirable, is thus exposed in public. It is not the first time the hamlet Roma have had valuables to offer, but it may be the first time they have valuables that are stable, legitimate and that may be bartered in public. Some of the implications for local power structure have been discussed. The mayor has much to gain in maintaining his good relationship with the bulibaša. As head of the formal power structure in the village, he and his employees may demand their fair share of the relief gift anyway, but as the organisation is directed towards helping Roma he is obliged to co-operate with the bulibaşa to get access to more than his due share. This may also mean that he must cultivate his relationship to influential hamlet Roma in general. The hamlet Roma have, by their monopoly of

Western clothes, become a power to count on in the village. From a Roma point of view the relief gift is the ideal object for exchange. It is obtained free, it is an object of desire to villagers and there is no fixed price, which leaves much room for a clever trader. In contrast to the petty barter of food for pans or buckets, for wild fruits, where the ţiganca humbly waits at the villager's gate to be let in, the barter of clothes makes the villagers come to the ţiganca's house or to her stand in the street where she sets the price as she knows that the demand is great. To see peasants fight over the merchandise of hamlet women was a provocation to many villagers, who either kept away from this event or said scornfully: 'Look at them (the ţiganci) now. Now they are the queens!'

The new resource has also made some Roma quite wealthy, although this is carefully hidden from the public eye. Some of this wealth is invested in prestigious objects like carpets, television sets, women's traditional skirts and new houses, some is invested in state bonds bought from peasants, and some is kept in the bank and used for weddings and funerals. All these investments have, however, one end: to strengthen a household's prestige and honour in the view of other Roma and to be better equipped for the competition for resources. To position oneself better in this competition may be achieved by marriage or other types of alliance, and in both instances wealth is prestigious because it may be shared. The hamlet Roma are famous for this luck that has fallen upon them, and Roma from all over the district want to have a share of their wealth. Many Roma accuse them of stinginess and shame because they fail to share their luck with their brothers. To obtain some type of alliance with them is however one way of entering into the group of 'sharing brothers'.

Thus this gift has implications for local political relations as it serves to challenge power structures, not by changing them but by bringing disorder into deeply embedded classification schemes and thus also to village identity and villagers' social position in postsocialist Romania. To the villagers it is a disturbing feature of the new democratic, liberal political economy. Everything is turned upside down as expressed in the very common comment: 'Now we have democracy and everybody may do as he chooses'. Even the despised but tolerated ţigan comes out of the shadows and demands to be called Rom. To the Roma it only confirms what they always knew; the Roma are cleverer, have more luck and are morally superior to the gaže.

Exchange, Domination and Resistance?

Nomadic Rejection

This chapter began by discussing how relations of power and domination between Roma and villagers are challenged and partially inverted through barter. It was then argued that the challenge to power structures expressed by the exchange of valuables and magic is not to be interpreted as 'resistance' in a counter hegemonic sense (Scott, 1990; Willis, 1977) but as an expression of competing cosmologies and a different hegemonic discourse that does not have as its object to destroy the village hegemony but to negotiate its relation to it. Seeing hegemony as fragmented questions the notions of domination and resistance as an analytical pair (Scott, 1990). Foucault's well known phrase: 'where there is power, there is resistance' implies, in my understanding, one overarching exercise of power and a secondary force opposing it (Foucault, 1976: 95). I have suggested that this idea cements the understanding of power relations in terms of a primary and a secondary force, and will argue that it is necessary to ask on what grounds this hierarchy of power is established.

In discussing gender relationships among hamlet Roma I have argued that male dominance is accepted by all Roma as a general principle, whereas its interpretations in actual social practices are not. What is seen as legitimate domination in different contexts is subject to negotiation and conflict between men and women. Male authority is thus not absolute but dependent on context. This claim is based on my interpretation of hegemony and power relations inspired by Ewing (1997) and by ideas expressed in the notion of nomadology (Deleuze and Guattari, 1985). From this perspective, different hegemonies representing different social groups are seen to intersect and provide motivation for different sentiments and social practices.

I see the Rom life and cosmology as a different mode of existence, in Deleuze and Guattari's sense, from the villagers' mode, although their modes are mutually interdependent. I consider the hamlet Roma to adhere to the idea of 'nomads' by their nonrelationship to property, their flexible, nonterritorialised organisation, their opposition to central authority and their refusal of state hegemony. The notion of nomadology was briefly discussed in the introduction. Deleuze and Guattari's idea about the relationships between different systems of power is metaphorically represented as the relation between the state and nomadic society. While the state is characterised by law, fixation and power centres, nomadic existence is characterised by fluidity, fate and the destruction of leadership. The state form and nomadic form, say Deleuze and Guattari, are interdependent in terms of coexistence and competition and in 'a perpetual field of interaction' (Deleuze and Guattari, 1985: 17). Based on these ideas I interpret the relationship between the Rom and the non-Rom societies as different cosmologies and communities with distinct but yet interdependent traits. My argument, then, is that the Rom mode of existence is not incorporated by the state. Hegemonic discourses in the village influence hegemonic discourses in the hamlet, but they are mutually constituted as oppositions to each other either in terms of dichotomies or as dualities. By rejecting the state institutions for control and domination of its subjects, the Rom mode of existence is relatively autonomous of state power and may be seen to constitute an alternative power system that is not to be understood as resistance.

Although the Roma accept the political domination of gaže in principle, they do not regard it as legitimate for their own social practices in general. This does not imply independence or any notion of 'freedom from power' but the possibility of alternative power projects, world views and organisational forms. The perspective of hegemony as fragmented allows us to suggest that the Rom world is represented in the village world and vice versa without any of them representing an overarching hegemonic discourse. My argument is that the Roma as nomads are precisely not incorporated into the hegemonic discourse of the state. By seeing the relationship between the Roma and the villagers as one example of the relationship between 'state', as a unicentred, static system of power based on territorialisation, and 'the nomads', as a multicentred, deterritorialised and flexible system of power, the idea that power and resistance are inherently asymmetrical is questioned.

The Rom mode of existence should rather be analysed as the unforeseen outcome of people forming communities based on a specific mode of subsistence, organisation, power structure and cosmology. By their social practices and discourses the hamlet Roma oppose state domination, not by any conscious strategy or purposeful intent, but by perpetuating the way of life they know and appreciate. By rejecting schools and by avoiding wage labour, by differentiating themselves from peasants and by several other social practices, the Roma avoid the central state institutions for incorporation of its subjects, and experience a certain degree of cultural autonomy. The way that Rom socialisation strategies 'vaccinate' the Rom child against abuse from the gažo society and that the rejection of schooling prevents the gažo cosmology from replacing that of the Roma, have been discussed earlier. The structural domination of the majority – the gažo – although inhibiting the Roma from resource competition, does not dominate the Rom self-perception. It is not a psychological or symbolic dominance, and is thus interpreted by the Roma more as an environmental obstacle than as subordination. I do not at all suggest that the individual Rom does not feel and experience the hate, oppression and injustice to which she or he is subject, only that the Rom cosmology creates a contemporary world where the Rom is King.

The Rom mode of existence is dependent on the state mode and challenges it at the same time by representing its inversion. The hamlet Roma never openly challenge the organisational and structural power of the state. Ethnic struggle is not a strategy they apply. It is by practice, by their cosmology and by their mode of existence, implying a struggle for autonomy and dependence, that they challenge the power of the state and thus the cosmology and power structure of the village. This represents 'the lines of flight' (Deleuze and Guattari, 1985: 121) from state hegemony. The hamlet Roma themselves are both consciously aware of their perpetual struggle for cultural autonomy and peculiarly unconscious of it as a struggle. It is expressed as culturally encoded signs and is naturalised as a way God created the world (*gade mukle les o Del*), a world consisting of coexisting Roma and gaže: 'is there any difference, really?'. This duality of creating difference and unity is, as I have argued, central to the perpetuation of relatively peaceful relations between Roma and villagers and expresses what I see as the central themes of gypsiness: dependence and independence; separation and exchange. The day the Roma become Romanian in a sociological and cultural sense, will be the day when they have the same to offer for barter as any other villager and exchange can no longer be a means of livelihood.

There are some interesting contrasts in the Rom and village cosmology concerning difference and interdependence. The Roma acknowledge difference between groups as constitutive of them, but not as static. In their model of society and their experience, the individual may transgress boundaries and transform himself. Roma may become gažo, Čurara may become Kelderara and the dead may cross the boundaries of the living. These border crossings are dangerous and may be secured by observing rituals of separation, but they are fruitful and should be exploited. This renders differences between groups dynamic and even ambiguous or dual, and opens up possibilities of incorporating gažoness and still being Rom. As stated earlier, all Roma know somebody who has passed into gažo society; many have witnessed the transformation in their own families. Difference between groups is thus only relative and is not seen in terms of biology and hierarchy. In fact, the Roma oppose the hierarchy of the gažo cosmology by creating their society of equality and brotherhood, by seeing 'Romness' and 'gažoness' as a matter of grade rather than as a dichotomy and by challenging their position in the gažo cosmology. Romanes; the Rom way of life, may be seen as a cultural model that allows relative peaceful coexistence with gaže while rejecting the gažo cosmology and inverting the relations of power implicit therein.

Barter: Incorporation and Duality

Exchange between Roma and villagers, although somewhat antagonistic and limited, not only constitutes the two social groups as 'different', it also, to a certain extent, constitutes them as villagers; people who do trust each other to a certain degree by generally reciprocating. There is a discrepancy between the discourse on ethnicity and the social practice of exchange. From an analytical point of view a certain degree of mutual trust is inevitable to carry out delayed exchange, and mutual trust creates a bridge for transferring cosmology. Even if Roma try to hold on to their ideology of negative reciprocity in exchanges with gaže and try to ward off domination by treating exchanges as purely economic, ideas, values and practices of peasant cosmology are incorporated with the food and objects received and accommodated into Rom cosmology. And even though villagers insist that țigani are not trustworthy and should be avoided, and in spite of villagers interpreting most exchanges with țigani as alms, the prestigious clothes pass through țigani hands before being obtainable to villagers. Receiving an annual gift from 'The West' is the kind of magic expected to happen to țigani, just as magic acts are only performed by țigani (and priests). I suggest that 'gypsiness' perceived of as magic, as opposition to order, as unrestrained desire, as lack of moderation and as shrewdness; the ability to transgress social boundaries, is part of what is presented to villagers as something desirable to be appropriated by exchange. This interpretation points to the understanding of individual and collective subjects as 'heterogeneous', incorporating significant 'otherness' (Kristeva, 1982). Julia Kristeva (1982) has introduced the concept of 'abject' to discuss this kind of rejected, but incorporated 'otherness', and I suggest that the abjected 'otherness' of țigani is appropriated by exchange and constitutes aspects of the peasant selves. This incorporation is explicitly expressed when Romanians say that there is a țigan in every Romanian. In a similar, but not the same, way, the Rom person is constituted as heterogeneous. I claim that the gažo does not represent an abjected part of the Rom person, but that 'gažoness' and 'Romness' are experienced as different aspects of 'humanness'. To be Rom does not imply rejecting relationships to gaže, as being Romanian implies rejecting relationships to țigani.

Power relations between Roma and villagers have always been dynamic and the focus on the political, economic and social 'transitions' that are discussed as a trait of all postsocialist states (Verdery, 1996) may undervalue the very turbulent history of this region. The relations between the different ethnic groups of Romania may be said to have constituted the Romanian State in the past and in the present. The relationship of exchange and power between Roma and villagers at the village level is perhaps an apt representation of aspects of the new role of the Roma in the Romanian figuration. The last chapter of this book will, based on the historical relations between ethnic groups in Romania, discuss the continuity of past and present for the understanding of the relations between Roma and villagers as an aspect of the Romanian figuration.

Notes

1. Of course there were exceptions, but they were generally explained in terms of people being 'poor and worthy' etc.

2. Transcribed from a tape recorded by Lars Gjerde.

3. The first weeks after the clothes arrived one could see Romnja in checked, pleated skirts and pink cardigans, and men in fancy T-shirts often with slogans in Dutch all over their chest. I observed children who changed clothes several times a day, from beautiful dresses to training gear and then into bikinis without their parents objecting. As time went by, more and more clothes were sold, and the rest were worn out. One can see shreds of clothes and single shoes all over the hamlet. The hamlet paths are literally paved with shreds from the yearly delivery of relief clothes.

Chapter 10

The Țigan as Signifier

Introduction

I introduced this book by arguing for the understanding of Roma in terms of gypsiness; a mode of existence that implies their relationship to non-Gypsies and the mutual ideas that govern this relationship. I hold that the different social groups of Romania constitute a specific ethnic figuration that is crucial for the understanding of power relations and ethnic identity in the region and that țigani hold a significant position in the Romanian figuration and in the collective identity of Romanians as ambiguous and stigmatised 'others'. By following some aspects of the life and strategies of Joska, the hamlet bulibaşa, and his 'people', I have discussed how the interdependency and power situation of Roma and non-Roma is handled and changed under new socioeconomic conditions. This last chapter will take a broader view and discuss the changing position of Roma as signifiers in the Romanian figuration.

The țigan in the Romanian Habitus

Assimilation of Roma into the Romanian, but also the Hungarian and German populations, has been a continuous process from the earliest times of țigan/gažo coexistence in Romania (Achim, 2004: 40,41). This process of transformation is very obvious in the rural setting of Transylvania. In villages and towns in this area one may observe all grades of ethnic transformation from Rom to gažo, or seen from the other perspective: from țigan to *Român* (Romanian). Most hamlet Roma had relatives that had married gaže, or had become Roma gažikanes or even gaže, while we never met a single Romanian that told us that they had țigani in their family. At the same time a flow of rumours about Romanians who 'really are ţigani', but pretend to be român, was present in public discourse both on the national and the village level. Ceauşescu is only one example; we were told about many prominent people in academic and political positions that 'really are ţigan'. This information was generally given in a hushed voice and with a contemptuous, but often also mischievous smile. Such rumours had some basis in historical facts. According to Achim, one of the princes of Moldova, Ştefan Răzvan, was the son of a slave woman who managed to become a boyar and later to occupy the throne for a period in the sixteenth century (Achim, 2004: 41). This indicates, says Achim, that social mobility was possible even for ţigani (Achim, 2004) and I suggest that many families in Transylvania and probably all over Romania have secrets containing ţigan ancestry. I suppose that marrying ţigani has been evaluated quite differently according to class and ethnic membership, but that it has been experienced as a shame in most families and has been denied when it has been possible. I suggest the secret shame of 'ţigan blood' in many Romanians is an apt justification of the Romanian experience of ţigani as abjects (Kristeva, 1982).

Shame and Civilized Bodies

Norbert Elias noted that the notion and experience of shame is a central technology of civilization.

> Considered superficially, it (shame) is fear of social degradation or, more generally, of other people's gestures of superiority. But it is a form of displeasure or fear which arises characteristically on those occasions when a person who fears lapsing into inferiority can avert this danger neither by direct physical means nor by any other form of attack. This defencelessness against the superiority of others, this total exposure to them does not arise directly from a threat from the physical superiority of others as actually present, although it doubtless has its origins in physical compulsion, in the bodily inferiority of the child in face of its parents or teachers. In adults however, this defencelessness results from the fact that the people whose superiority one fears are in accord with one's own super-ego, with the agency of self-constraint implanted in the individual by others on whom he was dependent, who possessed power and superiority over him (Elias, 2000: 415).

The insight of this passage is that the notion of shame is bound to the power relations that the individual is part of, and that shame is an expression of a hegemonic social opinion at least partly shared by the shamed individual.

As discussed in the first chapter, ţigan slavery was not only crucial to feudal economy, it also served to support the idea that even free peasants could fall from grace and be enslaved. Enslavement: becoming ţigani, thus served as a constant threat to ordinary peasants (Achim, 2004: 57). When țigani first entered the Romanian territories it was as prisoners of war: they were regarded as infidels in the Ottoman Empire and as the 'barbaric' representation of the enemy (Beck, 1989). This position has strengthened by the structural and organisational marginalisation of țigani in society up to present times. I propose that țigani have served the same function in the civilizing process in Transylvania and Romania that peasants served in the civilizing process in France, that of barbarians against whom the civilized person distinguishes himself (Elias, 2000a: 176,77). The continuous representation of țigani as 'slaves', as 'others within' and as 'the non-civilized' appears to have been important for the identification of Romanians as civilized. The self-representation of Roma as different from gaže has likewise always been important for their economic and cultural survival. For generations țigani have served this role as the counter-image of good, proper people in socialisation and everyday evaluation among villagers and town people.

Everything perceived of as gypsylike (*țiganesc*) was avoided and expressed in terms of shame. Married women dressed in dark and plain clothes, and as a middle-aged peasant woman explained, she preferred dark colours because she did not want to look like a țiganca. The young mothers in the village proudly told me they bottle-fed their infants, 'because', they announced, 'we have no milk', in sharp contrast to the constantly breastfeeding țiganci. From a very young age village children have been disciplined by arguments such as: 'Behave yourself, don't act like a țigan. Look how dirty you are, do you want to be a țigan? Shut your mouth or the țigani will take you away!' The undisciplined body of the child has been equated with the undisciplined țigani, and the process of socialisation has been aimed at ridding the child of antisocial and hence țiganesc behaviour. Thus the stigma of the țigan is embodied as shame in the village child. The shame of breastfeeding, the shame of uncontrolled behaviour and that of a dirty appearance derive from the fear of not belonging socially to the Romanian village community, but lapsing to the inferior status of the țigan and recognising oneself as inferior (Elias, 2000: 415). Thus the Romanian child develops a different sense of shame from that of the Rom child. The Rom child is praised by his or her significant others for the ability to behave like a gažo among gaže when that is necessary, but shamed for expressing a gažo personality towards other Roma. The ability to present both Rom and gažo behaviour is important in dealing with gaže. Thus these parallel and different regimes of shame have also contributed to the development of different personality structures and moral habitus of Roma and Romanians. In spite of their structurally inferior position, the Roma are generally not shamed by Romanians as their alleged superiority is not in accordance with the Rom superego, in Elias's sense.

Perhaps more than ever before are the ţigani today important to Romanians as negations of modernity and civilization in order to maintain their idea of themselves as relatively modern and civilized. But the ţigan is significant for the Romanian personality structure and collective identity in another sense as well. As abjects, they also represent desires, powers and possibilities that have been rejected in the civilizing process as they represent a rejection of civilization itself. The ambiguity towards everything foreign, expressed among villagers, influences their relationship to ideas like modernity, civilization and democracy. Even if they admire the West for its economic achievements and for what they see as its superior level of civilization, villagers reject what they see as moral inferiority as part and parcel of foreignness and civilization. By rejecting civilization, ţigani thus express the villagers' own suspicion and fear towards everything foreign. In that way even ţigani may be seen to represent the villagers' own resistance to a civilization that brings efficiency and modernity, but that they also accuse of bringing stinginess, calculation and a cold heart. In the first chapter I indicated that Romanian villagers seemed to see the relatively more modern and civilized Hungarians as more 'strange' and threatening than the ţigani. With the ladder of civilizaţie as moral parameter, Romanian collective identity struggles to find its form between the cold and hard Hungarians representing foreignness and civilization, and the bad and immoral ţigani, representing the uncivilised, but none the less Romanian barbarian. The symbolic dependence of Romanians on the ambiguous image of ţigani makes every change in the relations between the categories and every change in the image of ţigani relevant for the collective identity of all 'nations' of Romania. This challenge to Romanian village identity took many interesting turns during my fieldwork.

Classification Crisis

Romanians as a Bunch of Italian Gypsies

The constant village emphasis on the inherent difference between themselves as Romanians or Hungarians, and the ţigani seemed particularly strange because of covert exchange that became quite overt after a while. Little by little I started to interpret this in terms of a classification crisis, brought out by the new political system, but also by my husband's and my own unusual presence in the village and our intangible position in between villagers and Roma. Another trait strengthened my suggestion: several Romanians in and outside the village from different social layers of the Romanian society complained about how ţigani were confused with Romanians and vice versa in the mass media in Western European countries and by West Europeans in general. Two examples were always presented: When the Romanian national football team had played at the world championship in the U.S.A. in 1994, reporters had commented that they played fairly well for a 'bunch of Gypsies'. A famous Russian politician was interviewed about some event concerning Romanians and Romania and had referred to Romanians as 'Italian Gypsies'. A general complaint was that ţigani had spoiled the reputation of Romanians abroad either by seeking asylum in Germany and presenting themselves as Gypsies persecuted by Romanians, or simply by presenting themselves as Romanians and behaving so badly that they were expelled and thus violated the chances of decent Romanians to seek asylum in Germany. The complaint that ţigani ruin Romania's international reputation has also been expressed as a threat to Romania's chances of membership of NATO and the European Union (Berge, 1997).

Ethnic Violence: Burning Down ţigani Houses

Paired with this accusation of ţigani ruining the reputation of Romanians was a complaint of the international world's misinterpretation of the relationship between ţigani and Romanians. Many villagers saw the general interest in the conditions of ţigani by international organisations like the Council of Europe and the Human Rights Watch, and the general interest of donor organisations, as a criticism of Romanians based on a false understanding of the condition of ţigani. The very complex and ambiguous relation between Romanians and Roma in rural Romania is generally interpreted by international organisations in terms of discrimination and oppression, thus missing out the mutuality and interesting relations of power that I also see as a trait of the relationship. The problems ţigani are seen to pose together with the power they are felt to exercise in many contexts are thus rejected. In human rights reports (Helsinki-Watch, 1991), Romanians are generally portrayed as aggressors and Gypsies as victims; the inversion of how many Romanians see the relationship. This is experienced as an injustice by many Romanians and the blame is partly directed towards ţigani.

Some friends in the village had relatives from a distant town visiting, and asked us to come over and meet them. The conversation quickly turned towards ţigan/român relations and towards the incidents when several Rom houses were set on fire by Romanian neighbours. We asked them to tell us more about these events because they had happened in their region and they seemed vaguely to support the arson. They assured us that they were very strongly against such actions, but that one should try to understand the people who had set fire to the houses. The burnt houses had belonged to ţigani who had sought asylum in Germany and had come back very rich from welfare money, black-market labour and theft. They had returned to their villages and built houses bigger than the village church with shining tin roofs. Not only had they ruined the reputation of Romanians in Germany, but they also mocked the poor, thrifty Romanian villager by splashing their undeserved wealth around for everybody to see. On this ground, they argued, one should understand the anger and frustration of villagers.

Although the family distanced themselves from the burning down of ţigan houses, which seemed to have been sparked by an instance of violence between the groups, they supported the Romanian villagers' right to feel anger and frustration. This anger was a legitimate reaction to what they saw as the ţigani's illegitimate claim to asylum and to an undeserved position as 'rich' with the arrogance to display their wealth in a poor neighbourhood.

Symbolic Violence: Drinking Village Money

A sociologist at the University in Cluj that studied ţigan/român relationships in several Romanian villages, argued, in a private conversation, that the ţigani exercise symbolic violence in their relations to villagers. He supported his claim by pointing to what he saw as the public display of wealth among ţigani, which he interpreted as a demonstration of their public inversion of village values. I found this interpretation interesting both empirically and analytically. My suggestion is that much of the Rom public demeanour is interpreted by villagers in terms of aggression and attack; as an exercise of power. One episode in the village led me to see their point.

As Christmas was approaching, Joska told us he had seen the mayor to ask for welfare money for all families in the hamlet to celebrate Christmas. As we looked a little sceptical he added that many families did not have money for proper food and drink to celebrate Christmas. We knew that all families had earned much money from the sale of clothes a couple of months earlier, but said nothing. A few days before Christmas we passed one of the village bars and heard the shouting and singing of many people. We were called in and found the bar full of hamlet Roma drinking champagne and liqueurs. We asked if they were celebrating a baptism or something and Joska answered, laughing, that they were celebrating Christmas with the welfare money they had received from the mayor. I felt my indignation rise and asked in a rather moralising way why they did not buy food. Joska answered that they had only received about 15,000 lei (US$2) per household, which was so little that one could just as well drink it up together! (One day's minimum wage in Romania at that time.) All villagers knew about this event, and although I never heard any comment I do suppose their general feeling of having to 'feed the ţigani' was strengthened. I also suggest that villagers interpreted this event as an affirmation of the țigani's new position in the village as the mayor's 'favourite poor'. Such episodes, although confirming the general view of țigani as immoral spenders and as children, are also interpreted as signs of the new chaotic situation of present-day Romania that often is experienced as aggression. Physical violence is about violating boundaries of the body. Rejecting Romanian values, attacking the hegemonic order of the village community and violating the reputation of Romanians abroad may all be experienced as aggressive acts violating the social body that constitutes the village and Romanian society. This does not excuse violence and aggression in any sense, but it does challenge the perception of simple relations of oppression.

The Present Challenge – Ethnicity and Modernisation

An Ethnic Hall of Mirrors

Romania, but most prominently Transylvania, constitutes what one may metaphorically term an ethnic 'hall of mirrors' where different categories of people who claim different origin and mother tongue see their own image in that of the others. But as in a hall of mirrors, every mirror is different, twisting and parodying the image in different ways. Thus the image of gypsiness is different seen from the Romanian, German, Hungarian or Rom point of view, but all images contribute to each other in different combinations. The Rom self-image is thus made up of historical experience and cultural traits, as well as the other groups' images of them. Every image of self tends to be seen as negation of the others: Romanians are what țigani, Hungarians and Germans are not, Romanians characterise țigani in the same way as Hungarians characterise Romanians etc. But as the collective identity of Roma is dependent on that of gaže and on the power relations between them, so is the collective identity of Romanians dependent on those of țigani, Hungarians and Germans and the same power relations. My argument has been that the Romanian figuration based on power relations between ethnic groups and on ideas of civilization constitutes a hierarchy that links class, ethnicity and concepts of race together (Beck, 1986), and that ethnicity in this context takes on a specific meaning.

Although the ethnic plurality is greatest in Transylvania, the historical struggle of Romanians between two major empires – the Ottoman representing 'the East' and the Habsburg, representing 'the West' – has been politically exploited in the creation of the Romanian nation since the nineteenth century and in the creation of the modern Romanian state (Verdery, 1990). As the German minority has never had the political power in any part of Romania, and as the German population decreased drastically in the twentieth century, it was the relationship to Hungarians, the Magyar, which stirred the nationalist feelings of most Romanians. The Magyar represented the former rulers and landowners who tried to retrieve what they saw as their land: Transylvania, and even succeeded in 1940–1944 (Verdery, 1996: 100). Thus Transylvania became a symbol for Romanians in general of who was to be master of the house. History was to prove who was entitled to rule and to own Transylvania, and the people who had most far-reaching records of having occupied the territory were seen as the true Transylvanians. The threat of 'the Magyars' taking back Transylvania is a fear expressed not only in political rhetoric but also by peasants in the villages. The nationalist propaganda about the Romanian roots of Transylvania launched in state-controlled television during the Ceauşescu era seems to have struck a chord in most Romanians, not only in the urban middle class and the intellectuals.

The historical position of the ţigani as a social category, not a nation, and hence never a threat to the nationalist ideology or to power relations on a national level may have come to an end. In their new national position as Roma; an ethnic minority, they are establishing a new position in the postsocialist Romanian figuration that posits them as a threat not only on the village level, but possibly also to the nation.

Ethnicity, Nationality and Resistance

After the 1989 revolution, NGOs and political parties claiming to represent the Rom population mushroomed in Romania as in other east European countries. This was not altogether a new phenomenon, but this effort was now supported by a global discourse on ethnicity, a European preoccupation with human rights for minorities and a democratic agenda set up by the new government. Like the educated Vlachs of eighteenth and nineteenth century Transylvania, the educated Roma of twentieth century Romania demand to be regarded as one naţie with its own language and equal rights with other ethnic minorities. The Rom political parties are not made up of village Roma, but of Roma who (like intellectual Romanians in the preceding centuries) had changed their language and way of life and that had acquired a social position in the Romanian society through education. I will claim that this represents a new and threatening situation for many Romanians. That a few ţigani wish to be acknowledged as Roma and be treated as equals is not disturbing in itself. What may be experienced as disturbing is the unpreceded visibility and support to claims of equality this process may bring to the millions of village ţigani who still live in close economic interdependence with villagers. The prospect of the wretched ţigan claiming equal status with Romanians, Hungarians and Germans, for that matter, will have to change the collective identity of those categories, but especially that of Romanians at the bottom of the ladder of civilizaţie. On the national level, the experience of țigani as a threat to Romanians may be expressed by the many conflicts and violent attacks by Romanian villagers on țigani hamlets and on the generally aggressive sentiment towards țigani in public opinion; often expressed unmasked as the desire to exterminate all țigani (Verdery, 1996: 99). The idea of țigani ruining the economy and of monopolising business and crime, the idea often presented that țigani are a threat to Romanian's inclusion in the European Union, and the fear that foreigners do not see the difference between Romanians and țigani, are all general expressions of these challenging changes. I suggest that all these traits constitute the new significance of the țigani in the Romanian collective identity. The țigan is emerging from the marginal and shady position and with him the secret, shady and shabby side of the Romanian self. Caught by the Western gaze, the Romanian is ashamed of revealing this secret or uncivilised aspect of himself and his society and thus losing esteem in front of what he has been taught to consider his superiors, West Europeans. And he turns round and blames the țigan, the abject and cause of his shame and repulsion.

I do not expect violence or extermination to be the Romanian solution to this conflict: ambiguity and ambivalence are far more prevalent traits of the român/țigan relationship in Romania than repression and hatred. Țigani are considered far more 'indigenous' and Romanian among most villagers, than Hungarians are. The fear and threat posed by Hungarians have their root in a memorised past and in the political propaganda about the threatening Hungarian state. This is the fear and hate of the powerful oppressor and much more dangerous to express than the fear and hate of the village țigan. Țigani may very well have served and still serve as a buffer between the two main 'nations' of Romania on the village level; by expressing contempt and aggression towards țigani, the relationship between Romanian and Hungarian has survived at the village level.

The Politicisation of the Rom Elite

The politicisation of Rom ethnicity expressed by political organisations, such as the *Partidul Rromilor*, the *Rromani CRISS* (The Rrom Center for Social Intervention and Studies) and others active after 1990, may be seen as an act of political resistance by one stratum of the Rom population. This presents a radical break with what I have termed the nomadic mode of existence as a parallel, competing, but not incorporated system of power. Although it may be experienced as threatening to the Romanian collective identity, the bulk of Romania's țigani or Roma are not part of this resistance. The main policies of Rom organisations and parties are for formal access to political participation at all levels of the Romanian political system together with practical access to education, better housing and living standards. These issues are important to large sections of the group termed 'țigani' (and lately Roma) who are in a process of social mobilisation and assimilation where education is the necessary capital. This is not, however, in the present interests of the rural and urban Roma who subsist on different strategies of begging, barter and trade. This adaptation makes formal political struggle based on ethnic belonging dubious. What rights should the begging and bartering village Roma fight for? In order to maintain their subsistence strategies the hamlet Roma would have to argue for the right not to be politically and culturally incorporated in the Romanian state, for instance, by not having to send their children to school.

The Roma were officially acknowledged as a national minority in Romania in 1989. The idea of Roma as a people, as some kind of unified group, which is fundamental to the political struggle of Roma elites, is a very vague idea among most Roma. The hamlet Roma know very well that there are Roma all over Romania and even all over the world. The notion of '*sa ciganie*' (all gypsies) may imply the actual local settlement, the networks of inter-related Roma or the idea of the Roma world-wide. But they only identify with Roma they know and are related to by bilateral kinship and the Roma who share their way of life and language (Gay Y Blasco, 1999). The question is whether they would include the intellectual elite in this group.

Modernisation and Democratisation

The discourse on modernity is an important civilizing device and, in contrast to the Romanian discourse on civilizaţie, it does not appear to exclude anybody on the basis of ethnicity or nationhood. The young generation of villagers is eager to present themselves as modern and that implies wearing Western clothes, starting some kind of business, moving into town and not engaging in subsistence farming. Westernisation and modernisation may be seen as parallel processes thus making them explicit as civilizing processes that contribute to increased economic, cultural and political corporation and interdependence of the European states as a social figuration. Western ways of life shall, together with market economy and participation in the European Union, transform Romanians into Europeans. Modernity should not be treated as one overarching, hegemonic force, but as many diverging and sometimes even opposing discourses according to contextual interpretation (Ewing, 1997). Thus even hamlet Roma regard them selves as modern in many contexts.

I expect that the transformations of Romania within the European figuration will change the relations and interdependence of social and ethnic groups in Romania in unforeseen ways. What will happen to the uncivilised ţigani in this process? The subsistence of the hamlet Roma was, as I have argued, based on on forced wage labour in the Ceauşescu era and later on the relatively affluent, self-sufficient peasant community. When forced wage labour was abolished after the revolution, the advent of the relief gift prolonged the Roma's adaptation to rural life. When this source dries out and farming is modernised in Romania as a condition and/or effect of Romania's participation in the European Union, there will no longer be rural communities of ţigani living off the peasants' surplus.

This does not mean, however, that all ţigani will give up their rural mode of subsistence and what I have termed Rom mode of existence, only that those will change. I suggest most hamlet Roma will either stay in the village and slowly be assimilated into the village community as peasants, become itinerant merchants or move into the nearby towns or to other European countries and develop new peripatetic strategies there. Some prosperous and/or intellectual Roma may gradually constitute a new ethnic minority with special rights and privileges as Roma. I have argued that the systems of exchange developed in villages between Roma and peasants are based on ideas of both inherent difference and interdependence between them. The political efforts of the Rom elite are to change this state of affairs and make Roma economically independent, but politically and culturally dependent on the gažo society. By adhering to the rhetoric and strategy of ethnicity and by claiming equality with other naţie in Romania, the Rom elite thus seeks to be acknowledged as equal based on sameness, not on difference. They strive for the independence of the Roma from the gaže rather than interdependence. The question is whether such a status is possible for the Roma without acquiring a 'higher level of civilization' in the Romanian sense. This would probably mean being culturally and politically incorporated into the state; precisely the domination the hamlet Roma try to avoid by their mode of existence. One probable scenario that emerges from the struggle for ethnic equality is that the negative aspect of difference and otherness that defines the ţigan today will cling to the civilized future Rom. This negative otherness may overshadow the present positive aspect of interdependence and 'sameness' between Roma and gaže and create the future Roma as independent but still despised.

Epilogue

Since leaving the village in the summer of 1997, we have been back three times.

The first visit was in 1999 when we spent one week there and could ascertain that no major changes had occurred since we had left. A group of young men from different families had, however, left to work in Turkey, a journey that probably was possible because of the money most families had saved from the sale of clothes. The next visit was in 2001 when we spent most of our stay in hospitals and at deathbeds as both Viorel, our Romanian host, and Varga, the Romni of one of our closest friends in the hamlet, were severely ill with cancer. Varga died in her bed, while we were there, in the tiny hut she used to live in with her husband and their six children. The only room was filled to the brim with family members comforting her in the last hours of her life. The only visible changes in the hamlet on this visit were several newly built houses; the hamlet seemed to have expanded. Viorel died later, also in his bed, with his small family present, I expect.

Before our third visit in 2004, we were told that Joska and Kurva and most of their familia had converted to Pentecostalism and had joined the Romanian Pentecostal congregation in town. We were also told that Joska had been appointed consultant to the mayor in Rom questions. When we arrived in the hamlet another remarkable change caught our eyes: the Romnja, who for the most part had been sturdy and strong-looking women when we stayed in the village and hamlet, had grown fat. Even the women who had been skinny were now rather chubby. When I commented on this change they laughed and told me that they now lived better than before. A closer look revealed at least two features that may be seen as a consequence of changes due to the NGO gift. We noticed that the pigs and piglets that usually roamed between the houses and on the plains were gone. The Roma commented on this change like this: 'No, we don't have pigs any more; we are modern now and raise chickens'. This of course meant that women no longer had to go scavenging to find bread to feed the pigs. Instead of the long walks three times a week in town, the women now stayed at home and only visited the village. The second change was that most families had refrigerators. A refrigerator makes it possible to buy or gather food only twice a week and store it; the daily walks to scrape together provisions were thus not necessary anymore. The hamlet Roma had become modern, fat and apparently very happy about it! How these changes influenced the relationship to villagers is, however, another story.

The last change to influence the life of Romanian Roma is a result of changing relationships between European states; the abolishment of visas for Romanians to western Europe. In the last two years, more and more Romanian Roma have begun to tour Europe as musicians, shoe shines, flower vendors and beggars. In the streets of Norway's towns, from Oslo in the south to Tromsø in the far north, one may meet street beggars that look like characters in historical movies. On their knees, with crutches, trembling and singing, Romanian (Rom) beggars imbue in Norwegian citizens the same mix of contempt and pity that they imbue in Romanians. Cries demanding a ban on 'foreign beggars' have already been raised. A women's magazine recently wrote a reportage about a Romni beggar in Oslo and even interviewed her back in her town in Transylvania. There, she proudly showed off the four cows that she had bought with the money she had received begging in Norway and that were herded by a Kaštale family. This example may signify a last large-scale Gypsy migration from Romania and other ex-socialist countries into Western Europe and may well challenge the Norwegian self-perception as a democratic and tolerant people.

BIBLIOGRAPHY

Abu-Lughod, L. (1986) *Veiled Sentiments*, University of California Press, Berkeley.

Achim, V. (2004) *The Roma in Romanian History*, CEU Press (Central European University Press), Budapest and New York.

Ariés, P. (1996) *Centuries of Childhood*, Pimlico, London.

Appadurai, A. (ed.) (1986) *The Social Life of Things: Commodities in Cultural Perspective*, Cambridge University Press, Cambridge.

Appadurai, A. (1996) *Modernity at Large: Cultural Dimensions of Globalisation*, University of Minnesota Press, Minneapolis.

Baban, A. and H.P. David, (1997) 'The Impact of Body Politics on Women's Bodies', in *Women and Men in East European Transition* (eds Feischmidt, E. Magyari-Vincze, and V. Zentai), Editura Fundatiei Pentru Studii Europeene, Cluj-Napoka, pp. 156–70.

Barth, F. (1955) 'The Social Organization of a Pariah group in Norway', *Norveg Journal of Norwegian Ethnology*, 5, pp. 125–43.

Barth, F. (1971) 'Role Dilemmas and Father-Son Dominance in Middle East Kinship Systems', in *Kinship and Culture* (ed. Hsu, L.K.), Aldine Publishing Company, Chicago, pp. 275–83.

Bauman, Z. (1995) *Life in Fragments: Essays in Postmodern Morality*, Blackwell, Oxford.

Bauman, Z. (1997) *Postmodernity and its Discontents*, Polity Press, Cambridge.

Beck, S. (1986) 'Indigenous Anthropologists in Socialist Romania', *Dialectical Anthropology*, 10, pp. 249–64.

Beck, S. (1989) 'The Origins of Gypsy Slavery in Romania', *Dialectical Anthropology*, 14, pp. 53–61.

Berge, T. (2000) *Forurensning eller arbeidsløshet: Reaksjoner på industriforurensning og industrinedleggelse i byen Copşa Mica, Romania*. Solum Forlag, Osler.

Bloch, M. and J. Parry (eds) (1982) *Death and the Regeneration of Life*, Cambridge University Press, Cambridge.

Bourdieu, P. (1986) *Outline of a Theory of Practice*, Cambridge University Press, Cambridge.

Bourdieu, P. (1990) *The Logic of Practice*, Polity Press, Oxford.

Buchowski, M. (1996) 'The Shifting Meaning of Civil and Civic Society in Poland', in *Civil Society Challenging Western Models* (ed. C. Hann), Routledge, London, pp. 79–98.

Carsten, J. (2000) 'Introduction', in *Cultures of Relatedness: New Approaches to the Study of Kinship* (ed. J. Carsten), Cambridge University Press, Cambridge, pp. 1–36.

Chelcea, I. (1944) *Tiganii din România: Monografie Etnografică*, Editura Institutului Central De Statistică, Bucureşti V, Splaiul Unirii 28.

Clastres, P. (1977) *Society against the State*, Urizen, N.Y.

Cohen, A. (2000) 'Introduction: Discriminating Relations: Identity, Boundary and Authenticity', in *Signifying Identities* (ed. A. Cohen), Routledge, London, pp. 1–13.

Cohen, A.P (1994) *Self Consciousness: an Alternative Anthropology of Identity*, London, Routledge.

Cohen, A.P. (1985) *The Symbolic Construction of Community*, Routledge, London.

Counihan, C.M. (1999) *The Anthropology of Food and Body: Gender, Meaning, and Power*, Routledge, New York and London.

Crowe, D. (1991) 'The Gypsy Historical Experience in Romania', in *The Gypsies of Eastern Europe* (eds D. Crowe and J. Kolsti), M.E. Sharpe, Inc, New York, pp. 52–61.

Crowe, D. and J. Kolsti, (eds) (1991) *The Gypsies of Eastern Europe*, M.E. Sharpe, New York.

Das, V. (1998) 'Masks and Faces: an Essay on Punjabi Kinship', in *Family, Kinship and Marriage in India* (ed. Uberoy, P.), Oxford University Press, Calcutta, pp. 185–229.

Deleuze, G. and G. Guattari (1985) *Nomadology*, The Athlone Press, London.

Douglas, M. (1966) *Purity and Danger: An Analysis of the Concepts of Pollution and Taboo*, Ark Paperbacks, London.

Eidheim, H. (1977) *Aspects of the Lappish Minority Situation*, Universitetsforlaget, Oslo-Bergen-Tromsø.

Elias, N. (2000) *The Civilizing Process*, Blackwell Publishing, Oxford.

Elias, N. (2001) *The Society of Individuals*, Continuum, New York and London.

Eminescu, M. (1999) *Poezii Poems*, Teora, Bucuresti.

Evans-Pritchard, E.E. (1940) *The Nuer*, Clarendon Press, Oxford.

Ewing, K.P. (1990) 'The Illusion of Wholeness: Culture, Self, and the Experience of Inconsistency', *Ethos*, 18, pp. 251–78.

Ewing, K.P. (1997) *Arguing Sainthood: Modernity, Psychoanalysis and Islam*, Duke University Press, Durham and London.

Fardon, R. (ed.) (1990) *Localizing Strategies: The Regionalisation of Ethnographic Accounts*, Smithsonian Institution Press, Washington DC.

Fog Olwig, K. and K. Hastrup (eds) (1997) *Siting Culture: The Shifting Anthropological Object*, Routledge, London and New York.

Foucault, M. (1976) *The History of Sexuality, An Introduction*, Penguin Books Ltd., London.

Fraser, A. (1995) *The Gypsies*, Blackwell Publishers, Oxford (U.K.) and Cambridge (U.S.A.).

Frisby, D. and M. Featherstone (1997) *Simmel on Culture: Selected Writings*, Sage Publications, London.

Gal, S. (1991) 'Bartók's Funeral: Representations of Europe in Hungarian Political Rhetoric', *American Ethnologist*, 18, pp. 440–58.

Gay y Blasco, P. (1999) *Gypsies in Madrid: Sex, Gender and the Performance of Identity*, Berg, Oxford.

Georgescu, V. (1991) *The Romanians, A History*, I.B. Taurus & Co. Ltd. Publishers, London.

Giddens, A. (1991) *Modernity and Self-Identity: Self and Society in the Late Modern Age*, Polity Press, Cambridge.

Gilmore, D.D. (1987) 'Honor, Honesty, Shame: Male Status in Contemporary Andalusia', in *Honor and Shame and the Mediterranean*, 22 (ed. D.D. Gilmore), Special Publication of the American Anthropological Association, Washington DC, pp. 90–103.

Gjerde, L. (1994) *The Orange of Love and Other Stories: The Rom-Gypsy Language in Norway*, Scandinavian University Press, Oslo.

Godelier, M. (1999) *The Enigma of the Gift*, The University of Chicago Press, Chicago.

Gropper, R.C. (1975) *Gypsies in the City*, The Darwin Press, Princeton, NJ.

Gupta, A. and J. Ferguson (1992) 'Beyond "Culture": Space, Identity, and the Politics of Difference', *Cultural Anthropology Journal of the Society for Cultural Anthropology*, 7, pp. 6–23.

Gupta, A. and J. Ferguson (eds) (1997) *Anthropological Locations: Boundaries and Grounds of a Field Science*, University of California Press, Berkely.

Hann, C. (1996) 'Introduction. Political Society and Civil Anthropology', in *Civil Society Challenging Western Models* (eds C. Hann and E. Dunn), Routledge, London and New York. pp. 1–27.

Harris, O. (1981) 'Households as Natural Units', in *Of Marriage and the Market: Women's Subordination in International Perspective* (eds K. Young et al.) SCE Books, London, pp. 136–55.

Haugen, I. (1978) 'Om forvaltning av utilgjengelighet', *Tidsskrift for Samfunnsforskning*, 19, pp. 405–14.

Haukanes, H. (2001) 'Anthropological Debates on Gender and the Post-communist Transformation', *Nora* 9, pp. 5–20 (16).

Helsinki-Watch (1991) 'Destroying Ethnic Identity: The Persecution of Gypsies in Romania', *Helsinki Watch Report*, New York.

Hirsh, E. and M. O'Hanlon (eds) (1995) *The Anthropology of Landscape: Perspectives on Place and Space*, Clarendon Press, Oxford.

Howell, S. (1986) 'Formal Speech Acts as One Discourse', *Man*, 21, pp. 79–101.

Humphrey, C. and S. Hugh-Jones (1992) 'Introduction: Barter, Exchange and Value', in *Barter, Exchange and Value* (eds C. Humphrey and S. Hugh-Jones), Cambridge University Press, Cambridge, pp. 1–20.

Hübschmannová, M. (1998) 'Economic Stratification and Interaction: Roma, an Ethnic Jati in East Slovakia', in *Gypsies: An Interdisciplinary Reader* (ed. D. Tong), Garland Publishing, Inc., New York. pp. 233–271.

Høgmo, A. (1986) 'Det tredje alternativ: Barns læring av identitetsforvaltning i samiske områder preget av identitetsskifte', *Tidsskrift for samfunnsforsknng*, 5, pp. 395–416.

Jameson, F. (2000) 'Marxisme og dualisme hos Deleuze', *Agora*, 2-3, pp. 74–97.

Kaminski, I.-M. (1987) 'The Dilemma of Power: Internal and External Leadership: The Gypsy Roma of Poland', in *The Other Nomads* (ed. A. Rao), Bölaug Verlag, Köln Wien, pp. 323–56.

Kligman, G. (1988) *The Wedding of the Dead: Ritual, Poetics, and Popular Culture in Transylvania*, University of California Press, Berkeley.

Kligman, G. (1994) 'The Social Legacy of Communism: Women, Children, and the Feminization of Poverty', *in The Social Legacy of Communism* (eds J.R. Miller and S.L. Wolchic), Cambridge University Press, Cambridge, pp. 252–271.

Konstantinov, K. and T. Thuen (1998) 'Outclassed by Former Outcasts: Petty Trading in Varna Comments and Reflections', *American Ethnologist Journal of the American Ethnologist Society*, 25, 4, pp. 729–45.

Kristeva, J. (1982) *Powers of Horror: An Essay on Abjection*, European University Press, New York.

Lacan, J. (1977) *Écrits: A Selection*, Tavistock, London.

Lan, D. (1989) 'Resistance to the Present by the Past: Mediums and Money in Zimbabwe', in *Money and The Morality of Exchange* (eds J. Parry and M. Bloch), Cambridge University Press, Cambridge, pp. 191–208.

Levi-Strauss, C. (1987) *Anthropology and Myth: Lectures 1951–82*, Oxford, Blackwell.

Lucassen, L., W. Willems and A.Cottaar (eds) (1998) *Gypsies and Other Itinerant Groups: A Socio-Historical Approach*, Macmillan Press, Houndsmill.

Marcus, G.E. (1995) 'Ethnography in/of the World System: The Emergence of Multi-sited Ethnography', *Annual. Review of Anthropology*, 24, pp. 95–117.

Marian, S.F. (1995) *Nuntă la Români*, Editura Grai si Suflet – Cultură Natională, Bucureăti.

Matras, Y. (2002) *Romani: A Linguistic Introduction*, Cambridge University Press, Cambridge.

Melhus, M. (1990) 'A Shame to Honour A Shame to Suffer', *Ethnos*, 55, pp. 5–25.

Mennell, S. and J. Goudsblom (1998a) 'Introduction', in *Norbert Elias: On Civilization, Power and Knowledge*, (eds S. Mennell and J. Goudsblom), The University of Chicago Press, Chicago. pp. 1–46.

Mennell, S. and J. Goudsblom (eds) (1998b) *Norbert Elias: On Civilization, Power and Knowledge*, The University of Chicago Press, Chicago.

Miller, C. (1998) 'American Roma and the Ideology of Defilement', in *Gypsiness: An Interdisciplinary Reader* (ed. D. Tong). Garland Publishing, Inc., New York and London, pp. 201–209.

Moore, H.L. (1994) *A Passion for Difference*, Polity Press, Cambridge.

Naterstad, S. (1996) *Spre Communism in Zbor*, Unpublished Master's Thesis, Klassisk Romansk institutt, University of Oslo.

Okely, J. (1975) 'Gypsy Women: Models in Conflict', in *Perceiving Women* (ed. S. Ardener), Malaby, London, pp. 55–86.

Okely, J. (1983) *The Traveller-gypsies*, Cambridge University Press, Cambridge.

Okely, J. (1994) 'Constructing Difference: Gypsies as "Other"', *Anthropological Journal on European Cultures*, 3, pp. 55–73.

Østerberg, D. (2000) 'Gilles Deleuze differensfilosofi', *Agora Journal for Metafysisk Spekulasjon*, 2–3, pp. 165–81.

Parry, J. (1986) 'The Gift, The Indian Gift and "The Indian Gift"', *Man*, 21, pp. 453–73.

Pecican, O. (1997) 'Romanian Masculine Model', in *Women and Men in East-European Transition* (eds M. Feischmidt, E. Magyary-Vinze, and V. Zentai), Editură Fundaţiei pentru, studii Europeene, Cluj-Napoca, pp. 201–12.

Piasere, L. (1987) 'In Search of New Niches: the Productive Organisation of the Peripatetic Xoraxané in Italy', in *The Other Nomads* (ed. A. Rao), Bölaug Verlag Køln, Wien.

Raduly, J. (1997) 'Women and Birth in Romania', in *Women and Men in East-European Transition* (eds Feinschmidt, M.E. Magyary-Vinze and V. Zentai), Editură Fundaţiei pentru, Studii Europeene, Cluj-Napoca, pp. 171–82.

Recentamentul dîn 1930. Populaţiă statornică în 1930. Vol. II Partea 1, Judeţul Bihor.

Rudie, I. (1993) 'The Ritual Work of Malay Marriage as a Field of Debate', in *Carved Flesh/Cast Selves Gendered Symbols and Social Practices* (eds V. Broch-Due, I. Rudie and T. Bleie), Berg, Oxford/Providence, pp. 173–195.

Sahlins, M. (1988) *Stone Age Economics*, Routledge, London and New York.

Scott, J.C. (1990) *Domination and the Arts of Resistance*, Yale University Press, New Haven and London.

Seim, J. (1994) *Øst-Europas historie*, Aschehaug Forlag, Oslo.

Simmel, G. (1955) *Conflict and The Web of Group Affiliation*, The Free Press, New York.

Spülbeck, S. (1996) 'Anti-semitism and Fear of the Public Sphere in a Post-totalitarian Society: East-Germany', in *Civil Society: Challenging Western models* (ed. C. Hann), Routledge, London, pp. 64–78.

Stewart, M. (1993) 'Mauvaises Morts, Prêtres Impurs et Pouvoirs Récupérateur du Chant: Les Rituels Mortuaires chez les Tsiganes de Hongrie', in *Terrain: Carnet du Patrimoine Ethnologique*, Mars/20, pp. 21–37.

Stewart, M. (1997) *The Time of the Gypsies*, Westview Press, Colorado.

Stewart, M. (1999) '"Brothers" and "Orphans": Images of Equality among Hungarian Rom', in *Lilies of the Field: Marginal People Who Live for the Moment* (eds, S. Day, E. Papataxiarchis and M. Stewart), Westview Press, Colorado and Oxford U.K.

Strathern, M. (1992a) 'Parts and Wholes: Refiguring Relationships in a Post-plural World', in *Conceptualizing Society* (ed. A. Kuper), Routledge, London, pp. 75–104.

Strathern, M. (1992b) 'Qualified Value: the Perspective of Gift Exchange', in *Barter, Exchange and Value: An Anthropological Approach* (eds C. Humphrey and S. Hugh-Jones), Cambridge University Press, New York, pp. 169–91.

Sutherland, A. (1975) *Gypsies: The Hidden Americans*, The Free Press, New York.

Tsing, A.L. (1993) *In the Realm of the Diamond Queen*, Princeton University Press, Princeton, NJ.

Turner, V. (1967) *The Forest of Symbols: Aspects of Ndembu Ritual*, Cornell University Press, Ithaca.

van de Port, M. (1998) *Gypsies, Wars and Other Instances of the Wild*, Amsterdam University Press, Amsterdam.

Verdery, K. (1983) *Transylvanian Villagers: Three Centuries of Political, Economic, and Ethnic Change*, University of California Press, Berkeley.

Verdery, K. (1990) 'The Production and Defense of "the Romanian Nation", 1900 to World War II', in *Nationalist Ideologies and the Reproduction of National Cultures* (ed. Fox, R.), American Ethnological Society monograph series (2), Washington DC, pp. 81–111.

Verdery, K. (1991) *National Ideology under Socialism: Identity and Culture Politics under Ceausescu's Romania*, University of California Press, Berkeley.

Verdery, K. (1996) *What Was Socialism and What Comes Next?* Princeton University Press, Princeton, NJ.

Voiculescu, C. (2002) 'Identity Formation at Sangeorgiu de Mures' Roma Population', *Sociologie Romaneasca/Romanian Sociology*, 2002 (4). «www.sociologieromaneasca.ro», Annual English Electronic Edition.

Waldrop, A. (1997) 'Fornuft og følelser i husholdet', *Sosiologi i dag*, 4, pp. 77–104.

White, J. B. (1996) 'Civic Culture and Islam in Urban Turkey', in *Civil Society Challenging Western Models* (eds C. Hann and E. Dunn), Routledge, London, pp. 143–54.

Willems, W. (1995) 'The Shortcommings and Pitfalls of Gypsy Studies', *Gypsy Lore Society*, Leiden, Netherlands.

Williams, P. (1983) 'L'affirmation tsiganes et la notion d'authenticité', *Etudes Tsiganes Paris*, 28, pp. 9–17.

Williams, P. (1984) *Marriage Tsigane: Une Cérémonie de financailles chez les Rom de Paris*, L'Harmattan, Selaf, Paris.

Williams, P. (1985) 'Marriage Tsigane. Une cérémonie de fiancailles chez les Rom de Paris', *Etudes Tsiganes*, 31, pp. 11–24.

Williams, P. (1993) *Nous, on n'en parle pas: Les vivants et les morts chez les Manouches*, Edition de la Maison des sciences de l'homme Paris, Paris.

Willis, P. (1977) *Learning to Labour: How Working Class Lads Get Working Class Jobs*, Westmead, Saxon House, London.

Wolf, E.R. (1982) *Europe and the People without History*, University of California Press, Los Angeles.

Woodburn, J. (1998) '"Sharing is Not a Form of Exchange": an Analysis of Property Sharing in Immediate-return Hunter-gatherer Systems', in *Property Relations: Renwing the Anthropological Tradition* (ed. Hann, C.M.), Cambridge University Press, Cambridge, pp. 48–63.

Yannaras, C. (1991) *Elements of Faith: An Introduction to Orthodox Theology*, T&T Clark, Edinburgh.

Index

Okely, Judith, 11, 13, 50, 55, 65, 68, 126, 134, 140
omul nou, 31
oppression, 189, 197, 199
Orthodox Christianity, 16
otherness, 12, 13, 50, 191, 203
Ottoman Empire, 26–33, 195

patrilineal descent, 76
peasant ideology, 151
Piasere, Leonardo, 49, 53, 58, 59, 101
pollution, 127, 128, 140, 141, 152
power relation, 111, 185
practical kin, 79

rasa, 2, 92
reciprocity, 64, 164, 168, 169, 178, 179
    negative, 60, 173, 191
reflexivity, 126, 135,
    self-, 20,
relatedness, 85, 91, 93, 94, 112
ritual
    death, 131, 134, 141
    gift-exchange, 116, 166
    meals, 131
    pollution, 127, 128, 130, 132, 140, 154, 157, 158
    separation, 131, 134, 138, 158
    work, 126, 127
Roma gažikane, 138, 160, 178, 194
Romanes, 140, 5
    cosmology, 45, 57, 125, 134–36, 145, 140, 141, 190
    language, 2, 9, 21, 33, 37, 44, 60, 67, 78, 79, 97, 112, 127, 130, 135–41, 160
Romanian figuration, 1, 13, 17, 24–32, 39, 192, 193, 199, 200
Romanianness, 24, 29, 30, 145
royal serfs, 34

Saxon, 27, 31
scavenging, 42, 44, 45, 50, 53, 54, 63, 64, 66, 82, 91, 94, 113, 138, 204
school, 4, 55, 56, 102, 116n, 121, 138, 139, 147, 148, 202
sedentarism, 18
self-sufficiency, 49, 57, 58, 68, 113, 149, 153, 154, 156, 164–69
serf, 27, 34, 35,
shame, 25, 55–58, 62–73, 79, 82, 99, 104, 108–111, 114, 125–31, 135–37, 140, 160, 187, 194–96, 201
sharing, 49, 56–60, 69, 87, 90, 94, 95, 100, 104, 105, 121–23, 135, 137, 139, 154, 165, 169, 173, 178, 187
shifting selves, 15–20, 65, 87
signifiers, 181, 193
šjogoro, 75
slave, 2, 27, 29, 33, 34, 194
sliminess, 184, 185
sociability, 8, 137, 141, 153
social landscape, 5
spurcat, 128
state, 3, 4, 11, 28, 30, 31, 34, 35, 38, 115, 119, 123, 136, 153, 169, 170, 187, 200, 201, 202
    mode, 18–20, 170, 188
    nation-, 24,
    power, 18–20, 149, 161, 164, 170, 178, 188, 198–81, 203
stealing, 50, 55–58, 63, 66, 102, 169, 172, 175, 178, 179
stigma, 56, 195
strangers, 7, 13, 25, 35, 150, 161–64, 173, 174, 178, 184
striated space, 18
subject positions, 14, 15, 19, 65, 68
subjectivity, 14,
suffering, 155, 156
superego, 196